Business Bestsellers in a Nutshell

Devanshu Darmora

UNICORN BOOKS BUSINESS

F-2/16, Ansari Road, Daryaganj, New Delhi-110002

☎ 011-23275434, 23262683, 23250704 • *Fax:* 011-23257790

E-mail: info@unicornbooks.in • *Website:* www.unicornbooks.in

Branch : Mumbai

23-25, Zaoba Wadi, Thakurdwar, Mumbai-401002

☎ 022-22010941, 022-22053387

E-mail: rapidex@bom5.vsnl.net.in

Showroom :

★ **PM Publications,** New Delhi

- 10-B, Netaji Subhash Marg, Daryaganj
  New Delhi-110002
- 6686, Khari Baoli, Delhi-110006

ISBN 978-81-7806-329-4

Business Bestsellers in a Nutshell

Edition: 2013

Disclaimer

This book contains the author's subjective opinions and views about the subject matter given in the considered bestseller books. The material contained in this book is general only and has been prepared without taking into account yours' objectives or needs. It is not intended to be a substitute for the original books. The readers are advised to read the original books for definitive professional advice.

No representations are made to the accuracy, completeness or reasonableness of the statements in this publication. Further no responsibility is taken for omissions, errors or contrary interpretation of the information provided in this publication. The author and publisher cannot be held responsible for any loss incurred as a result of reliance placed on the views and opinions expressed in this book.

Some of the product names and Company names included in this book have been used for identification purposes only. The author, editor and publisher disclaim any affiliation, association or connection with, or sponsorship or endorsement by such owners. Trademark and service mark terms used in this book are the property of the trademark holders. Use of a term in this book should not be regarded as affecting the validity of any trademark or servicemark.

Printed at : *Param Offsetters, Okhla, New Delhi-110020*

meet the author

Devanshu Darmora honed his marketing finesse at IIM A and has been the recipient of Carnegie Mellon University's Prof. David Lamont certificate of 'Academic Excellence'. He is currently working as a Senior Researcher with one of the leading marketing consulting firms in the world. This pink city lad is a dreamer to the core and a keen observer of business, society, economic environment & innovation. He has helped guide strategic marketing initiatives and consulted with several global heavyweights like DuPont, PepsiCo, KPMG, Google, Bharti, Nokia, AT Kearney, Zain & others.

Besides his obsession with honing the science of measuring marketing performance, Devanshu spends his spare time socializing at Cafe Lounge and watching 'Bollywood' films. Following the fortunes of Ferrari and the Indian cricket team is another passion with him. Being a regular viewer of ESPN Live, he claims to nail all sports where height does not make a difference... But most of all, this self-help junkie loves reading business bestsellers. 'The Tipping Point' by Malcolm Gladwell has been his all-time favorite.

Dedication

For some, this is the toughest part of writing a book. Thanks to my unmarried and kidless status, the choice came rather easy...

"So,  my rockin' mom & dad."

In addition to this rather hackneyed dedication, there are perhaps thousand other better reasons why I deserve to be tagged as a copycat. But for me, the end always justifies the means. Going by the same theory of consequentialism, I thought what better way of honoring my parents. They're my real life role models and deem more worthy of this dedication than anyone else. Also, when it comes to simple cause and effect, they are really the ones who wrote this book!

One glitch, though...
I had to miss out my awesome bros – Himanshu & Shivam

Contents

The Making of *Business Bestsellers in a Nutshell*

As a consultant, I have always touted the importance of "customer voice" and to this end scripting *Business Bestsellers in a Nutshell* was like a purposeful endeavor towards meeting the demands of a modern day reader. A useful starting point for me was to connect the loose ends by understanding why most people despite their intention don't end up buying the highly recommended must read self help books.

Voice of people from readership survey.......

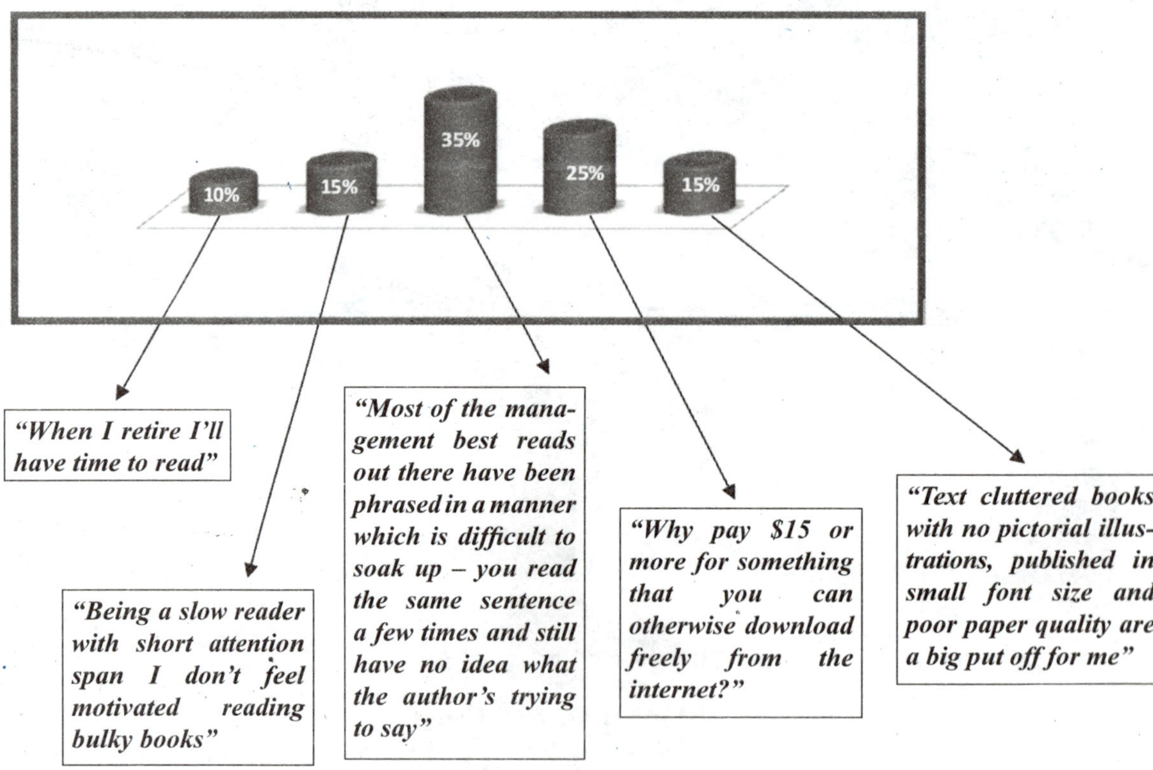

Another interesting finding was that more than 70% of readers embarking on a journey into a new book feel they have to hack through hundreds of pages of dense overgrowth before their conscience allows them to give it up as a lost cause. About 25% of all the buyers actually read the book cover to cover and others ostensibly absorb some knowledge.

It doesn't have to be this hard!

Taking a cue from the survey results and fitting in my own experiences I decided to write a ready reference, fun to read and easiest to understand self help book of less than 200 pages which could be comfortably digested by all types of readers from entry level to CEOs. A book with no-fluff summaries of books that matter, logically structured to get the maximum out of your reading time, thereby justifying its purpose of cutting through the clutter and spreading the learnings of best business literature to the widest audience possible.

A Few Last Words

It took me about two years of re-writes to finally pen an ending I was satisfied with. You don't need to reinvent the wheel. All said & done............

Readers of *Business Bestsellers in a Nutshell*	Readers of *other books*
Profit by the juicy wisdom nuggets sampled out in the book and stay on the top of best in business knowledge. Unlike their counterparts, they do not spend long nights trying to finish that last chapter. Neither do they go through the pain of re-reading the entire book if they have to revisit some of the important concepts which they might have forgotten over time.	Retain merely the dregs of what they read and are content to get through a book for the sake of getting through their time. They have a great collection of unread hardcovers & downloaded ebooks - making it terribly difficult for them to decide which new book to crack open next. This in turn makes them feel guilty and overwhelmed.

BOOK TALK

LESS IS OFTEN MORE

In the age of '3 minute elevator pitch', there is much to be said about the discipline of packaging information into bite (or is that byte?) sized chunks. No more can we afford the luxury of one week off-sites. Today's time-starved professionals need tasty and easy to swallow knowledge capsules (of course without the side effects of boredom) to keep their business blood pumping.

To tell you frankly, I was never a speed reader myself and like all other mortal souls I use to hesitate reading the tomes available in the bookstores about financial freedom or the habits of highly effective people. Most of the time, it would take me weeks to finish a book because more often than not, I found it going down the list of my priorities. Despite the inner drive, I would avoid reading simply because it was too heavy on my grey cells. I knew I would have to wade through a lot of chaff to find the occasional gems and that's precisely what years after, motivated me to author this book. The purpose of writing *Business Bestsellers in a Nutshell* was to fuse together the collective wisdom from chart-topping business books of all times on the topics of marketing, human resource management, customer satisfaction, business strategy, leadership & personal finance and build it into an information architecture that is interesting and easier to understand, pretty much like a multi starrer movie with Oscar winners from all categories. Again, the reason behind such an extensive breadth & diverse choice of subject coverage was that I wanted this book to be the most effective & holistic learning experience of your life. A book which gives you an ROI that is many times over!

Positioned as an antidote to information overload, this book is geared for people like you and me who are tired of reading cluttered books that stray too much from their otherwise interesting premise and are overburdened by factoids. It distills insights from more than 1800 pages of bestselling management literature in less than 200 odd pages making it an ideal resource for the business owners, executive class, business students and anyone curious about self-betterment. If having these condensed success secrets at your fingertips saves you from that one fatal mistake then it's definitely worth it. And when it prepares you for long term business success, it becomes truly invaluable for your freedom, wealth and ultimately a successful life.

So, grab your café au lait & set out to conquer the world.

Happy Reading!

Devanshu Darmora
05/01/2013

A Snapshot of
THE ONE MINUTE MANAGER

When most people become a manager for the first time, they are more than a little unsure of themselves. Naturally, they often use speech and ways of doing things that they have seen others use. That's great if their role models are good, but can be terrible otherwise. "The One Minute Manager" provides a positive role model for those who have not yet seen one, and good reinforcement for those who have not seen one lately.

The One Minute Manager

—Inspired by Kenneth Blanchard & Spencer Johnson

"If you pick the right people and give them the opportunity to spread their wings—and put compensation as a carrier behind it—you almost don't have to manage them."

—Jack Welch,
Former CEO of General Electric

Most managers while dealing with their subordinates grope forward with all the cocksureness of a foot soldier crossing a foggy minefield. As per the authors, our difficulty with learning how to be a manager is probably not to do with "management" per se, but the way the learning is presented to us and the different ways in which we all like to learn. One minute management is a perennially popular, internationally proven approach to effective management that both in a philosophical and practical sense, strikes at the very roots of achieving significant, overall managerial performance and productivity. Like a piece of blotting paper, it absorbs in simple yet profound ways the essence of managership.

After going through this book, you'll master a powerful leadership style that helps you find the strengths in your people and bring out their full potential to achieve much more with far less time and resources. The lessons are imparted in the form of an interesting parable about a young man who has set out looking for world-class management skills. In his search, the aspirant manager gets caught between the two extremes of the scientific and human relations schools: some managers get good results (but at a price that a few colleagues and subordinates seem willing to support) whilst other managers (whose people really like them) have results that leave much to be desired. As luck would have it, this young man comes across the One Minute Manager, a willing mentor who unlike other conventional managers seems to have things well in control. During the course of the story that follows, the One Minute Manager teaches three simple precepts, which he establishes with his employees: One Minute Goal Setting, One Minute Praising, and One Minute Reprimands. In doing so, he debunks the myth that management has to be hard, or that you can only be a nice guy or a 'company' guy. You can be both. The parable finally ends with the ambitious manager adopting and exploiting the OMM philosophy and gradually attaining great success and fame, like his tutor.

Maybe you are a first-time manager or one with 20 years of experience, whatever your professional life-stage, you no longer have to feel stressed and work all those extra hours. Comparable to a Chicken Soup for the Managerial Soul book, OMM is a great relational management tool to build upon. The secrets revealed below are not contrived, artificial mechanisms that interfere with our natural personalities. Instead, the entire idea can be implemented by following a few simple behavioral modifications that feel natural and are easy to adopt and maintain.

The First Secret: Set 1-minute goals with your subordinates

OMM requires regular meetings between managers and their staff where goals are agreed on, written down in a brief statement, and time and again reviewed to ensure that productivity is adhered to. Most managers know what they want their people to do. They just don't bother to tell their staff in a way they would understand. They assume their subordinates should know. One should never assume when it comes down to goal setting. Say, for example, if you ask your housecleaner to clean your room, she would not know whether to sweep the room, place everything in order, arrange the books in the shelf or do all the three. On the other hand, if you ask her to sweep the room and arrange the books, she would know exactly what she needs to do. As a result, both you and your cleaning lady are satisfied with the job. One could argue that the direct reports should ask but they don't want to look stupid in front of their bosses and aren't you always busy rushing here and there anyway. So instead of clarifying, these poor fellows decide to find their own answers or lose enthusiasm because they simply don't understand the rules of the game. It's the same as watching football. How many people would sit in front of their televisions sets and watch two teams run up and down the field if there were no goals to shoot at or any way to score?

> One of the most important aspects of effective goals, which often gets lost in the planning process, is that they should inspire. Martin Luther King didn't say, "I have a strategic plan." He said, "I have a dream." Everything his followers did was a step to achieving his dream.

It is amazing how often people are told about the power of goal setting, yet how some times there is agreement between what a person says their job involves and what their manager says it involves. Perhaps you should try a little experiment. Pick two members of your team - a star and an average performer. Next, ask them to write down what their main goals for their jobs are, what their responsibilities and accountabilities are, and what are the important tasks they do that contribute to those goals. Then you do the exercise yourself for their roles and compare the lists. You're definitely in for a surprise. In fact, research proves that of all the Pareto's vital few variables that impact employee productivity, performance planning figures at the top. So, there's no getting away from it. As a manager, it is your responsibility to clarify goals of each and every person who reports directly to you and to approve goals for the employees at the next level down. Identify what the present level of performance is on each goal and then what level is desired. The discrepancy between the actual and the desired goal becomes the area for improvement. Then choose a pragmatic deadline for reaching that new level. The secret of one-minute goals is simply to agree on your team's goals upfront so that you know what a good performance would look like. Also, once you have pinned down your goals, ensure that you write out each of them on a single sheet of paper or index card and make several copies of it so that you and your subordinates can refer to them daily for continued clarification.

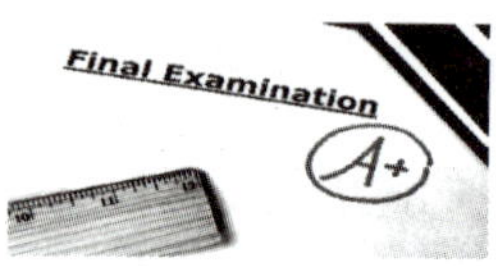

Setting people up for success

Ken Blanchard shares one of his own experiences as a college professor. As a teacher, Ken was always in trouble. What drove the faculty crazy more than anything was that at the beginning of every semester, he gave his students the end semester exam. When the faculty found out about this, they called him in and asked, "What are you doing?" Ken said, "I thought we were supposed to teach these students." The faculty said, "You are, but don't give them the final exam ahead of time!" Ken said, "Not only will I give them the final exam ahead of time, what do you think, I'll do throughout the semester? I'll teach them the answers so that when they get to the final exam, they'll get A's." In Ken's mind, helping students to get an "A" was more important than evaluating their performance. He was more concerned with making sure they learned the material than ranking them along a normal distribution curve for grading purposes.

Leading people to be their best also means that your staff should be so prepared for accomplishing their goals that, if need be, they can go on autopilot. What it does is - it frees them up mentally to be alert to the possibility of making something big happen. They must also be so prepared that when the big play comes, they should want the ball coming their way. Nobody wishes for a defensive halfback who's praying that the opponent throws the ball to the other side of the field. A prepared employee craves for the action coming his or her way. If an important customer must be served, he wants to be the one to take on that challenge.

Delivering well-crafted, targeted feedback

Employees need specific and descriptive feedback, if they are going to master a skill or achieve a goal. But this type of one-to-one feedback is in short supply in most organizations. The reason is twofold. First, managers avoid giving feedback because they do not have a clear process to follow, and second, they are concerned that without such a process, the conversation might be perceived as evaluative and judgmental. The result is hesitation on the part of the manager, that results in the feedback session never occurring. On the other hand, most managers, who do give occasional feedbacks, base it on their own need to be seen as an expert or to control the environment. To address this, OMM recommends that managers ask themselves, "Is this my need to give this feedback or am I giving this feedback because the other person's performance will actually benefit as a result of it?" Once a manager is clear on the purpose of the feedback, the next step is to provide the type of feedback that will best meet the needs of the recipient. The secret to helping an employee excel through well-crafted feedbacks lies in the details: the best way to capture the details is to meet frequently and informally, while the specifics of a success or a disappointment are fresh in the memory. But you can't achieve this by merely sitting inside your corner office. You have to be out and about, talking to your staff and co-workers, and seeing and hearing what's going on out there. It's called "Management By Walking Around", or MBWA. If you're new to MBWA, your staff won't know how to react and you may get stiff, monosyllabic answers at first (no one wants the boss standing over them and watching what they do). Persevere and show genuine interest, MBWA does require high amounts of emotional intelligence, awareness, and acuity to gauge where people are. And while it takes time initially, it doesn't have to be time consuming. When employees feel that a leader is building their skills, moving them towards autonomy, and acting as a teacher, mentor, and career champion, it creates a connection. It is this connection that impacts an employee's engagement level and all facets of an employee's performance. Just a few minutes on a regular basis can make all the difference.

The Second Secret: Use 1-minute praising when goals are achieved

One can't say enough about the importance of praising. Yet most people are still managed by being basically left alone until they make a mistake that's noticeable, thereupon to be ridiculed by their bosses. You can call this a "leave-alone zap" management style or "Seagull management." Seagull managers fly in, make a lot of noise, dump on everyone, and then fly out. Wannabe One Minute Managers should instead put accent on the positive and catch people doing something right. And then praise them publicly for it where others can overhear it. Those who overhear will remember that doing the right thing, even if it is only a normal part of the job, brings praise. And they will aspire to mimic the behavior.

OMM insists that relaying feedback is the number one motivator. To support their argument, Ken Blanchard and Spencer Johnson give the following behavioral examples:

- Can you imagine standing a child up and saying "you walk" and when he falls down, pick him up and spank him and say, "I told you to walk." No, you stand the child up and the first day he wobbles a little bit and you get all excited and say, "He stood, he stood," and you hug and kiss the child. The next day he stands for a moment and maybe wobbles a step and you are all over him with kisses and hugs. Finally, the child, realizing that this is a pretty good deal, starts to wobble his legs more and more until he eventually walks.
- Think back the first time we ever asked for water, did we say "Could you please pour me a glass of water, I'm rather thirsty?" No. First we said, "wahha." And we were praised and cheered for that. Mom and dad jumped up and down, called grandma and grandpa and all that good stuff. Then, because our parents didn't want us ordering "wahha" when we were adults, what was "praised" was altered until it became closer to the desired result.
- Do you think that Sea World went into the ocean, held a rope out of the boat and magically found whales that would jump over it? Of course not! They capture a whale; bring it to the pool, then put a rope on the bottom of the pool. As and when the whale swims by the rope, it gets fed. Then they raise the rope. If the whale swims under it, it's not fed; over it and it gets fed. They continue raising the rope until it's above the water level, and guess what? The whale is jumping out of the water and splashing the first 10 rows of gleefully wet families.

These examples illustrate that the most important thing in training somebody to become a winner is to catch doing something right - in the beginning, something approximately right and gradually moving them towards the desired behavior. Yet, most firms are notorious for throwing their newly appointed recruits to the wolves, many times failing to provide even the most basic management training. We welcome them aboard, take them around to meet everybody and then we leave them alone. Not only do we not catch them doing anything approximately right; but periodically we haul them over the coal just to keep them moving. It's the most popular leadership style of all but indeed a wrong one.

One minute praising works well when you:

1. Tell people right from the start that you are going to let them know how they are doing.
2. Praise people immediately. Don't save praising for a holiday.
3. Praise in person, specifically pointing out what was done well. Just saying to someone, "good job," is nice but it is not very helpful because they do not know specifically what is good so that they could do it again.
4. Tell people how good you feel about what they did right, how it helps the organization and the other people who work there. Shake hands and touch people in a way that makes it clear that you support their success in the organization.

5. Be consistent—even if you're having a tough day/week, praise the positive. If the praise is delayed, insincere, or random, then the employee may think that the manager is being sarcastic or ungrateful, or is giving false praise.

> A one minute praising might sound like this: "Let me tell you how much I liked the report you turned in yesterday afternoon. It was right on target. I appreciate the close analysis of the resource implications, the long-term projections and the point-by-point attention to all the targets. This will help all of us to move the project ahead, which feels just great. Thanks!"

Such properly administered praising will positively reinforce the desired behavior and will keep your staff motivated and achieving.

What gets in the way of managers catching their people doing things right more often?

Most managers instinctively know that recognizing their people is important, but they are challenged by the dilemma of choosing between importance and urgency. For busy managers, the focus is on execution and performance, and reward and recognition take a back-seat. However, not taking the time to recognize and reward people can be shortsighted. Recognition is a deep-seated human need. If people aren't receiving the recognition they need, then trust, credibility, and connection with their leaders will diminish. Once that happens, performance suffers—slowly at first, in small, almost imperceptible ways—but then it starts to build. Eventually, you have people staying at work physically, but emotionally quitting.

Don't skimp when it comes to reward and recognition

These days, leaders are preoccupied with figuring out new strategies for cost control and revenue growth. Everyone is so focused on ensuring a successful recovery. While you do all the right things to lead your organization strategically and operationally out of these tough economic times, don't forget to take a minute to recognize the people working so hard alongside you.

A culture of praise and recognition needs to be established at the top. People at all levels in the organization need to feel cared for and recognized for the work they are doing. That's one of the keys to building a motivating culture. And that's one of the differentiators that will separate successful organizations from unsuccessful ones as we move along the path towards economic recovery.

Reward & Recognition on a Limited Budget

Just because money is tight, that doesn't mean you should put your company's reward and recognition efforts on hold. While money is important, it's not the only thing you have at your disposal. Listed below are some easier and low-cost ways of puffing up your employees:

1. E-mail from the president.
2. Allowed to attend a seminar of their choice.
3. "Highlighting Employee" section in company newsletter.
4. "Well Done" pens.
5. "Attaboy or Attagirl" stickers.
6. Paid time off.
7. Gift certificates to local restaurant or theater.
8. Flex time.
9. Selecting the workplace radio station for a week.
10. Care package to spouse or children of the employee.

Rewarding others for their effort is key to building rapport with your team and having them enjoy working with/for you. It works on all employees, whether they are newly assigned, in training, in transition from one position to another, or most senior and experienced. Sometimes, however, you see more problems than things going right. That's where the third leg of the OMM comes in.

The Third Secret: Use 1-minute reprimands when goals are not achieved

Most associates will hear some form of rant from their boss from time to time, although there are some who won't say anything and just store things up until the formal appraisal. Often it's water off a duck's back. Because employees don't have clear responsibilities and duties and because they don't receive one-minute praisings, they assume that the criticism during annual performance evaluation is just the way bosses act. That's no way to manage. While avoidance may be an appropriate course of action in some select cases, more often it is a managerial default position because the skills, or will, are not there to have the conversation that is needed. As managers feel that they lack the skills to have challenging conversations, they are concerned that they will do more damage to the relationship or to the project by addressing it openly, so they stew on all their negative responses and choose to avoid the problem and hope it clears up on its own. While the feeling of reluctance in delivering tough feedback is normal, managers have to be on guard that it doesn't lead to "avoidance syndrome." When this happens, a manager will shut down or withdraw from a situation instead of confronting it directly. This strategy may keep the lid on a situation in the short term, but in the long-term, damage is usually substantial with drops in productivity and morale due to ongoing conflict and disagreement. As per the authors, being honest with those around you also involves reprimanding them when a wrong has occurred, which means that you as a manager have to hold people accountable for their goof ups. Garry Ridge, President of WD-40 is so emphatic about this concept that he fired a poor performer's manager rather than the poor performer when he found out that the manager had done nothing to help that person and coach him.

But don't reprimand in public, save the negative comments for a more private time and place. Also never come down on learners or else you'll immobilize them. If you are dealing with somebody who knows better, who has performed a similar task well in the past, only then a one-minute reprimand might be appropriate. Job familiarization has made these workers aware of their ability to perform assigned tasks. However, managers need to exercise caution when considering reprimands for people who are new to the job, still in training, or simply inexperienced in handling a new task. In these instances, a one-minute manager will revise goals rather than reprimand. Bear in mind that people have the best of intention and that they are always doing the best that they can, given the information, skills, and competencies that they have at their disposal. So, never blame the person. One-minute reprimand separates the person from his behavior. Feelings are discussed so that behaviors can be analyzed and corrected. These discussions are intended to illustrate that the individual is not just his behavior, but he is the person managing his behavior. Thus, managers should not deal with their subordinate's last mistake as if it were representative of his entire behavior pattern.

A one minute reprimand might sound like this: "I want to give you a specific reaction to the report you turned in yesterday afternoon. I worry that the report lacks long-term projections. I'm disappointed that it doesn't take up all the targets point by point. In order to move the project ahead, we really need a finer-grained analysis. But, look, you do fine work for the group. I remember the initiative last month, which moved forward really well. Let's take another pass on this one and we will be there."

The author's definition of a one-minute reprimand also entails reassurance, both being equally important. This means, you have to play a drill sergeant first and then be an equally good cheerleader. You can't really afford to leave the latter out.

The first half of the reprimand:

1. Reprimand people immediately.
2. Tell people what they did wrong -- be specific.
3. Tell people how you feel about what they did wrong and in no uncertain terms.
4. Stop for a few minutes of uncomfortable silence to let them notice how you feel.

The second half of the reprimand:

5. Shake hands, or touch them in a way that lets them know you are honestly on their side. Touch is a very powerful message. People know immediately when you touch them whether you care about them, or whether you are just trying to find a new way to manipulate them.

6. Do not forget to remind how much you value them.
7. Reaffirm that you think well of them but not of their performance in this situation.
8. Realize that when reprimand is over, it is over. Don't bring it up again, not during that work day, not a few months later. Just let it lay and trust that one reprimand was enough. Imagine how demoralizing it is to an employee who is trying his best, messes up once, then works well for a month, only to have a mistake thrown at his face after he had atoned for it already.

The emotional deposit through second half of the reprimand makes the employee realize that you mean them no harm. What you are really delivering is tough love and trying to help. The beauty of one-minute reprimand is that as opposed to other establishmentarian ways of confronting poor performance that lead to nothing but emotional buildups it actually makes your staff feel better about their work.

Partnering Skills

Frontline leaders need to accurately diagnose the individual competence and motivation levels of his or her direct reports—is the direct report an eager beginner with the task? An overwhelmed employee with moderate skills for the task? Or an experienced veteran who has routinely handled this task successfully in the past? Each of these employees requires a different management style.

When beginning a new task on which they have little, if any, prior knowledge or experience, most individuals should be led by a Directing style. They need to know what to expect and how to do the task at hand. As the employee develops expertise, his or her competence and commitment fluctuate. People at this stage need a Coaching style—high direction to continue to build skills—as well as high support to address their low commitment. As competence continues to improve, most individuals go through a self-doubt state where they question whether they can perform the task on their own. These individuals need a Supporting style—they need to be listened to and encouraged but do not need much direction, since they have demonstrated competence for doing the task. Finally, at the last stage of development, employees demonstrate high levels of competence and commitment. The corresponding leadership style to use is Delegating—giving the employee increased autonomy because he or she has demonstrated both competence and commitment in performing the task.

As employees move from the enthusiastic beginner stage on a task, through disillusionment, then on to capable, but cautious, performance, and finally, to self-reliant achievement, managers need to shift from a directing style to a coaching style, then a supporting style, and finally, to a delegating leadership style.

But how should leadership style be modified when faced with a decline in performance? Just as improvements in performance prompt forward shifts in leadership style, decreases in performance require a shift backward in leadership style. If a highly committed and competent employee starts to decline in performance, you first want to find out why. This means moving from a delegating style to a more supporting style, where you listen and gather data. If you both agree that the direct report is still on top of the situation and can get performance back on track, you can return to a delegating leadership style. However, if you both agree that this performance situation needs more attention from you as the leader, you now can go to a coaching style, where you can provide closer supervision. Seldom, if ever, do you have to go all the way back to a directing style.

Becoming more coach-like

People are promoted not because they have demonstrated any kind of particular management skill, but because they have demonstrated extreme competence in their roles as individual contributors. Too often what these new managers do is just continue to do what they did really well—which is not what's needed in their new role. For many managers, solving problems is part of where they get their value. So it's really hard for some mangers to shift from telling and solving to asking and drawing out.

The result of managers only giving direction and solving problems is that people working for these types of managers don't grow and develop as quickly as they could. Instead of gaining skills and moving on to other assignments within the organization, these people are held in place. It also stymies the organization by keeping people at a restricted level rather than moving them towards self-reliance.

So how can organizations encourage their managers to be more coach-like? Here are a few suggestions to consider:

1. **Change mindsets:** Encourage managers to see coaching as a part of their job instead of a threat. Unlike the athletic model, where a coach stands on the sidelines and yells, in the Blanchard model, coaching means making the shift from telling people what to do to asking people for their ideas. If managers believe it is their responsibility to do all the thinking, or to be the only one who comes up with options, they won't get the benefit of others' ideas and solutions. But, if managers believe it is their responsibility to draw out options from others, they will benefit from the creative ideas that result when people are asked for their opinions rather than being told what to do. Instead of dreading the loss of people (promotion into a new position) he had worked to develop, a good manager considers it part of what makes him a valuable leader.

2. **Model coach-like behavior:** Organizations can promote coach-like behaviors in frontline managers by encouraging senior leaders to be more coach-like. If senior leadership fully

understands what coaching is and uses coaching as part of their management style, they can help actively develop the managers below them, so that those managers can then coach the teams they are working with.

3. **Provide incentives for managers to develop their people:** Coaching impacts the bottom line of an organization by improving morale, efficiency, and productivity. In the same way that managers are tracked and evaluated on their ability to manage results, they should also be tracked, evaluated, and rewarded on their ability to develop people. Managers, who develop people, feed the leadership pipeline. Many companies know they are going to be short on leaders in three to five years. If so, anyone, who can develop people that will feed into the succession pipeline, is hugely valuable.

Goal setting is all about making sure employees understand perfectly what their duties are, what is expected of them and that there are no surprises."

"The best minute I spend is the one I invest in people."

"Everyone is a potential winner. Some people are disguised as losers...Don't let their appearances fool you."

"If you are going to take out a long-term car loan, don't buy a short-term car."

"How on earth can you get results if it's not through people?"

"You really have only 3 choices as a manager":

1. First, you can hire winners. They are hard to find and they cost money.
2. Or, second, if you can't find a winner, you can hire someone with the potential to be a winner. Then you systematically train that person to become a winner. It's ironic; most companies spend 50%-70% of their money on people's salaries. And yet they spend less than 1% of their budget to train their people.
3. If you are not willing to do either of the first two (and I am continually amazed at the number of managers who won't spend the money to hire a winner or take the time to train someone to become a winner), then there is only the third choice left - prayer."

What kind of manager are you? Are you genuinely happy for your associates when they experience success, or are you always peering around the corner hoping no one is more successful than you? Are you secretly happy when they fail and get "egg on their face?" When this is the case, organizational productivity is certain to suffer. Why is it so difficult to be genuinely happy for the success of others? As children, we cheered for our teammates when they scored the winning run. With our own children we're always celebrating their achievements at soccer games, plays and spelling bees. The pity in corporate world today is that most of us die before we are fully born. Bear in mind that a good manager is not simply an observer but an active participant seeking not only his own growth but the development of those around him.

Short-sighted managers are the curse of any organization. They are constantly looking over their shoulders to see if anybody is gaining on them.	**Evil vs. Good**	The best managers delight in the success of their teams. They realize that their success depends on the achievements of everybody, and that the more the group achieves, the more they will grow and develop.

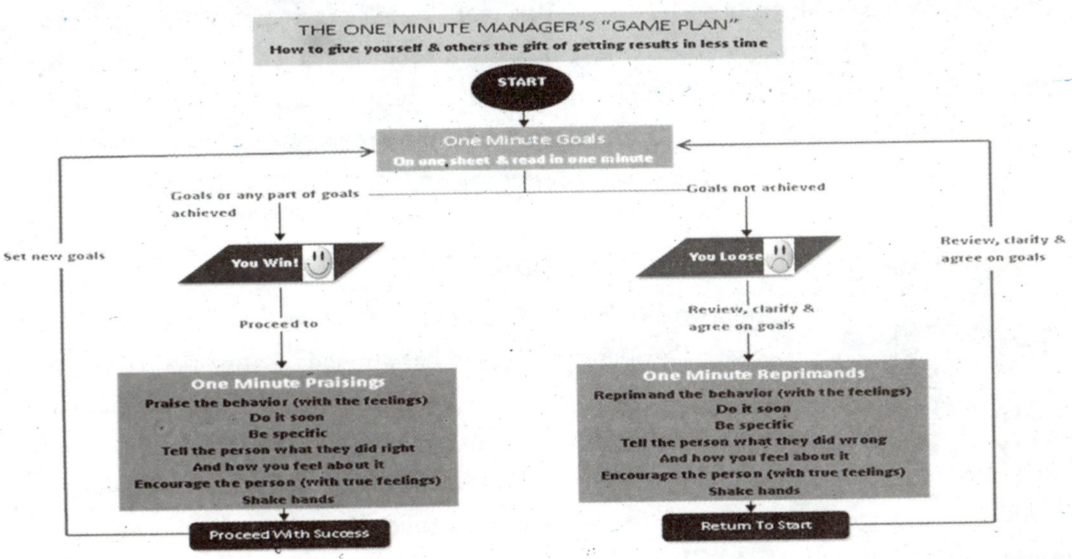

Lessons from the dog training book

Let's say, you have a dog named 'Rover'. When his behavior is good, you give him a reward. Sit Rover. Good boy! Here's a treat. Give the treat over and over and pretty soon Rover will sit the moment you ask him to plop down. But, you must keep repeating the treat. Have you ever watched handlers of show dogs in the ring? No matter how well the dog is behaving or how many dog shows they've been in, the dog always gets his treat. This means lots of petting, praising and excitement by the handler. Treats and recognition combined feed two of the animal's strongest needs: reward and affection. Contrastingly, what's your response when Rover refuses to conform? You grab his snout and hold it shut and say stuff like "No" or "Bad Dog", with a facial expression that shows disappointment and anger. Maybe he'll run away and avoid being around or he'll aggressively growl and snap. What do you do then? You take him to task and lock him up in his kennel. If you do that every time your dog gets into mischief, he will sooner or later stop and understand what "No" means.

Okay, let's translate these rules to workplace. How often do you take out your employees for a treat? I bet they're lucky if it's once a month. Sometimes it's never. Repeated positive reinforcement is the best way to enjoy repeated good behavior. The treats don't even have to be large. You can also encourage good behavior at work by simple compliments that are directed to reinforce specific actions—"I really liked the way you handled that difficult customer." The occasional lunch out or small thoughtful gift provides the icing on the cake. Contrary-wise, what do you do to cope with an employee, who pays no attention? Most managers prefer shutting their eyes because it's uncomfortable to give constructive feedback. But that doesn't serve either the employee or you well. Go back to the dog training book. Just like the disobeying dog who gets grounded in his kennel, employees need to be held on the hook when their performance is less than ideal. And they need to know it immediately because if you punish your dog for a puddle on the floor long after it's been made, how will he know what you're upset about.

The one minute parenting

In his two books on parenthood (One minute father & One minute mother), Dr Spencer Johnson has applied what works best in managing companies to raising a family. He asserts that it is not sufficient for adults to make important decisions on behalf of and in the best interests of their children. If not involved in the overall decision-making process, they do not feel obligated to follow the rules. In the method of one minute goal setting as proposed by him, rules are not set by the parents alone. Instead, they are agreed upon in the family meetings where everyone participates and helps in the decision-making, even the youngest family members. Such strategies not only help build their self-confidence and esteem, but also train them to be responsible for their actions from an early age. Making children accountable for their decisions in turn involves them directly into their upbringing and takes a great deal of burden off the parents. It also makes it difficult for them to disobey and rebel against the rules; after all, they set the rules themselves. Of course, common sense dictates that not all issues be left to children's discretion. For example, if they refuse to take certain medication because they do not like its taste, we should give it to them regardless. However, many issues can be resolved more easily and to the satisfaction of both parents and kids if children's views are taken into account. When you review the goals during the family meeting, or anytime you notice your children are getting closer to achieving their goals, you call them and give them a one-minute praising. This simple yet very effective method lets them know that their efforts are noticed and appreciated, and the good feeling it gives encourages them to do even better. On a different note, while the one-minute reprimand makes children feel chastised and punished, it also tells them that although their behavior made you angry, you still love them and you believe they have the ability to exhibit better behavior in future. They are left feeling that their behavior was bad, not them, that they have their parent's love and confidence, and that they can do better.

If we accept that we can influence and empower our children, we will no longer feel that we must ground them and make them mind by taking away their privileges. With a strong, loving foundation in place, we can begin to give our children the opportunity to make choices and decisions, all the while providing a structure on which they can build, increasing their responsibilities and decision-making opportunities as they grow.

If a hammer is the only tool you have, every problem starts looking like a nail

OMM does not mean that it takes a minute to do all the kinds of things you need to do as a manager. It is just a way to say that being a manager is not as complicated as people would have you believe. The problem is that all too often we seem concerned about the husk of management and disregard the kernel. Not so with OMM. A One Minute Manager does not cloak himself in the garb of a crusader going off to do battle in search of the Holy Grail. Diametrical to other perturbed managers, he gives little advice, provides options, gets to know his subordinates on a gut level and is capable of having solid relationships with them. He believes that employees must be accountable for their work lives, but he does not live their lives for them. He thinks of himself as the sixth man in a basketball team. When his subordinates want to call him into the game, he is happy to play, but if they don't need him, he is also happy to stay on the sidelines and cheer.

You must, just for once, have a shot at One Minute Management. For all you know, you may like it. You may even find it doing wonders. To begin with, try to visualize what your gut instincts would have been in the same situations the One Minute Manager describes. Otherwise, you may miss the point of how much your behavior needs to change. The first time I read The One Minute

Manager, I remember thinking "If only I could remember all these good ideas and what to say and what questions to ask". On rereading it, I can say "Yes, I do these things naturally". That is why this McDonaldized fast food approach to coaching people is so powerful. It describes what effective people in business do naturally.

❑❑❑

IMPORTANT NOTE

This summary culls the content of the book - "The One Minute Manager" down to its essence so that even an average reader can sensitize himself to it, sparing him with the time consuming details. In case you feel a need to further explore this topic, the author recommends reading the original work published by "Harper Collins".

A Snapshot of
THE TIPPING POINT

Spreading a marketing message, promoting political change and solving social ills all require a deep understanding of human behavior. 'The Tipping Point' to this end purports to answer two questions, "Why is it that some ideas or behaviors or products start epidemics and others don't? And what can we do to deliberately start and control positive epidemics of our own?" It's a fascinating book that makes you see the world in a different way.

The Tipping Point

(Inspired by Malcolm Gladwell)

Intro

"It takes a big idea to attract the attention of consumers and get them to buy your product. Unless your advertising contains a big idea, it will pass like a ship in the night. I doubt if more than one campaign in a hundred contains a big idea".

—David Ogilvy,
Founder Ogilvy and Mather, Acknowledged as 'Father of Advertising'

From time to time, we all confront a social or cultural enigma. A cheesy game show that lets contestants call their friends or poll the audience for answers, becomes the biggest thing on television. A once obscure book gets to be all the rage. For Malcolm Gladwell, such phenomena are not merely the result of luck, fat budgets, and changing demographics. Instead, a distinct set of factors and players help to create what he calls a "tipping point" that turns an idea, person, or product into the object of a hot trend that the author likens to an epidemic. What's really fascinating about this book is that Gladwell takes a series of historical events which we all know, and then, based on his theoretical underpinnings, he illustrates how they're largely unconscious contagions with far more subtle undercurrents at work. Thus, showing us a road map to change, with a profoundly hopeful message that one imaginative person applying a well-placed lever can move the world and shape and engineer the course of social epidemics.

The Tipping Point, whilst applying social psychology to "real world" situations, neatly explores the notion of simple cause and effect. Derived from the ideas in epidemiology (study of the spread of viruses/diseases), it's a commonsensical way of making sense of this maverick world. To understand the concept better, let's take the example of a flu epidemic, as provided by Gladwell. Assume that a standard flu has a transmission rate of about 2%, meaning that one in fifty people, who interact with an ill person in the course of his disease, will catch the bug himself. Suppose, fifty is also exactly the number of people an average Manhattanite in the course of riding the subways and mingling with colleagues at work comes into contact with every day. What we have, then, given the recovery rate, is a disease in equilibrium. Every day, each carrier passes on the virus to a new person. And the next day those thousand newly infected people pass on the virus to another thousand people but the overall proportion of flue infected people in the population remains the same.

Now imagine that the Christmas season arrives. The subways and buses get more crowded with tourists and shoppers, and instead of running into an even fifty people a day, an average Manhattanite now has close contact with, say, fifty-five people a day. That may not sound like much of a difference, but for our flu bug, it is critical. The number of people a single flu victim infects now increases to fifty-five divided by fifty, or 1.1. So for every ten flu victims, an extra person is infected. Eleven infect 12.1. 12.1 infect 13.3 and so on up, the figure rises higher every day, until Manhattan has a full-blown flu epidemic on its hands by the Christmas Eve. In the language of epidemiologists, fifty would be the "tipping point" for this epidemic, the point at which a low level flu outbreak turns into a public health crisis.

Every epidemic has its tipping point, and to fight an epidemic, you need to understand what that point is. Take AIDS, for example. Since the late eighties, the number of people in the United States, who die of AIDS every year, has been almost steady at forty thousand, which is exactly the same as the number of people who are estimated to become infected with H.I.V. every year. In other words, AIDS is in the same self-perpetuating phase that our flu epidemic was in, early on; on the average, each person who dies of aids infects, in the course of his or her lifetime, one new person. If the number of new infections increases just a bit—if the average H.I.V. carrier passes on the virus to slightly more than one person then the epidemic can tip upward. On the other hand, even a small decrease in new infections can cause the epidemic to nosedive. That's the surprising thing about epidemics. They don't behave the way we think they will behave. Suppose, the number of new H.I.V. infections each year was a hundred thousand, and by some heroic aids—education effort you managed to cut that in half. You would expect the size of the epidemic to also be cut in half, right? This is what scientists call a linear assumption—the expectation that every extra increment of effort will produce a corresponding improvement in result. But epidemics aren't linear. Improvement does not correspond directly to effort. All that matters is the tipping point, and because fifty thousand is still above that point, all these heroics will come to naught. The epidemic would still rise. This is the fundamental lesson of non-linearity. When it comes to fighting epidemics, small changes like bringing new infections down to thirty thousand from forty thousand can have huge effects. And large changes like reducing new infections to fifty thousand from a hundred thousand, can have small effects. It all depends on which half of the tipping point the epidemic is presently trending. So, whenever confronted with an outbreak, the starting point should always be a number crunching exercise aimed at estimating its tipping point.

Gladwell argues that the best way to understand the emergence of fashion trends, the ebb and flow of crime waves, the unexpected transformation of an unknown movie made, on a shoestring budget, into a blockbuster hit, making hundreds of millions of dollars or any other mysterious changes that mark our everyday life, is to view them as epidemics. If you carefully analyze why some trends achieve exponential popularity while others sputter and fade into oblivion, you will find that everytime the patterns and processes involved are strikingly similar. Building on to this argument, the book begins by discussing the inexplicable resurgence of then-terminally-uncool Hush Puppies shoes among a handful of hipsters in Manhattan's cutting-edge enclaves in the 1990s, a trend which soon spread across the United States and resulted in exponential increases in the company's sales. Using this case as an introduction to the book's analytical theme, the author states that he will identify, dissect and explain the mechanisms by which certain trends take hold, while others crash.

Chapter 1: The Three Rules of Epidemics

There is more than one way to tip an epidemic. Epidemics are a function of the people who transmit infectious agents, the infectious agent itself, and the environment in which the infectious agent is operating. And when an epidemic tips, when it is jolted out of equilibrium, it tips because something has happened, some change has occurred in one (or two or three) of those areas. These three agents of change are what Gladwell calls the Law of the Few, the Stickiness Factor, and the Power of Context.

The Law of the Few: It contends that the spread of any new product or service is determined by the initial adoption patterns of a small group of socially infectious early-adopters. Drawing from social network science and research into the diffusion of innovations, Gladwell explains how a combination of word of mouth advocacy and the copycat effect allows connected and respected early-adopters to drive product diffusion and act as gate-keepers to mass-market adoption. The infectious power of this special subset of early-adopters can be explained by their position as social hubs in peer networks, connecting everybody to everybody by *six degrees of separation, thereby connecting businesses to their mass market. This network centrality combined with an early-adopter profile provides these socially infectious connectors with a viral capability similar to that of celebrities and expert opinion leaders.

The few that lead you to the many…… (Target Marketing Redefined)

It follows from The Law of the Few that we, as marketers, should be seeking to develop special relationships with the socially infectious connectors, focusing innovation on preferentially satisfying their needs rather than simply pandering to the fickle desires of the mass-market herd itself.

> The target audience for any marketing campaign is typically defined by factors such as age, sex, geographic location and income. But what if those factors aren't enough? Furthermore, what if they're not relevant to reaching the tipping point?

'Focus your energies on the trendsetters, the socially promiscuous & those with the power to influence and the mass will follow' is the Tipping Point marketing mantra. By recruiting these 'consumers that count' into research partnerships and panels, just as Procter and Gamble are doing with their ground-breaking Tremor panel, marketers can help generate the goodwill, involvement and positive word of mouth necessary for a new product or service to spread contagiously through a target population. And keep in mind—this concept applies as much to the internal marketing programs your company directs at its employees as it does to the external campaigns it promotes to consumers and other businesses. Gaining buy-in to a new initiative among the inner circle of employee influencers can be the difference between success or failure of that program.

"Six Degrees of Separation" study by social psychologist Stanley Milgram

Milgram distributed letters to 160 students in Nebraska, with instructions that they be sent to a stockbroker in Boston (not personally known to them) by passing the letters to anyone else that they believed to be socially closer to the target. The study found that it took an average of six links to deliver each letter. Of particular interest to Gladwell was the finding that just three friends of the stockbroker provided the final link for half of the letters that arrived successfully.

The Stickiness Factor: The second factor that influences the spread of any infectious agent through a population is its intrinsic contagiousness. Gladwell calls this 'The Stickiness Factor', borrowing from the media term used to describe how 'sticky' a channel or program is, which depends on how 'glued' to it we are. The stickiness factor says that there are specific ways of making a message memorable. Think about a song that you couldn't get out of your head or that television commercial you still remember from when you were a kid. Can you pinpoint what it is you think made them "sticky"? If you pay careful attention, you will notice that relatively simple changes in the presentation and structuring of information can dramatically enhance the stickiness of any message. Relevance, telling a story, eliciting interaction and repetition are a few of the key factors that lead to 'stickiness.' All said and done, connections and the personal character of the people trying to spread a message can certainly help it spread, but if the message is not worth spreading, it will go in one ear and out the other.

The Power of Context: Thirdly and finally, products and behaviours spread far and wide only when they fit the context in which they are launched. For example, the wave of crime in New York subway came to an abrupt halt by simply removing the graffiti from trains and clamping down on fare-dodging. The context changed and so did the people. We must understand that most human behavior is situational, contrary to the commonly held belief that behavior is attributable to one's innate character, disposition, personality or genes. Consumers are contextual chameleons and will adopt your product if it fits the context, situation or occasion in which they find themselves. For example, if Gladwell were to buy a used vinyl jacket from a thrift shop, many young people might look at him like he stepped out of a time machine. But, put those same young people in New York City, and have them witness a bunch of east village hipsters wearing that same jacket, and all of a sudden, the jacket is cool and sought-after. The jacket hasn't changed, only the context of the environment, in which the jacket was seen, has changed.

These three rules of epidemics provide us with direction for how to go about reaching a tipping point. The balance of this book summary will take these ideas and apply them to other puzzling situations and epidemics from the world around us. How do these three rules help us understand teenage smoking, for example, or the phenomenon of word of mouth, or crime, or the rise of some TV shows? The answers may surprise you.

Chapter 2: The Law of the Few: Connectors, Mavens, and Salesmen

In making his case for "The Law of the Few," Gladwell reveals the surprisingly large role a small cadre of influencers play in reaching tipping points. Each of these players, whom he calls Connectors, Mavens, and Salespeople, can serve to ignite a cause in their own unique way – whether it's introducing a new product, enrolling others in a project, or getting the word out about an important issue—but first you have to identify them, then you need to create the right marketing message, and then you need to communicate that message to them in an appropriate and effective way. With any luck, you'll infect them with your message and they'll take care of spreading it to the rest of the population.

- **Connectors** embody the maxim "it's not what you know but who you know?" Connectors are socialites who have ties in many different realms and act as conduits between them, helping to engender connections, relationships, and "cross-fertilization" that otherwise might not have ever occurred. They are rare in society, but maintain many more times the number of relationships than an average person does. In networking terms (as described by Granovetter) connectors are the master of "weak ties" – that is, they consistently interact with what we might call acquaintances. As information travels through networks, two things tend to happen. First, the information is highly likely to come in contact with a connector—much more likely than coming in contact with someone who is not so connected. Second, if the information engages the connector's interest, he or she will distribute it to a huge number of other individuals in a short period of time, creating a tipping point. Gladwell cites the example of one such connector named Paul Revere, who, during the American independence movement, rode north of Boston one night warning that "the British are coming," and this was enough to get the people mobilized and ready to resist the British advance the next day.

A similar errand to other towns by his countryman, William Dawes that same night did not yield any result.

- **Mavens** are the databank; they know everything there is to know about a certain topic. But they have two additional features that make them different from ordinary experts: they love to share information and are trusted by those who know them. They're not necessarily a hub in a network like a connector is, we can view, This is why Gladwell focuses most of his practical suggestions for spreading messages on finding Mavens. Connectors can then transfer the advice of a maven across social boundaries that a maven might not be able to breach. Gizmodo is one such example of a gadget maven. It is a blog that gives juicy inside info about a variety of electronic devices, as well as all sorts of things gadget geeks might enjoy. Started in 2002, Gizmodo has grown to be Gawker Media's largest blog, bringing in upwards of 100 million page views a month in traffic.

- **Salesmen** are the quintessential persuaders, who can get people to make decisions and take actions that they ordinarily wouldn't take if left to themselves. Their ability to persuade makes them strong carriers of infectious ideas, concepts, trends and changes. Think about the last time you were in a store and what you liked or didn't like about the retail person assisting you. Have you ever felt suckered into buying something and recognized the only reason you bought an item was because of the person selling it to you? They aren't all in retail, of course. I was sold on market research as a professional career choice by my brilliant teacher, who was also in his own ways a salesman. By the same token, if Barak Obama were to step back in time to the 1800's, he would have been one of the most prolific snake oil salesmen of all times. He could have convinced any crowd that his product could, cure baldness, help women get pregnant, cure arthritis, mixed in feed fatten cattle overnight, help the skinny gain weight and the fat lose it.

Food for thought: What would you describe yourself as - a connecter, maven or salesman? Think of the people you know and who out of them best exemplifies these categories and why. Is the word-of-mouth phenomenon a strictly organic process or can it be manipulated? Do products circulate via word-of- mouth solely based on their merit and impact on the consumer or is it possible for marketers to create buzz from people paid to do so? Would this work or fail as soon as the 'word' got beyond the 'fixed' transmitters?

Are Connectors Really Contagious? An Experiment

In December 2003, Paul Marsden of the London School of Economics tested the idea that connectors are indeed socially infectious in a field experiment on the preferences for Coke or Pepsi. To do this a student connector was recruited using a simple screening questionnaire based on the ACTIVE profile, to which were added two further criteria for social infectiousness from the psychology of influence - elevated social status among peers and physical attractiveness. The connector was then asked to administer 100 street corner questionnaires in Houghton Street, London, to investigate student opinion on the UK government's new plans to introduce variable university fees. Whilst administering the first 50 questionnaires, the supposedly infectious connector was instructed to be visibly drinking a can of Coke and for the final 50 questionnaires a can of Pepsi, although no mention of this or the brands was to be made. At the end of each interview, the connector was asked to offer a free can of Coke or Pepsi to participants as a thank you for participation.

Would mere exposure to the visible adoption of Coke or Pepsi by our connector (independent variable) have an infectious influence on the choice of respondents (dependant variable), or would, as the null hypothesis suggested, their preferences be unaffected by what the connector happened to be drinking?

Results As expected, when the socially infectious connector was drinking Coke, more people chose Coke (72%), and when he was drinking Pepsi, more people chose Pepsi (54%). The extent of the infectious influence was significant, even reversing the overall pattern of preference for Coke or Pepsi. A chi-square test (chi-square value = 6.986) rejected, with a very high level of significance ($p < .01$), the possibility that this outcome could have been produced by chance, allowing us to add further evidence in support of the Tipping Point model that connectors do indeed have a significant infectious influence on the preferences of those exposed to them.

To further verify that this infectious power of suggestion is specific to connectors, the experiment was replicated the following day, this time using a non-connector (without an ACTIVE profile) as the interviewer. As expected, the non-connector had no significant infectious influence on respondents; in fact people were less likely to choose Coke when exposed to the interviewer drinking Coke and less likely to choose Pepsi when exposed to the interviewer drinking Pepsi. The implication for marketers is uncomfortable but clear: Not all consumers are created equal. Some are more equal than others. By preferentially partnering the infectious 'Few', we will be focusing on the 'consumers that count', addressing the right needs of the right people who have the power to unleash an epidemic of demand for our products and services.

Chapter 3: The Stickiness Factor: Sesame Street, Blue's Clues & the Educational Virus

The non-stop blitz of advertising messages has created a stickiness problem. Media Dynamics (a New York based firm), estimates that an average American is exposed to 254 different commercial

messages in a single day. There are billions of websites vying for your browsing time. Cable systems routinely carry hundreds of channels of programming. A glance inside the magazine section of any Barnes & Noble bookstore will reveal the thousands of magazines and periodicals that come out each month. In the face of such information overload, consumers simply don't remember much of what they are told, read or watch. But there are simple ways to enhance and engineer stickiness into your marketing collateral, reveals Gladwell. The trick is to package information so as to engage your target audience in ways that they find to be informative and entertaining. This is how the National Milk Mustache "got milk?" Campaign became one of the most recognized and respected advertising campaigns, having earned a place in the US advertising history. As the "umbrella" campaign for print, radio and TV advertising, as well as public relations, promotions and other initiatives, the "got milk?" message is one that's on everyone's lips across the U.S. Since its inception over 10 years ago, this fun and compelling message has helped boost awareness of the nutritional aspects of milk, and was the impetus to expand the availability of milk to more consumers than ever before. Likewise, many of such stick worthy advertising campaigns have become part of our collective consciousness and have in fact taken on a life of their own. But advertising slogans are not the only things that rely upon stickiness for success. Teachers look for ways to provide stickiness in their lessons. Television shows try to find ways to get viewers hooked. Columnists try to change readers' opinions on policy issues. People trying to make changes in organizations hunt for ways of presenting the change so that its features become contagious. All kinds of potential fads exist around us, but only sticky ones survive the test of clutter.

Big Bird, meeting First Lady Pat Nixon at the White House in 1970.

An interesting element of stickiness is the fact that it is often counterintuitive, or contradictory to the prevailing conventional wisdom. To illustrate this point, Gladwell undertakes an in-depth discussion of the evolution of children's television between the 1960s and the 2000s. The creators of children's educational television Sesame Street and the Blue's Clues had some powerful intuitions about how to reach and influence young minds. But when they made the effort to measure the impact of their intuitions, they discovered many important cases where they were wrong. You will be surprised to know that initially, the child psychologists advising Sesame Street said that mixing fantasy and reality would confuse children. To investigate this further, the Sesame Street creators came up with a way to measure the attention paid by children to the show. They set up a shiny blinky light show next to the TV and noted when the kids were distracted by it. When there were just people talking to people, the kids were easily distracted. When the muppets were brought in and interacted with the people, the kids paid attention. The producers literally called up their psychologist advisors and told them they were going to go against advice. Imagine what Sesame Street would have been like without Big Bird talking to Mr. Hooper? Chances are if they'd not made that courageous break with the best intuition of the time, we'd not have a Sesame Street to remember.

Years later, Blue's Clues did Sesame Street one better. Based on the research of theorists like Daniel Anderson of the University of Massachusetts (who served as a consultant for Blue's Clues), the producers set out to develop a show that took advantage of children being intellectually and behaviorally active when watching television. Research since Sesame Street had changed how attention span in young children was perceived. Sesame Street was developed with the understanding that children have short attention spans, so the show was designed in a magazine-like format, in which each episode was made up of a variety of segments and the content was presented pretty much on a one-way conversational format. However, Blue's Clues creators found out that if children were more involved in the action of what they were viewing, they would attend to its content longer than previously expected and learn more. Direct, qualitative evidence from watching kids as they watched the TV programs also showed that kids learn better through repetition. But, kids don't always like repetition. Whatever they are watching has to be complex enough to allow repeated exposure for deeper levels of comprehension. At the same time, it should not be so complex that it baffles the children and turns them off. So, Blue's Clues dropped the traditional magazine like narrative format and instead decided to tell one story, beginning to end, camera moving left-to-right like reading a storybook, transitions from scene to scene as obvious as the turning of a page. Every episode of Blue's Clues was structured in this way. Its pace was deliberate and its material was presented clearly. One way this was done was through the use of pauses—"long enough to give the youngest time to think, short enough for the oldest not to get bored." The creators of Blue's Clues provided their viewers with more authentic learning opportunities by placing problem-solving tasks in the context of storytelling techniques, slowly increasing the difficulty of these assignments, and by inviting their direct involvement.

Steve and Blue with friends, Mr. Salt, Mrs. Pepper, and Paprika.

Like Sesame Street (a multi-Emmy-Award winning American educational children's television series and a pioneer of the contemporary educational television standard), Blue's Clues was also a "smash hit." Within eighteen months of its premiere, "virtually 100% of preschoolers' parents knew about Blue's Clues," an awareness comparable to "top-tier" shows like the 30-year-old Sesame Street. It became the highest-rated show for preschoolers on commercial television and its "dubbed" American version is now shown in over sixty countries. The show's extensive use of research in its development and production process has inspired several research projects that have provided evidence for its efficacy as a learning tool.

Most of us think of Sesame Street and Blue's Clues as purely the result of the creative genius of people like Jim Henson and Frank Oz. But the truth is that they were carefully and painstaking engineered, down to the smallest details. Also in both cases, the tweaks that both sets of creators used were counterintuitive. For "Sesame Street," crossing the assumed line between fantasy and reality by placing Muppets and people on the screen together made the content more compelling to kids. In the case of "Blue's Clues," the tweak was a scheduling change that went against the grain. By airing the same show five days in a row as opposed to running a new show every day, Blue's Clues built confidence among kids over time and became more compelling as the week advanced. Media Planners should take a cue from the two TV shows and do what they can to obtain direct qualitative evidence on environments that have the potential to be sticky. They may want to take a few steps back in creating plans or reconsider their potential benefits from a fresh perspective and try to identify the places where a little tweak can create bigger marketplace impact for their brands.

Food for thought: We have become overwhelmed by marketers clamoring for our attention. Has the excessive amount of choice proved counter-productive for consumerism? For instance, walking down the cereal aisle at the supermarket, do you:

A. Buy way more than you need after spotting 3 new attractive, discounted products.

B. Head straight to your regular brand, walking out with the same cereal you have had since you were a kid.

C. Become paralyzed with indecision and leave after 2 hours with a loaf of bread.

What are some of the desperate measures taken by advertisers, publicists and celebrities to get noticed and stay in the limelight? How has the level of shock tactics used to grab public attention escalated and changed over time? What about the commercial we dislike and we only recall because it irritated us so intensely? Haven't the advertisers fulfilled their purpose by the sheer fact you remember their commercial? Does this mean that the cliché "even bad publicity is good publicity" is right? If something gets noticed and sticks in the viewer's mind, then does the nature of the message not matter? And finally, do we risk to become totally desensitized as a culture, immune to the eyebrow-raising, attention-grabbing ploys of marketers?

In my mind, Al Gore is a star student of Malcolm Gladwell. The man who introduces himself in his film by saying, "Hi, I'm Al Gore, I used to be the next president of the United States," was able to do for his viewers what the makers of Blue's Clues & Sesame Street did for kids. Using illustrative flow charts and expert interviews, he finally found a way of making climate change understandable and, therefore, real.

Chapter 4: The Power of Context (Part One): Bernie Goetz and Rise and Fall of New York

The Power of context infers that epidemics are sensitive to the conditions and circumstances of the times and places in which they occur. Think of examples of human behavior as a function of social context. Are certain individuals more sensitive to their environment than others? How often or to what extent does the environment dictate your behavior, i.e., your conduct when at the opera versus being at a baseball game?

If the environment or historical moment in which a trend is introduced is not right, it is not as likely that the tipping point will be attained. To illustrate power of context, the author takes on the historic 1990s New York City crime decline. Although Gladwell acknowledges that a wide variety of complex factors and variables likely played their role in sparking the dramatic dip, he argues convincingly that it was a few small but influential changes in the environment of the city that allowed these factors to tip into a major reduction in crime rate. Inspired from the mid-1980s work of James Q Wilson & George Kelling, a number of New York City agencies began to make decisions based on the Broken Windows theory, which held that minor, unchecked signs of deterioration in a neighborhood or community could, over time, result in major declines in the quality of living. Thus, even relatively trivial problems like graffiti, public disorder, and aggressive panhandling are all the equivalent of broken windows and communicate a lack of control, emboldening criminals, upsetting law-abiding citizens, and plunging the neighborhood into a downward "spiral of urban decay." To reverse these trends, city authorities started focusing on seemingly small goals like painting over graffiti, cracking down on subway toll skippers, and dissuading public acts of degeneracy. And the results were astonishing—violent crime declined by more than 56 percent in the city, compared to about 28 percent in the nation as a whole. Property crimes tumbled by about 65 percent as against 26 percent nationally.

The shooting incident on the subway between Goetz and the four youths had very little to do with the psychological pathology as well as with their background and poverty. It had everything to do with the message sent by the graffiti on the walls and the disorder at the turnstiles.

Obviously murder and graffiti are two vastly different crimes. But they are part of the same continuum, and a climate that tolerates one is more likely to tolerate the other.

Food for thought: Most conservative theories say that the criminal is a personality type whereas the Broken Windows theory and Power of Context suggest the opposite – the criminal is actually someone acutely sensitive to his environment and who is prompted to commit crimes based on his perceptions of the world around him. Which theory do you believe? How does one explain certain exceptional figures like Gandhi and Mandela, who were subject to the most brutal and atrocious conditions, yet immerged seemingly uncorrupted? The essence of the Power of Context is that our inner states are the result of our outer circumstances. But then, how does this work with or against the idea that our inner states ultimately create our outer world –that perception is reality or that if we change the way we look at things, the things we look at change?

How can we arrest non-conformance to the traffic norms? Broken Windows theory suggests that if broken windows in a building were not repaired, there is a tendency for the tenants to break more windows. Likewise, bad driving behavior is both learned from and reinforced by our surroundings. Unchecked tailgaters, drivers who don't signal, speeders, highway lane weavers, red light runners, etc. epidemically invite further violation of traffic rules. Which means traffic tickets alone would have fixed the problem and done a lot good, if implemented honestly.

How often do we as media planners really step back and try to understand the message environment? We do a significant amount of work to identify where messages should be placed, but not a lot to understand what it looks like when we get there.

A broken window in business happens when someone isn't paying attention to details. For example, a poorly located sale item, a randomly organized menu, s or an employee with a bad attitude are all examples of the broken window phenomenon. It can be physical, like a faded, flaking paint job, or symbolic, like a policy that requires consumers to pay for customer service. When the waiter at a Chinese restaurant is named Billy Bob, that's a broken window. When a call for help assembling a piece of furniture results in a ten-minute hold on the phone (playing the same music over and over), that's a broken window. When a consumer asks why she can't return her shirt at the counter and is told, "because that's the rule," that is a broken window. They're everywhere. Except at the really sharp businesses.

Chapter 5: The Power of Context (Part Two): The Magic Number One Hundred and Fifty

Gladwell makes a convincing case that there's a natural optimization of socialization and information-sharing that happens when groups reach 150 or so members. According to him, groups of less than 150 members usually display a level of intimacy, interdependency, and efficiency that begins to dissipate markedly as soon as the group's size increases over 150. Thus, groups under the size of 150 are more effective as they can better exploit the bonds of memory and peer pressure. To further bear out this point, Gladwell traces the path of the novel –"The Divine Secrets of the Ya-Ya Sisterhood" from regional cult favorite to national best-seller. The one-of-its-kind content of this novel appealed strongly to small reading groups of middle-aged women in Northern California, and that these women were uniquely well-positioned to catapult the book to national success as a result of an informal campaign of recommendations and advocacy. As the book started to take off, its author Rebecca Wells cancelled everything else and for over a year, she toured the country giving talks, meeting with existing Ya-Ya Sisterhood groups, helping organize new ones, like the carpet bag preacher of religious movements, who rode from town to town, meeting with congregations until they could organize their own churches and bring in their own minister. In both cases, the lesson is that small, close-knit groups have the power to magnify the epidemic potential of a message or idea.

Another good example of our hard-wired social limits is Gore Associates, a privately-held multimillion-dollar company responsible for creating Gore-Tex fabric and all sorts of other high-tech computer cables, filter bags, semiconductors, pharmaceutical, and medical products. What is most unique about this company is that each company plant is no larger than 150. When constructing a plant, they put 150 spaces in the parking lot, and when people start parking on the grass, they know it's time for another plant. Each plant works as a group. There are no bosses. No titles. Salaries are determined collectively. No organization charts, no budgets, no elaborate strategic plans. Wilbert Gore—the late founder of the company, found through trial and error that 150 employees per plant was most ideal. "We found again and again that things get clumsy at a hundred and fifty," he told an interviewer some years ago.

The consequense of magic number 150 is that groups above this size are unstable compared to sub-150 groups. These groups need more control and structure, and formalized knowledge-sharing, than sub-150 groups. Before you hit the magic number, you can rely on personal trust and relationships to solve the groups, problems. Beyond this the group starts to split up into smaller clans, with their own agendas.

Chapter 6: Case Study: Rumors, Sneakers, and the Power of Translation

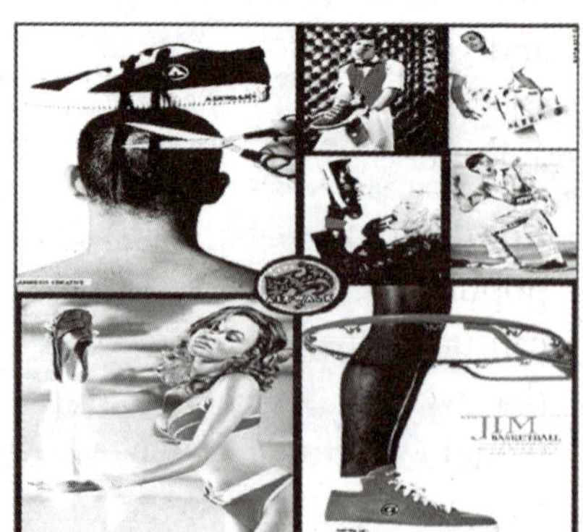

Gladwell argues that epidemics tip when the information or products the innovators experiment with are translated by mavens, connectors & salesmen into something the early majority can accept and work with. Airwalk tipped in 1990s primarily because its advertising campaign was founded very explicitly on this principle of epidemic transmission. It was originally geared towards skateboarding subculture of Southern California, but sought to transcend this niche market and attain national recognition. At the start, working with only a small budget, the creative director of Lambesis (the ad agency hired by Airwalk), Mr. Chad Farmer, came up with a series of dramatic images—single photographs showing the Airwalk user relating to his shoes in some weird way. In one, a young man is shown wearing an Airwalk shoe on his head, with the laces hanging down like braids, as his laces are being cut by a barber. In another, a leather-clad girl is holding up a shiny vinyl Airwalk shoe like a mirror and using it to apply lipstick.... As Airwalk grew, Lambesis went into television. In one of the early Airwalk commercials, the camera pans across a bedroom floor littered with discarded clothing. It then settles under the bed, as the air is filled with grunting and puffing and noise of the bedsprings going up and down. Finally, the camera comes out from under the bed and we see a young, slightly dazed-looking youth, holding an Airwalk shoe in his hand, jumping up and down on his bed as he tries unsuccessfully to kill a spider on the ceiling. The commonality across all these advertisements was that Lambesis ruthlessly honed in on and exploited several timely avatars of coolness, such as Tibetan Buddhism, pachuco gang culture, and hipsters' ironic embrace of preppy culture, rendering Airwalk shoes cool by association in the process. In doing so, it dropped the extraneous details and exaggerated others so that Airwalk's crazy ads acquired a deeper meaning and connect with the mainstream customers.

Can you think of other current products that have exploded onto the market with an equally impressive advertising assault? Would Apple computers and the iPod phenomenon, for example, be as popular if it didn't have its signature marketing campaign?

Next, Gladwell touches on the Translation Factor. Translator takes ideas and information from a highly specialized world and translates them into a language the rest of us can understand. The most sophisticated analysis of the process of translation comes from the study of rumors. In the book, *The Psychology of Rumour,* Gordon Allport relates the story from 1945 of a Chinese teacher who asked directions which ultimately got spread as a rumour that a Japanese spy had gone up the hill to take pictures. The rumour developed through three phases. Firstly, it was levelled – all kinds of details were removed, such as the exact nationality of the visitor. Second, it was sharpened – some details were made more specific, as sightseeing became espionage. Finally, assimilation took place and the story was changed so it made sense to those spreading the rumor – most people in the town at that time had a relative or friend involved in the war. So, what mavens, connectors and salesmen do to an idea in order to make it contagious is they simply rumourize it in a way that specific details are dropped and others are exaggerated so that the message itself comes to acquire a deeper meaning; thus causing a "tip".

Food for thought: How do weird, idiosyncratic things that really cool kids do tip into massive popularity? They are translated from a highly specialized world into a language the rest of us can understand. So, when we judge things as being weird and idiosyncratic, are we really saying that we just don't understand it? It's not the product but our interpretation of it that is limited. Could everything, if 'sugarcoated' in a way we recognize, ultimately, become palatable and even enjoyable?

Chapter 7: Case Study: Suicide, Smoking, and the Search for the Unsticky Cigarette

In another case study, Gladwell discusses the relationship between a sudden, alarming rise in suicide among adolescent males in Micronesia and the persistent problem of teen smoking in the United States. In doing so, he takes a pressing social issue such as teenage smoking, and breaks it down and analyzes what an epidemic approach to solving that problem would look like.

In the 1970's and 1980's, Micronesia had teen suicide rates ten times higher than anywhere else in the world. Teenagers were literally being infected with the suicide bug, and one after another, they were killing themselves in exactly the same way under exactly the same circumstances. What could have possibly tipped this pattern? Citing the studies of a University of California sociologist, who found that suicides increase after reports of suicide appear in the newspapers, Gladwell suggests that even extreme behaviors, such as suicides can be contagious. Suicide stories are a kind of natural advertisement for a particular response to your problems. The deaths of people in highly publicized suicides give others "permission" to die – serves as the tipping point in suicide epidemics. Precisely the same way, the tipping-permission-givers in smoking are often parents who smoke, or even grandparents. They leave an indelible and powerful print on the young smokers-to-be teenagers, who are inherently, perhaps even genetically, predisposed to imitate others and try on new behaviors and attitudes during adolescence. Gladwell calls it a contagious epidemic of self-destruction, engaged by youth in the spirit of experimentation, imitation and rebellion...it becomes an important form of their self-expression. He further points out that the quest to cure addiction by reforming character is usually a wild goose chase. Decades of psychometric research have blown the "addictive personality" theory out of the water, and we now know that most of what we label character traits, such as the honesty/dishonesty axis, is predominantly situational. If we follow Gladwell's analysis, we need to look at addiction as an epidemic, much like the HIV plague, and try to find the Connectors, the Mavens, and the Salesmen, who drive it. Are there people who have a wide network of connections and who promote heavy smoking and drug use? Of course, there are. Is anything being done to identify these people, to reach them, and to try to change their message or shut them down? Are there mavens of drinking and drug use? Yes, there are such people. Is anything being done to identify them, to study their appeal, and to undermine their message? Are there Salesmen of addiction? We know there are, and many of them are hired by the tobacco & beverage companies to work their emotional charisma on television. Together, the connectors, mavens, and salesmen of addiction are a social scourge comparable to the promiscuous carriers of STDs, who infect hundreds of others and cause isolated small problems to escalate into major epidemics. But powerful economic interests have and will always prevent governments across the globe to launch effective countermeasures against these networks. Gladwell finally wraps up the discussion with the idea (proposed by two leading nicotine researchers) that since it's impossible to prevent kids from following their cool peers in experimenting with forbidden substances, why not reduce nicotine levels below a tipping point at which few will become addicted even at a pack and a half a day?

Food for thought: Do you agree that instead of fighting experimentation, which is a natural and unavoidable fate of growing up, we should be rather focusing on diminishing the consequences of that experimentation? For example, instead of forbidding your child from consuming alcohol, when he goes out or proselytizing about the dangers of under-age drinking, should parents rather ensure there is a sober, designated driver at one of their parties? Try thinking of other similar examples.

Chapter 8: Conclusion: Focus, Test, and Believe

In this chapter, Gladwell concludes with an account of the type of solution that reflects an understanding of the concept of the tipping point: A nurse seeking an effective, low-cost way to raise awareness of breast cancer and diabetes among African-American women shunned traditional routes and enlisted the help of hairstylists. In this environment, she reasoned, most women are relaxed and receptive to new information in a way that no other education efforts can duplicate. She changed her context from church to hair and beauty salons. She changed the messenger to the stylist. She changed the message to fit the conversational approach, trained the stylist to deliver it in compelling manner and provided constant updates. And unlike the previous conventional attempts that fell on deaf ears, her approach worked! Gladwell asserts that such solutions are the very type of cumulative, low-key approach that can, over time, build to a tipping point of massive popularity and influence.

From Tipping Point Dream to Tipping Point Reality

What underlies successful epidemics, in the end, is a bedrock belief that change is possible, that people can radically transform their behavior or beliefs in the face of the right kind of impetus. The reason we all suspect that it cannot be this simple is because we are prisoners of a linear mindset. We expect output to be linearly proportional to input. For example, imagine a sheet of paper folded in half, and then in half again, and so on for 50 folds. How tall do you think the folded stack would be? The thickness of a telephone directory perhaps.

Although tipping point model is scientifically informed by both evidence and theory, the proof of pudding for many business managers will lie in its demonstrable capacity to impact favourably on the bottom line. Given below are a few examples that manifest how a number of corporates, including the bigwigs like 3M, Pfizer, P&G and Microsoft, have successfully implemented tipping point marketing initiatives to kick-start their epidemics of demand.

Post-it Notes: Saved by Connectors

Although post-it notes were around long before the publication of *The Tipping Point,* the story behind the little yellow stickies is a powerful example of the Tipping Point marketing in action. In 1968, Dr. Spence Silver, a research scientist for 3M, was trying to invent a new super-sticky glue. He failed, and did so quite spectacularly, coming up with precisely the opposite to what he had been looking for: a super-weak glue.

Abandoned in an R&D lab for some six years, the failed invention was eventually put to use six years later by another 3M product development researcher, Art Fry. Fry was also a chorister at St. Paul's church, Minnesota, and was frustrated by the loose bookmarks that kept falling out of his hymnbook and preventing him from turning quickly to the appropriate page during the service. He decided to experiment with the abandoned glue, using it to coat one side of his bookmarks, in the hope that they would stay in place, and not damage the hymnbook. It worked. Fry had seen the light, and set about with the fervour of a new convert convincing 3M management of the commercial worth of his new, as yet unnamed, temporary sticky bookmarks.

This first part of the 3M post-it notes story may be familiar to many, but what is really interesting is what happened, or rather didn't happen, next. Post-it notes didn't work. They worked fine functionally, but they did not work with consumers. They failed in concept testing, failed in prototype testing and even failed in a test launch. The failed fruit of an R&D department had failed in the market. However, just before pulling the plug on the whole sad affair, 3M gave post-it notes one last chance. They conducted a special seeding research project that put the product in the hands of highly connected secretaries to CEOs in large corporations. Specifically, each of these 'connectors' was sent entire boxes full of the yellow stickies, asked to share them with their colleagues, and then feedback on any potential uses that could be found for them. This 'product placement in real life' conducted in both the spirit and name of research changed the fortunes of post-it notes. By generating goodwill, involvement and positive word of mouth emanating from a few right people in the right place, the research project triggered an epidemic of demand. Almost immediately, post-it notes started appearing on senior internal memos, on drafts, desks, and in reports, and the copycat effect ensured that the little yellow stickies spread infectiously through companies like a virulent virus to become the 5th largest selling office-supply product in America.

Microsoft: Unleashing a Computer Virus of the Mind

Another gold-standard of 'seed marketing' is the Microsoft's record-breaking launch of Windows 95 which involved trialling and 'beta-testing' of its soon-to-be-launched OS version. Microsoft recruited 450,000 early-adopters to trial their new software just prior to its final launch, ensuring that one out of every 189 PC users in the US had a pre-release copy. This enabled Microsoft to capture critical pre-launch feedback for the mass market launch whilst giving the 'consumers that count' a unique preview of their product that would generate a word of mouth epidemic of demand. When the final product was launched on the stroke of midnight on August 24, 1995, one million copies of Windows 95 were sold in the very first four days, making it the fastest selling software of all time, thrashing the previous record of 40 days to sell a million copies. All the subsequent windows editions have been launched in a similar fashion.

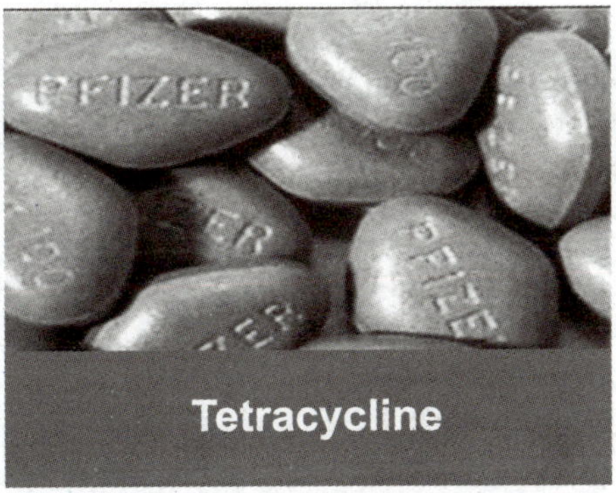

Pfizer: Infecting People to Fight Infections. To launch a new drug, pharmaceutical companies have to go through three rounds of mandatory trials; Phase I trials involve testing for safety, usually in a small number of healthy people, Phase II trials involve testing for efficacy, usually in a slightly larger number of sufferers, and Phase III trials assess comparative efficacy against competitors and determines side-effect profiles. However, there exists a fourth round of trials that, whilst not mandatory, lie behind the success of virtually every blockbuster drug. Phase IV trials are the pharmaceutical industry's equivalent to Microsoft's beta-testing programme. This use of tipping point strategy as a PR masterstroke, which has now become a common practice in the pharmaceutical industry, was first made famous by James S. Coleman, Elihu Katz, and Herbert Menzel's 1966 study of the diffusion of tetracycline, a new medical drug, among physicians. The investigation began when the director of marketing at the Pfizer drug company approached the three sociologists, then at Columbia University's Bureau of Applied Social Research, with a request to determine the effectiveness of Pfizer's tetracycline advertising in medical journals. This rather humdrum marketing question was converted into a particularly influential diffusion study by Coleman, Katz, and Mendel. They collected data via personal interviews with virtually all of the medical doctors in four small communities in Illinois. Prescription data were also collected from pharmacies, so they knew the date when each doctor first prescribed the new drug. This represented an important methodological improvement—observed actual adoption—over the usual diffusion investigation, which depended upon respondent accuracy in recalling the date at which an innovation was adopted. Further, doctors were asked sociometric questions to determine their interpersonal network links.

As one would expect, the results showed that the rate of adoption of tetracycline followed an S-shaped curve. But the most interesting revelations of this study was that doctors, who were linked in more interpersonal networks, adopted the innovation more rapidly than did more isolated doctors. Even though tetracycline had been scientifically evaluated in numerous clinical trials, which were reported to all physicians through medical journals, and even though Pfizer salespeople gave them free samples, they evaluated the innovation mainly through the personal experiences of their fellow doctors. An early adopting doctor told his office partner, a social friend, or a golfing partner, "Look doctor, I prescribed tetracycline to several patients of mine last week and it acted like a miracle drug. Perhaps, you should try it." This meant that interpersonal communication channels with peers had a strong influence on the adoption process and hence the interpretation that diffusion of an innovation is essentially a social process that occurs through interpersonal networks.

Procter and Gamble: Connector Panel that Walks the Customer Advocacy Talk. Indeed, no major corporation has embraced word-of-mouth marketing as aggressively. P&G is the only such company to have developed its own in-house business units devoted to it, and it has the nation's largest legion of connectors. The effort started in 2001, when P&G launched Tremor, its connector panel of 200,000 infectious teens, which was used to seed new products. Although only set up in 2001, controlled studies have already shown that the panel can produce an increase in sales volume of 14% (Klepacki 2003). Through this tipping point initiative, instead of marketing at teens, who no longer want to listen, the Cincinnati consumer product giant is listening to them, putting new products in their hands and onto their conversational agendas. Furthermore, it collects the rich e-mail feedback which it receives from the youngsters, condenses it into actionable consumer insights, and evaluates them for its innovation management, making Tremor a complete end-to-end marketing solution that includes intensive consumer research, message development and campaign execution.

At the end of 2005, P&G complemented Tremor by a similar panel called Vocalpoint for mothers with children aged 19 or under. Vocalpoint works in a fashion analogous to Tremor. It recruits mothers who possess a strong network and are very communicative. Today 500,000 Vocalpoint moms are advocating P&G brands across USA. That's not all. Apart from the word-of-mouth tools like Tremor and Vocalpoint, P&G maintains various websites as communication platforms, whose discussions it can tap into. Examples of these web sites are the girls website beinggirl.com or capessa.com, a website for women which is produced by P&G for Yahoo's health section. They facilitate an understanding of what the consumers in these target groups like or dislike, and what is really important for them in the various stages of their lives.

Marketing during a recession: (A Gladwellian take by the author)

It is well documented that brands that increase advertising during a recession, when competitors are cutting back, can improve market share and return on investment at lower cost than during good economic times. I believe, marketers with deep pockets would be able to negotiate favorable advertising rates and lock them in for several years. Also, with declension of marketing budgets, social media marketing might as well be tipped into the mainstream. Similar to the large search engines, possibility exists for the popular social networking websites like Facebook to provide national or global advertisers with a scalable and relevant platform for matching consumer interest to their products and services, while also offering even the smallest local advertiser (still an untapped potential) the ability to reach the 16 people in Topeka Kansas, who are into model airplane collecting, for example. And it's just not limited to reach, Facebook offers a number of creative ways for brands to learn more about their customers—understand what they like, who they know, what they support, etc. One option is to create a community in Facebook, with links to conventional online surveys, hosted outside Facebook. This approach is being used, for example, by Skittles Bubble Gum, with a group of over 4291721 Facebook members. You can also talk to your raving fans directly and when I say talk, I mean talk—there's a great voice chat application for Facebook called Vivox Voice Chat, which I've used. The sound quality rivals Skype. And guess what? It's free. Interestingly, a recent study on MySpace members revealed that thirty percent of frequent social networkers trust their peers' opinions when making a major purchase decision, but only ten percent trust advertisements. This again is a huge opportunity area given that most of the marketers today are still unconvinced about social networking as an advertising tool and none of them actually have been able to build a masterful social media practice just yet. But, of course, there is an ethical underpinning to this. Marketers would have to learn to engage their audience, educate them and earn their trust and respect instead of trying to manipulate them. The young internet social surfers might value the opinions of their peers over advertising, but they are also good at spotting an attempt to pass off commercial content for genuine sentiment.

To sum up, don't forget that it was the early adopters who made most of the money in the Gold Rush of 1849. Winners will emerge and knock your socks off with their social media campaigns. Heck, not even just "campaigns." They will add social media directly into their corporate DNA!

TAKEAWAYS

It's hard not to be fascinated by fads. Fads remind us of the potential for disorder always lying behind the placid surface of daily life. Economists study fads for examples of speculative mania—Dutch tulips, perhaps today's Nasdaq that inevitably result in depressions. Sociologists teach that in the middle of a fad individuals are more likely to be swayed by crowd psychology than by their own wants. Satirists find in fads human foibles writ large; Melville's "Confidence man" and Twain's "Man that corrupted hadleyburg" are built around the illusions that lead people to deny what their eyes see in favor of what their hearts desire. However, unlike previous observers of fads, Gladwell does not emphasize what they teach us about human irrationality. He does the exact opposite. Fads, he claims, are not really fads at all, but are the result of small things, well-timed, well-placed, and well-articulated to bring about their 'contagiousness.' Using some of the best and most provocative behavioral research studies in recent years, Gladwell run us through the hows and whys of taste, fashion, hipness, and other varieties of social contagion and convincingly illustrates how complex behaviors like smoking, suicide or crime show that we are suggestible in the face of what we see and hear, and that we are acutely sensitive to even the smallest details of everyday life. That's why social change is so volatile and so often inexplicable because it is the nature of all of us to be such.

If there is bizarreness and volatility in the world of the Tipping Point, there is also a large measure of hopefulness as well. Merely by manipulating the size of a group, we can dramatically improve its receptivity to new ideas. By tinkering with the presentation of information, we can significantly improve its stickiness. By finding and reaching those few special people, we can engineer the course of social epidemics. The world may seem like an immovable, implacable place, but it is not. With the slightest push in just the right place, it can be tipped.

❑❑❑

IMPORTANT NOTE

This summary culls the content of the book - "The Tipping Point" down to its essence so that even an average reader can sensitize himself to it, sparing him with the time consuming details. In case you feel a need to further explore this topic, the author recommends reading the original work published by "Hachette UK".

A Snapshot of
RAVING FANS

The good news according to Bain & Company is that companies can boost profits as much as 255% by retaining merely 5% more of their existing customers. But the bad news is that in today's demanding business environment, providing good service on time every time is no longer good enough. Unless your customers rave about your service, they are likely to be poached by an aggressive competitor. In this exclusive book about legendary customer service, Blanchard reveals who these "Raving Fans" are and how you can get them. Towering head and shoulders over your competitors has never been so easy!

Raving Fans

Inspired by Ken Blanchard and Sheldon Bowles

"There is only one boss-the customer. And he can fire everybody in the company from the chairman on down, simply by spending his money somewhere else."

- Sam Walton,
Founder of Wal-Mart

Customer satisfaction is a high priority for most companies. Many know from experience what research has declared statistically: it costs five times more to Jacqui being a new customer than it costs to get business from an existing one. While this is interesting, what really dumbfounded me was the Harvard case study that showed little correlation between satisfied customers and their retention. As per the findings from this research work, customers who rate themselves as 'highly satisfied' are likely to be loyal, while the ones who scale themselves just 'satisfied', are ripe for takeover. The case was indeed an eye-opener, but its statistics kept turning in my head, so I decided to further dig up the subject and grabbed a copy of 'raving fans' from my neighborhood bookstore. To my fortune, I did get the explanation I was seeking. According to the Blanchard & Sheldon Bowles, customer satisfaction may be the rage, but here's the stark truth—Satisfied customers may not complain and may not quibble about payment, yet you can bet your bottom dollar they will try and get a better deal at a better price somewhere else next time. So, forget about satisfying customers because satisfying them won't help you make it in the increasingly competitive business world. To do that, you need to create 'raving fans'.

The notion of 'raving fans' brings to mind a screaming crowd at some Beatles concert. From a marketing standpoint, raving customers are in no way different. They sing from the roof-tops about your awesomeness and are so devoted to your products and services that they wouldn't dream of taking their business elsewhere. To this end, the idea is also pretty much similar to the concept of family. Family implies loyalty, no matter what. Have you ever heard the expression,

'You can choose your friends, but you can't choose your family'. You can screw up here and there, but your family is with you for the long haul.

Story Background

The new Area Manager is wondering on what could be done to retain his customers and his job. To the rescue comes 'Charlie'—(a guardian angel with a penchant for golf), who guides him and takes him around to businesses that create raving fans through exemplary customer service. On one such visit to a departmental store, our Area Manager is looking for a book to be gifted to this wife on her birthday. Upon arrival, he and Charlie are greeted by the sales staff, who pin a complimentary white carnation on their suits. The store has a superb play area for children. The rest rooms are glittering and the towels are neat and crisp. The book he is looking for is not available at this store but the lady at the books section dispatches her assistant to procure it from a neighbouring shop, gift wraps it and hands it over to her customer—at no extra cost. Our Area Manager is amazed. How can they afford to do this? Pat comes the reply from the man who runs the business—"How can you afford NOT to do this?" The duo then visits several of Charlie's star pupils' businesses and encounter outstanding service in a variety of business settings. Thus unfolds a charming story that teaches how to define a service vision, learn what a customer really wants, institute effective systems, and make stunning customer service a competitive advantage—not just another 'flavor of the month' program.

This book summary includes startling new tips and innovative techniques that can help anyone create a revolution in their workplace and turn their customers into raving, spending fans. Follow along as I share with you Blanchard's secrets to mind-blowing customer service that will help you seduce customers into becoming walking and talking billboards for your business.

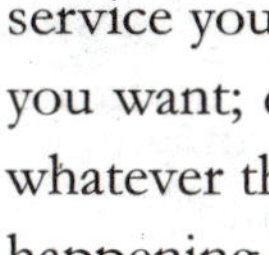

Secret No. 1 – Decide what you want

Create a vision of perfection centered on your customers. This means establishing what the vision of your company's relationship with its customers should be. For example imagine the 'perfect' service you want to give, the 'perfect' bank, law firm, airline etc. for your customers. Decide what you want; does everything you do in your practice epitomize your vision of the ideal service—whatever that is to you? Then bring the vision of perfection down to the level of what is actually happening and see where the bumps & warts are.

But isn't it all about customer? Why does your vision even matter? The customer's vision (to be covered under Secret 2) might change your window, but if you don't have your own vision to start with, you'll never put the necessary limits in place.

On deciding what you want to become for your customer remember to:

- Make it easier for customers to do business with you, e.g., advertise discounts, put up information kiosks, use websites and other technologies to help customers shop.
- Make doing business with you a warm and pleasant experience for your customer. Train your staff to be attentive, warm and knowledgeable, so that customers feel they are getting good value for their money. Offer free coffee, warm greetings and clean restrooms. Make customers feel happy to come back for more.
- Think "how can I not afford to do these things" instead of "how can I afford to do these" for the customers. But, never try to give your customers everything, all at once. It doesn't work.

Again, we can't be everything to everybody, Walmart doesn't sell Rolexes......may be Bolexes. Rolex doesn't sell affordable watches either, at least not to Walmart's standard of affordability.

When Sheldon was running a petrol station in Winnipeg, he realized that no one chooses to go a petrol station and aimed to make the experience as swift and exciting as possible—rather like a Formula One pit stop. Staff dressed in red jump suits and raced towards the cars as they came into the forecourt. One pumped petrol, another checked tyre pressures and another cleaned windscreens. It was at the time when everyone else was going self-serve and Sheldon had no competition!

Secret No. 2 – Discover what your customers want

Many companies don't listen to their customers because they fear the consequences. But there are two parts to listening. The first lies in understanding what the customer is saying; the second is in deciding whether or not you want to do what they suggest. This may sound heretical to customer service, but you must also learn to ignore what customers want if they do not match your vision. While it's easy to get excited about closing a sale, closing the wrong prospect will damage your credibility. The wrong prospect may receive some value from your product or service, but that's not enough. He will soon become a bad client & there is always an opportunity cost associated with dealing with problem clients. Every minute spent trying to satisfy them (in what may be a losing battle) is time not spent building stronger relationships with your best prospects & clients.

It really boils down to choosing to do business with those prospects that have the potential to be raving fans. The bottom line is that success is found only within the window you've defined in your vision, not in looking after every whim of any customer who shows up to your door.

Identify who your potential raving fans are and match your vision with theirs

Knowing what you want first helps you understand what your customers want. Imagine an airline wanting to be the best carrier in the whole world and then trying to reach out to flyers around the world without first deciding whether it will be a long haul, international long-haul carrier or a domestic, 'no-frills', low-cost provider.

Find out what your customer wants, not what you think they want and not even what they say they want

Have you ever been to a restaurant with high hopes of a delicious meal, only to come away disappointed with the food, the service or the whole experience and vowed never to set foot in their doorstep again. Chances are, you complained to your partner and maybe your work colleagues and neighbors, but not to the restaurant staff. If so, you join the overwhelming 96% who say nothing about poor goods or services—they choose to 'vote with their feet' and simply don't return.

Listen to your silent customers. Your service may be so bad that customers feel unwanted; they don't even bother to complain. What's worse, they may leave your company even without any viable competitor to take your place. Then there is this another group of customers who are as good as the buttoned up ones, they have been so accustomed to bad service that they rarely complain, and worse, reply 'fine' or 'satisfied' even when they mean the soup was cold, the line was too slow and long, etc. They are satisfied because they think nothing will happen even if they do complain.

How do you listen to the customer who isn't talking? Or to the one who says "Fine" or "Okay"?

You can't just leave "How are we doing?" cards on the table and expect to get useful information. You have to keep after customers in creative ways. The questions you ask are important. If a restaurant manager asks, "How was everything tonight?", what's the answer? "Fine." In that case, maybe it's the question that's not very good.

- Start asking sincere questions like: "What one thing could we have done differently tonight that would have made your time with us even better?"
- Past experiences have taught customers that chances are, you don't really want to know what they think or feel and that their complaints will be left unheard. Win their confidence. Take time to get the conversation going. Only when customers can sense you are serious, they will open up to you.

Encourage the other 4% of customers to speak up and appreciate what they are trying to say, listen to the music as well as to the lyrics—they may say one thing but mean another, e.g., clients say they like your low prices but their actual priorities are on-time deliveries and perfect quality.

If you don't catch the drift, you fail to give your customers what they need because you simply don't know what that is. Furthermore, you reject them, as if their thoughts had no value.

Sheldon had great feedback on his original vision but soon discovered customers would also like to buy coffee or a newspaper. By listening to their suggestions, he increased revenue and provided a better service.

Complaints!

Chicago retailer, Marshall Fields once said, "Those who buy, support me. Those who come to flatter, please me. Those who complain, teach me how I may please others so they will buy. The only ones that hurt me are those who are displeased but do not complain. They refuse me permission to correct my errors and, thus, improve my service."

Everyone dreads psyched out clients, but contrary to the belief held in common, an upset customer can be your biggest opportunity to excel. In fact, a complaint handled excellently does your business more good than what an ordinary satisfied customer does. Market research tells us that unhappy customers tell their stories to up to 10 of their friends. In fact, 13% actually spread the word to 20 or more people. The research also says that of the 4% cent who complain and have the matter resolved quickly, 95% stay with the supplier and are so satisfied that they pass this positive opinion onto five of their friends. This compares well with customers who have no complaints at all, but might only mention your business to one or two friends. So, make sure that you have a positive complaints policy, that customers are encouraged to tell you when things aren't right, and your staff are trained to handle their complaint to satisfaction. Complaints are invaluable customer feedback: if something isn't right, you need to know about it, and the last thing you want is for everyone else to know about it. Perhaps, you grew sick of complaints long ago, and stopped listening. Better change your habits. They come from customers who are actually trying to help you with your business.

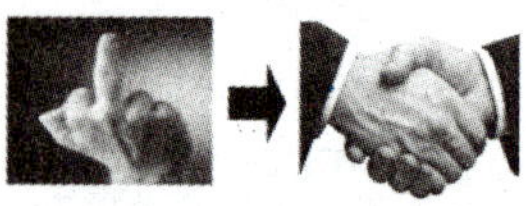

From the middle finger to the handshake

When someone swears at us or promises to see us fired, our immediate reaction may be to disconnect or to transfer the caller to the manager. In fact, your company may already have specific policies for dealing with out-of-control customers. But how can standardization be a solution to something which needs a customized approach? Good leadership implementation means turning over power to those closest to the customers—often those who are at the bottom of the organizational hierarchy. This is unbelievably simple and obvious; yet many businesses refuse to take this 'risk' and end up denying their front line staff the right to bring their brains to work or use their common sense in order to implement organizational visions and values.

Of course, this would require a lot of training. Here are some issues to consider:

1. Step into their shoes

   While it is easy to label abusive customers as lunatics, try to step into their shoes for a while. How would you react to their situation? If you had been on hold for an hour, transferred from agent to agent or had another rep disconnect from you, wouldn't you be furious? Most of us wouldn't react in a calm manner either if we were losing thousands of dollars every minute a system was down or when defective products were returned. If you see the problem from the customer's eyes, it will help you to have the right attitude which is paramount to working with enraged customers.

2. Focus on the issues

When someone is shouting at us, many of us get swept up into the emotionalism of the situation and begin to defend ourselves. It is very important to separate an objective argument from a personal attack. If a person is frustrated because a product or service has not lived up to its standard, it is essential for your company's representative dealing with the customer to realize that the customer is upset at the situation and not at him personally. Arguments often turn personal even when the people involved in the argument had nothing to do with the creation of the problem to begin with.

A customer can be totally wrong; however, most of the times they simply need education to better understand the situation at hand

3. Consider what you say and how you say it

(a) **Validate the customer's feelings.** Let the customer ventilate. If you feel you can, ignore any fowl language the first few times. Paraphrase what you hear the customer saying. Ask the customer if you got the story correct and if anything has been left out. Simply acknowledge that he or she's irritated. Example: "I can understand you are upset."

(b) **Assure customers you'll take care of them.** Let them know something will be done. Example: "I'm here to help you with this."

(c) **Make a 'sad-glad' statement.** This helps the customer realize you care. Example: "I'm sorry you experienced a problem. And I'm glad you told me about it!"

(d) **Ask the customers what will make them happy.** Don't let this scare you! Customer service experts say that most often the upset customer will ask for *less* than what you would have offered yourself. Example: "How can we make this better?" or "How can we make this up to you?"

(e) **Acknowledge that you'll do what they want, or make a counter offer.** (But always try to just give what customer wants! In the end, it will save you time and headaches, and avoid any bad word spreading about you.) Example: "I want to keep you as a customer, and we're going to honor your request." Or, "We can't do that as per our agreement, but we can... [counter offer here]."

Dealing with invective customer is hard, but do you think being intimidated by customers, who swear and shout, makes the situation any better? By being firm but sincere, by having the right attitude, watching our tone of voice and the way we phrase our comments, we can turn any bad situation around and force even the ugliest customer into becoming our raving fan.

If there are any complaints you receive on a regular basis, you should be taking them head-on. There's no way your business can grow with those landmines in your path. A perfect picture of customer service must include a built-in-recovery strategy. Always think proactively, looking around the corner. You should try to address concerns prior to you having to hear from the customer that something needs to be done. A simple example to this would be an Internet Service Provider informing its clients that a necessary upgrade to computer services infrastructure will temporarily disable internet access on x day at x time.

Everyone is responsible for delivering customer service

While some people in the organization may deal with external customers—front desk personnel, for example—others may have primarily internal customers—such as human resource professionals. And some people, like those in the accounts department, have both external and internal customers—they send bills and invoices to external customers, and they provide reports and information to internal customers. The point is, everyone has a customer.

Everybody's a spoke in the wheel

Today's customers do not want to hear that people need to "check with their manager", they are more demanding than that. Customers want the frontline person standing in front of them to meet their needs—and meet them now.

If we can change the mindset and get everyone to understand that customer service is a part of their job, and realize the importance of it, and believe in it, that's going to be a huge competitive edge for the organization. Or, it can be the beginning of a negative spiral down. If you don't address it in time, revenues start to go down. You lose good clients; you lose good employees—because people want to work for a good company. And if the company is not delivering good service and is having to constantly generate new business out there because customers are not happy with the way they are being treated, then their work gets even harder. They just feed off of each other.

Secret No. 3 – Deliver plus one percent

Once we have our vision firmly in mind, and we have listened to the customer's vision, we then can begin to blend these into key doables. To this end, "deliver plus one percent" is an action strategy that entails two aspects. Promise more only up to what you can consistently deliver and deliver using the Rule of One Percent.

First aspect

Delivering your product or service consistently time after time without failure is fundamental to the Raving Fans customer service. That means observe consistency in quality, timeliness, and results that you promise to deliver. When you're creating Raving Fans, you need to understand that in the beginning, it's a fragile relationship. They've been burned before and they don't trust easily. You're trying to pull them in and they're usually trying to resist. Consistency will overcome resistance, but, in the meantime, they're watching like a hawk for you to mess up.

How to Develop Consistency?

Don't commit the mistake of offering too much service. Go slow. Work on perfecting one or two of your visions or promises. Better find a small promise that you can consistently deliver than the myriad services you can seldom meet. Companies make the mistake of advertising new things even before they get the old ones right. Airlines, for example, promise sets of choice meals. However, when you fly, you oftentimes find that they do not have enough of each meal to make sure you get a choice. They also promise to fly on time but lose your luggage on the way. Focus on one thing, a small service that you can deliver consistently.

Put systems in place. At the heart of every excellent customer service is a network of systems. It is this system of people, roles, responsibilities and technology that guarantees delivery and not the "smiles" and "good mornings". Furthermore, when it comes to navigating those systems, emphasis has to be on the end result, which is fulfilling your customer needs. And, hence, systems need to be organized in ways that allow employees to respond quickly to customer needs, anticipate trends & get in front of them. Help your people deliver on what you have promised to your customer by putting them through training. If you'd like your staff to be warm, courteous and attentive, train them to be warm, courteous and attentive. Don't forget to empower your employees. Unless you do that, they cannot bring their talents to the table. Finally, congratulate your staff when they do well in exceeding customer expectations. Employee evaluations such as raises and bonuses can be tied to those who create Raving Fans. Disney Resorts create raving fans because they provide a vacation beyond all imagination. They accomplish this not through the miracles of animatronics or the amusement park atmosphere, these things can be found at hundreds of vacation destinations worldwide. Disney Resorts create raving fans by infecting their employees (known as cast members) with epidemic enthusiasm and pandemic pride.

Second aspect

Once you have mastered consistent delivery to meet your client's needs, improve your vision by adding "one percent" at a time. 1% may seem to be insignificant; the idea, however, is to improve your vision in small steps so as to allow you enough time to master consistency in delivering your new as well as existing commitments. If you try to do too much at once, it's likely that you will fail to deliver consistently; at the least, you'll feel frustrated or overwhelmed by the enormity of the job ahead. On

Why plus 1% ?

There are two main reasons. One, you have to continually improve because if you're not, your competitors are (especially if they know the triple D secrets – Decide, Discover & Deliver). Two, our expectations continue to rise. Remember the dial up days...now, if we have to wait more than a couple seconds for a page to load, we get a bit frustrated. Why? Our standards are higher than they were back then (the dial up dark ages).

the other hand, even if you improve by one percent each week, you will feel confident you can do the job and before you know it—by the end of the year, you would have already improved your product or service by more than 50%!

One percent improvement isn't the same as the marketing idea— "promise less than you deliver." Deliberately lowering your customers' expectations is cheating them of what you can actually deliver. It's like making better basketball players by playing with bigger basketball hoops. The extra one percent is designed to encourage continuous improvement, in small and manageable steps. Before you worry about exceeding expectations in some cases, you must make sure that you meet expectations every single time. It is not wise to spend millions on advertising multiple promises only to fail in the end and cut a sorry figure. Customers feel ripped off when they don't get what you promised.

The magic ingredient to the one percent rule is its flexibility. Why do apparel houses enforce a two-item limit on the number of clothes to try in the dressing rooms? Why not allow customers to bring as much as they can so they don't have to keep coming back? Apparel stores enforce this two-item limit to reduce the risk of shoplifting. However, if stores have exerted effort to guard against one bad shopper, why can't they strive to make shopping much more comfortable and easier for the other 99 honest shoppers? Such monolithic bureaucracies (impervious to changing conditions) are only acceptable if your customer service slogan is like everyone else's: "No worse than the competition". But the fact of the matter is that customer's needs continually morph & change. To this end, consistency alongside ongoing improvements (by one percent rule) allows you to accommodate for change—set a course but not follow it blindly.

More than just a product......... after all, it's all about the icing

Making customers feel special is part of the process of creating raving fans. If business was to be compared to a car, customers would be the fuel. No fuel and the car cannot go anywhere. Being in a true long-term collaborative partnership with my clients, I've gotten to know them and their businesses well and serve as another set of eyes and ears for them. Anytime that I am reading something that I think one of them might use, I forward it to that client, with a "I thought you might be interested" note attached. I occasionally even do this for clients with whom I'm no longer working.

Don't turn your raving fans into roving customers

Companies work hard to make their products work faster, last longer, look sharper, and taste better than others on the market. They go as far as to create high-tech systems, enabling customers to order items at lightning speed. This is all great, and it certainly can lead to a heightened customer experience; however, many companies get so wrapped up in the technological aspects that they neglect to focus on the human side of the product marketing mix, passing over opportunities to connect with their most enthusiastic customers.

My recent personal experience with a pizza joint highlights how a missed opportunity enraged rather than engaged a satisfied customer. It goes like this:

A few weeks back, in appreciation of my late night slog, I was treated by a large size Mexican green wave pizza from my boss's favorite restaurant, which turned out to be the best vegetarian pizza I had ever tasted. Now, if you are like me, you'll turn up your nose at anything resembling a pizza. This was different; it was a thick-crust pizza, crispy on the outside, soft and chewy on the inside, made with whole-milk mozzarella cheese with a hint of cheddar, and loaded with crunchy onions, crispy capsicum & vine-ripened California tomatoes. After sampling the very first piece, I was transformed into a raving fan. I had to have more. With the company's website clearly printed on the product label, I knew exactly where to go to alleviate my pizza craving. The online ordering process was straightforward and clear. At the end of the order, there was a section for comments. Being the enthusiastic fan that I was, I wrote a glowing note describing their pizzas as the best I had ever tasted. Smiling, I submitted my order knowing that I must have made somebody's day with my effusive comment. The response was an immediate confirmation of my order and the non-vegetarian pizza feast, which was later on delivered to me, was equally mouthwatering. So far so good, but the next day when I checked the website, there was no response to my comment. How could this be? Wouldn't they want to engage a delighted customer like myself? Despite the lack of response to my glowing compliment, I placed an even larger order a few weeks later. To give the company a second chance, this time I asked a question in the comment box. As I have been eating mass quantities of pizzas for the last couple of years, and since I am the health-conscious sort, I asked for calorie information on the pizzas I had ordered. Again, the response was a prompt confirmation of my order (as expected) and absolutely no acknowledgement of my question. Talk about adding salt to an already open wound! This raving fan was now perturbed. The company's website clearly states that they will respond to comments. I would have been happy with a simple "thank you" after my first note, and I really did want an answer to my question. I opened the door to a great opportunity for them to make me feel special and appreciated for my purchases and compliments. However, I ended up feeling ignored, frustrated, and unimportant. Needless to mention, I not in the least ordered from that pizza joint since.

What this episode tells you is that Raving fans will start roving if they feel they are not getting the service or the appreciation they deserve. Although customers may love your product and your company, it only takes one interaction (or lack of action) to swiftly change their loyalties

Learnings for the top leadership

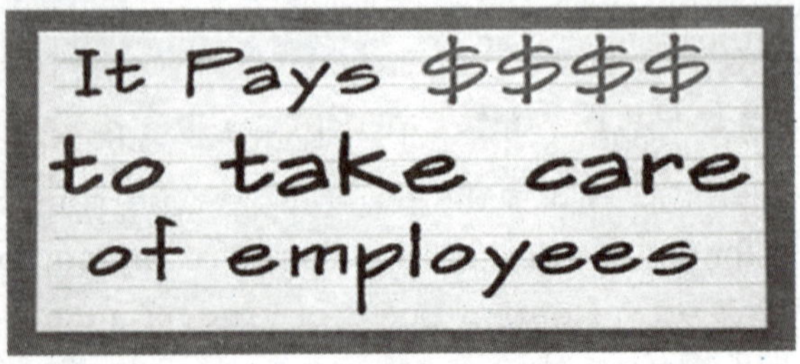

Recruiting and retention are hot topics in most HR circles. Ironically, a lot of people wouldn't be looking for jobs if their current employer was taking care of them. Companies need to attract them like a customer, and they need to retain them like a customer. So, in essence, all the rules of raving customers apply to raving employees.

Every corporate culture that truly understands the nature of great service has happy employees. And, that's because those employees are being serviced as well—they get the opportunity to be creative, innovative, and a part of the overall mission. When you engage people in a mission greater than the task, they become enthusiastic. And, who doesn't want enthusiastic employees?

- Ritz Carlton gives their frontline employees a discretionary cash fund to use if a customer is dissatisfied, or if the employee simply sees a chance to provide a higher standard of service. They can spend it entirely at their discretion, without fear of reprimand, and Ritz-Carlton has won countless Raving Fan Customers as a result.

- When Blanchard forgot his ID while checking in for an internal USA flight, he was relieved to be able to buy a copy of a book he wrote with the legendary National Football League coach, Don Shula from the airport bookshop because it had his photograph on the cover. He figured this was pretty good proof of identification. The Southwest Airlines Staff at the check-in desk yelled, "Hey, this guy knows Don Shula!" and came with him to the security inspectors to explain the situation. Having been given the power to make common sense decisions, they gave great customer service that he still raves about! The next airline forced him to visit five different levels of management and listen to long lectures on company policy before grudgingly allowing him on board. It's no surprise that they are now facing bankruptcy while Southwest is one of the few airlines still making money in America.

Good is only good. It is not excellent, it is not brilliant. Customers want to be dazzled, thrilled and wowed! It's that level of excellence which will raise you to the top of your niche market, will make your customers return to you, and become evangelical about you. Not easy! It takes something special to initiate such a major change, but once up and running the change will feed on its own success. Too many companies act like Ducks instead of Eagles. Ducks follow unnecessary rules and procedures and go 'Quack! Quack! Quack!' all the time while Eagles take the initiative, soar above the crowd and respond to customer's problems.

When it comes down to inventing your "secret sauce", revved up customer service is like a recipe that makes the relationship with your product or service stand out deliciously from all of the others. But this is only possible if you believe genuinely that the customer is "King" and focus on the customer in everything you do, from planning your company vision to developing business strategies and setting goals. Initiating a customer service program is a doomed exercise if you haven't already done this. A recent survey by Customer Management magazine showed that 60% of us think customer service is getting worse, despite the fact there is more media and management attention focused on this subject than ever before. If organizational culture and vision isn't intrinsically customer-focused and if customer service systems work against rather than in favour of the customer, no amount of talk or money put into a one-off 'customer service initiative' is going to change anything.

Creating this kind of organizational culture starts with the realization that everybody in a company has a customer. The Personnel department may not deal with anyone outside an organization but they still have 'internal customers' and need to turn them into 'Raving Fans.' How we treat our colleagues or internal customers has a huge impact on how an organization treats its external customers. When people are treated badly internally, ripples spread through the chains of command and poison the whole organization. If the Chairman is criticized by shareholders and the press and takes it out on his directors, they blame their managers, who take it out on the front line staff. And who are the only people they have left to whack? The customers. It's not easy being at the customer interface day after day and it's almost impossible to get excited about serving customers if you do not feel valued. Often, the first place businesses need to look if front line staff are not performing well is at the relationships these colleagues have with their managers. The golden rule is: treat your employees the way you want them to treat your customers.

Rapid technological innovation is also partly to blame. Failing to live up to its promise of making our lives easier, demands on our time have actually increased and sent stress levels soaring. In the old days, we would write a letter and not have to think about it for three or four days at the most until we got a reply. Now we have voice mail and email, people expect us to be on call and open for business twenty-four seven. It reminds me of the story of a little girl who asked her mummy why she hardly ever saw daddy. "It's because daddy can't finish his work during the day, so he has to work late," she was told. With childlike wisdom, she continued: "Why don't they put daddy in a slower group then?" The reality is there are no slower groups in our workplaces. Our work/life balance can easily shift in the wrong direction and organizations that care about customer service need to wise up to this. Our workplaces need to support and value colleagues in environments that enable them to do their job well, free from unacceptable pressure or bullying. Only when companies commit to creating this ethos in practice, the process of creating Raving Fan Customers by using the three secrets as revealed above, can begin.

All said & done, don't be penny-wise and pound-foolish. Someone else can always beat your price however hard you try, or they can offer a similar service. What they will find hard is trying to match the exceptional relationships you have built up with your customers. Invest in this area first—financially and practically. Put all your customers first, be they internal or external; turn power over to your front line staff; ensure that your organization values its people and you will get those Raving Fan Customers you deserve.

This book is written from a business perspective but the word 'customer' could easily be replaced with friend, coworker, spouse, etc. These same principles will help you form "Raving Fan" relationships.

❑❑❑

IMPORTANT NOTE

This summary culls the content of the book - "Raving Fans" down to its essence so that even an average reader can sensitize himself to it, sparing him with the time consuming details. In case you feel a need to further explore this topic, the author recommends reading the original work published by "Harper Collins".

A Snapshot of RICH DAD POOR DAD

Are you sick-and-tired of spending your best years in a cubicle, while life passes by? If you too are a prisoner with a salaried position in a corporate rat race then "Rich Dad Poor Dad" can be your escape map that will help you define the WHY & HOW of your Rat Race Escape and aid you in search of your buried cheese – Financial Freedom.

Rich Dad Poor Dad

(Inspired by Robert T. Kiyosaki and Sharon L. Lechter C.P.A.)

"How many millionaires do you know who have become wealthy by investing in savings accounts? I rest my case."

—Robert G. Allen,
Best-selling Author of Nothing Down & One Minute Millionaire

You may appear to be well off, but are you really earning enough to be financially independent? There is a difference, you know. Kiyosaki defines financial freedom as a person's ability to survive maximum number of days forward into the future, without compromising on their existing lifestyle, if they were to stop working today. To say that someone gets a handsome paycheck, then, is to say nothing about whether that person is wealthy enough. After going through this book summary, you will be able to evaluate your own thoughts and habits surrounding the topic of money, and consequently determine what you will need to be doing differently. Financial literacy is the key here, being raised in a poor or middle class family, most of us were never taught the fundamentals of personal finance. And consequently, in our drive to get rich, we try to build an Empire State Building on a 6-inch slab—a dream that is highly unlikely to materialize.

The story of "Rich Dad Poor Dad" revolves around two main characters: Kiyosaki's biological father—'the poor dad' and the father of his childhood best friend, Mike—'the rich dad'. Poor dad was highly educated and intelligent; he had a Ph.D. and had completed four years of undergraduate work in less than two years. He then went to Stanford University, the University of Chicago, and Northwestern University to do his advanced studies, all on full, financial scholarships. Rich dad, on the other hand, never finished the eighth grade. Both men were successful in their careers, working hard all their lives. Yet one dad struggled financially all his life and the other dad would become one of the richest men in Hawaii. One died leaving tens of millions of dollars to his family, charities, and his church. The other left a legacy of unpaid bills. Both men were strong, charismatic, and influential, but they did not advise the same things. Kiyosaki contrasts both his dads—their ideas, financial practices and describes how his real father, the poor and struggling but highly educated man, paled against his rich dad in terms of asset building & business acumen.

Poor Dad (highly educated but lacking the street smarts)

The author compares his poor dad to those people who are perpetually scampering in the Rat Race, helplessly trapped in a vicious cycle of paychecks. Poor dad believed in the traditional principles of working hard, saving money, and not buying material things that one cannot afford. He looked to education as the only passport to success and believed that having a good job with a solid company is what one should aspire for. Kiyosaki points out that his poor dad was always preoccupied with things like job tenure, social security, vacation & sick leaves, company insurance, salary raises and promotions. He worked hard incessantly but somehow never made it ahead financially. His approach to the subject of money was based on working hard to have enough money to pay the bills, in contrast to rich dad's approach to make his money work for himself.

Rich Dad (very little education, tons of street smarts)

It was from rich dad that the author learned not to say, "I can't afford it", but instead to ask, "how can I afford it?" Rich dad taught him that he shouldn't dwell on the fact that his wages are low, but instead ask "how can I make more money" because that is what stimulates the brain to take action. When someone says, "I can't afford it", his brain stops working. It, therefore, kills initiative and promotes passivity. The author adds that while his poor dad invested time and effort in education, he had a habit of putting his brain to sleep when it came to money matters. His rich dad, by contrast, was very skilled in the investment game because that's all he did. He always took a percentage off the top of any income he earned. He put that money into an investment account that went toward, purchasing his assets. While poor dad spent all his money first and never had any remaining for investments. The attitude of rich dad about money was manifested in the saying "the lack of money is the root of all evil"; poor dad, on the other hand, believed that the love of money is the root of all evils. He always said, 'I'll never be rich.' And that prophesy became his reality. Mike's father, on the other hand, always referred to himself as rich. He would say things like, 'I'm a rich man, and rich people don't do this.' Even when he was flat, broke after a major financial setback; he continued to refer to himself as a rich man. He would cover himself by saying, 'There is a difference between being poor and being broke. Broke is temporary, and poor is eternal."

It's often one of the very simple beliefs that we learn as kids or young people either held down from our parents, friends or school system that determine the outcomes in our life. Fortunately for Kiyosaki, having two dads as advisors allowed him the luxury of observing the effects that different thoughts have on one's life. He learns from both of his fathers but internalizes only what the rich dad taught him. These lessons are counterintuitive revelations that effectively undercut various popular myths.

Chapter 1: The Rich Don't Work for Money

At age 9, Robert and his best friend, Mike asked rich dad to teach them how to make money. The very first lesson Mike's dad made the boys learn was that instead of spending your whole life working to put a little money in your pocket and a bunch of money in someone else's pocket, you should have people work hard to put money in your pocket. He was able to achieve this by making the boys work in one of his grocery stores for ten cents an hour pay. After just 3 weeks of dusting cans, Kiyosaki was ready to quit. That's when the rich dad pointed out that you should never accept mediocre circumstances just because they're handed over to you. Rich people don't work for money. On the contrary, they find ways to put the money to work for them, even while they sleep. To achieve it, they almost always use two resources: either the time of other people (people who work for them) or the money of other people (for example, from the bank). They either own businesses or they invest money to receive residual income.

Next, Rich Dad puts the two boys to work, this time for nothing. Doing this forced them to think up a source of income, a business scheme. The opportunity came to them upon noticing discarded comic books in the store. The first business plan was hatched. The boys opened a comic book library and employed Mike's sister at 1$ a week to mind it. Soon they were earning $9.50 a week without having to physically run the library, while the neighborhood kids got to read as much comics as they could in two hours after school for only a few cents.

Kiyosaki goes on to say that opportunities in life come and go; the rich recognize them instantly and turn them into gold bullions while others are too busy seeking money and security and that's all they are ever going to get.

> Don't work for money. Work to learn. But not learning the stuff they taught us in school; learning about how to make money work for you.
>
> Picture this great analogy: A donkey pulling a cart and the owner dangling a carrot in front of the donkey's nose. The owner knows where they're going, but the donkey has no idea. It is simply following the carrot. So, at the end of the day, all the donkey gets is a carrot, while the owner actually gets something concrete accomplished. Each day, there will be a new carrot, and a new cart for the donkey. This is the 9-to-5 experience of working for someone else.

> *"Job is really a short-term solution to a long-term problem."*
>
> *-Rich Dad*

Chapter 2: Why Teach Financial Literacy

Rich dad always said, "if money is not first in your head, it will not stick to your hands." Simply put, money without financial intelligence is money soon gone. This explains why so many Americans are dead broke today despite belonging to the richest nation in the world. Their problem isn't credit cards—it's a lack of financial know-how. And at the root of that lack of knowledge is a school system, which teaches everything from Shakespearian literature to Newton's calculus but educates nothing about the subject of money. Clearly, advising people to cut up their credit cards won't solve the problem of excessive debt. A pair of scissors won't make anyone financially smarter, but some financial education just might.

Kiyosaki decries our antiquated educational system, which at best prepares kids to work and earn all their lives and does little to show them how to save, buy true assets and enjoy the returns. He argues that many of the skills essential to be successful in the financial world are not taught in school, which might explain why people like Bill Gates of Microsoft, and Ted Turner of CNN, and Thomas Edison left school early.

> *"One of the reasons the rich get richer, the poor get poorer, and the middle class struggles in debt is because the subject of money is taught at home, not in school. Most of us learn about money from our parents. So what can a poor parent tell their child about money? They simply say "stay in school and study hard" The child may graduate with excellent grades but with a poor person's financial programming and mind-set. It was learned while the child was young."*
>
> *—Robert Kiyosaki*

With the unfair advantage of financial knowledge the rich are going to get stronger and the poor & the middle class are just going to get weaker. There is going to be an ever widening gap. The rationale for teaching financial literacy is also supported by the fact that there is no real job security these days. Nobody is indispensible! Every year there are hundreds of thousands of fresh graduates marching into the corporate world; these graduates are more qualified in term of updated knowledge and skills. They are young, Especially after the economic slowdown of 2008 which saw many of us fired, most people have started rethinking their participation in the great economic rat race and are getting themselves financially educated. Some are doing this by choice, others by necessity.

Do you know the difference between asset & liability?

According to Kiyosaki, the key to achieving financial freedom is in understanding the difference between an asset & a liability, and learning to leverage it. "An asset puts money in your pocket and a liability takes money from your pocket," he explains. Things we own like cars, furniture, clothes and even collectibles, do have monetary value but they are not financial assets simply because they do not generate income, unless and until are sold for a profit. The rich understand this difference and buy assets, not liabilities, while poor people remain poor because they do just the opposite. They pile up on their liabilities and have zero assets.

Kiyosaki goes on to explain that any kind of debt is a liability for it is money owed to someone else. The classic example of a liability is credit card debt. When you use a credit card, you are, in actual fact, taking a loan from the bank or the company that issued the card. And with the loan comes interest payments. Most credit card companies, in general, do not require you to pay interest for the first credit card cycle, which can be up to 30-45 days. However, any amount not paid off in full after that first cycle will be subjected to interest. And if you have a balance due on your credit card, then all future charges are also subjected to interest. There will be no more first cycle grace period. As no money is exchanged in hands, the unwary are easily seduced into incurring more and more debt. On the same note, your primary residence is not really the asset you've been led to believe. Remember, when your banker advised you to avail a home loan and he kept on telling you that your house is the best asset that you will have, yes it is the best asset but not yours. It's the bank's asset since you will keep on paying the mortgage for years with interest to them. You will actually end up paying double or even triple the original value of your house as you pay your mortgage and interests for 10, 20 or even 30 years. What's worst, if you were not able to pay them on time, then they will foreclose it and you will end up paying for nothing. Even if you pay off the entire mortgage, your house does not qualify as an asset because it doesn't earn you any money, unless you sell it. And, don't forget the maintenance cost, property tax and insurance you pay every year.

The pattern of treating your home as an investment and the philosophy that a pay raise means you can buy a larger home or spend more is the foundation of today's debt-ridden society. This process of increased spending throws families into greater debt and into more financial uncertainty, even though they may be advancing in their jobs and receiving pay raises on a regular basis. It is high risk living caused by weak financial education.

It can be financially smart to carry good debt

Debt, in general, is a bad thing. However, Robert Kiyosaki explains that there is bad debt and good debt. When you borrow money to buy ego toys such as cars, clothes and electronic equipment, you are incurring bad debt. There is no financial gain from all these purchases. Good debt is when you borrow money to purchase assets. A classic example is money borrowed to buy rental real estate, where the tenant's payments are used to pay off the loan and generate cash flow. So, the root of the problem is not with debt itself, it is that people don't use debt as a tool for financial gain. Instead, they use debt because they fail to grasp the consequences of using it improperly.

Once you understand the difference between asset and liability, creating your own financial statement is the next step in gaining control over your personal finances.

A personal financial statement is like your report card after you leave school and measures how smart you are financially. As in a company FS, a PFS is made up of two accounting reports—the income statement and the balance sheet. The income statement records what types of income you are earning—active, passive or portfolio income, how much you are earning, and where your money finally goes (your outlays). It is a summary of all the money you earned and spent for a certain period of time. While assessing equity versus debt is done by way of a balance sheet. Just as an income statement measures one's short-term financial health through the comparison of income and expenses, the balance sheet measures long-term financial health through the comparison of assets versus liabilities. Thus, a PFS not just keeps you aware of your financial past and present, but it also shows the probable future.

> *"Too many middle-class people try to "keep up with the Joneses". The problem is… the Joneses are broke. They may have the big house, the nice car… but if you study their financial statements, you'll find that they own nothing, they have no assets, they are in debt."*
>
> *—Robert Kiyosaki*
>
> *"My banker has never asked me for my report card. He asks me for my financial statement."*
>
> *—Rich Dad*

Kiyosaki points out that the relationship between the income statement & the balance sheet is everything. To illustrate this association, he weighs the cash flow pattern of wealthy against that of the poor & middle class.

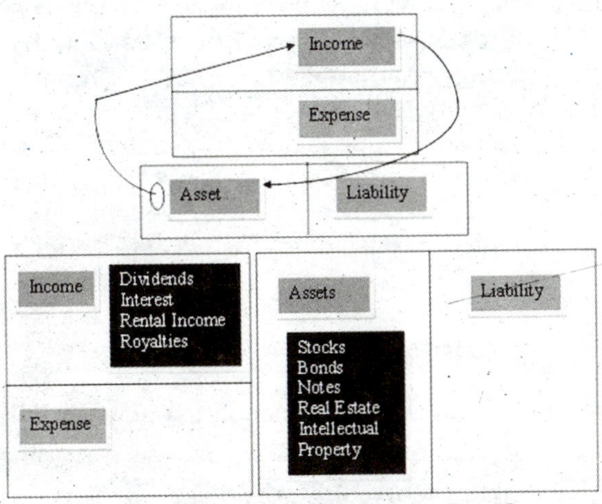

Cash Flow Pattern of Wealthy People

The rich buy assets first, so that they can eventually buy liabilities from the passive income that their assets generate. They gain control over their expenses, live below their means and have their assets work for them. And when their passive income starts exceeding their regular paycheck, they begin to use the excess to cover up the lifestyle expenses that they had till now put on the hold.

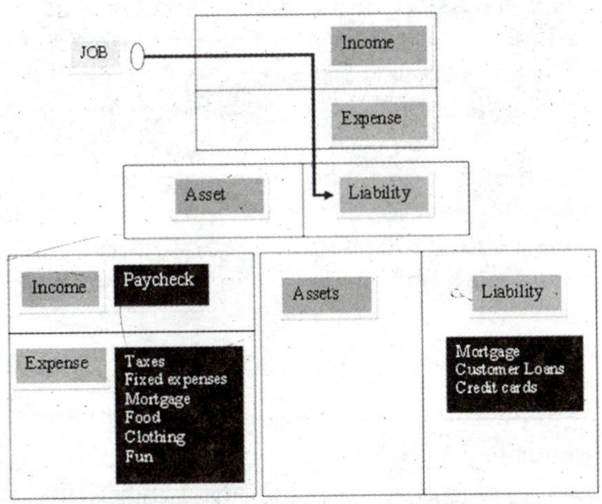

Cash Flow Pattern of Poor & Middle Class

The poor & the middle class fail to become rich because they use all their money to purchase liabilities first, till they have nothing left over to buy assets. They live a hand-to-mouth type of existence where any pay raises get swallowed up in trying to catch up, which they never do. It's is a surefire way not to eliminate debt and also happens to be the way most of us handle our money.

Which pattern does your financial statement reflect? What story does your financial statement tell? Are you in control of your expenses? Remember, financial freedom is not about how much money you make but how much money you keep, how hard that money works for you, and how many generations you keep it for.

The logic is simple. If you have an asset, then it generates income for you. With this income, you can buy more assets, which, in turn, will generate even more income! It's akin to a system with a positive feedback. Like when you put the microphone too close to a speaker, any little noise picked up by the microphone gets amplified out of the speakers. The amplified noise is again picked up by the microphone, which, in turn, gets amplified by the speakers. This process continues until the original tiny noise becomes an irritating screech. The good news is that in this context, spinning out of control means getting to where you want to be on your financial map. So, beef up your asset column and keep it strong. Once a dollar goes into it, never let it come out. Think of each dollar as your employee. Money in your asset column is money working for you instead of you working for money. The best thing about this money is that it works 24 hours a day and can work for generations.

The power of positive cash flow

Joe Spendsalot has been living paycheck-to-paycheck, making minimum payments on his $5,000 credit card debt. Joe brings in $2,500/month after taxes. He also spends $2,500/month, including $100/month to his credit card bill, which barely covers the interest. Because he spends as much as he earns, Joe's cash flow is zero. One day while running the numbers, Joe realizes it'll take him decades to pay off the credit card. So, he decides to increase his cash flow by taking a part-time job at the local comic book store, where he earns an extra $250 per month. At the same time, he cancels his cell phone, begins cooking more meals at home, and switches to store-brand groceries. This saves him another $250 per month. Joe is now bringing in $2,750 per month after taxes. He spends $2,250 per month. He has a positive cash flow of $500! It's now possible for him to pay off his credit card bill within a year. Once Joe has eliminated his credit card debt, he will have freed up an additional $100/month, raising his cash flow to $600. If he's smart, he'll begin saving and investing this money.

The only price of becoming rich—Delaying gratification!

As soon as the son of Kiyosaki's old-time friend turned 16, he started demanding a new car. His friends had all been given one by their parents, and he expected nothing less. But, it was not going to be that easy for the boy. His father believed in Kiyosaki's theory of Cashflow; so he gave his son $3,000 but forbade him from using it to buy a car just yet. At the same time, he gave his son a subscription to the Wall Street Journal. The father told his son that only once he had earned an additional $3,000 from his investments, could he then use $3,000 to buy a car. The other $3,000 would, of course, go into his college fund. "My friend said it was the best $3,000 he ever spent," says Kiyosaki. Not only had his son gained a new respect for the power of money, the 16-year-old also learned to spend money wisely instead of letting money burn holes in his pockets.

Chapter 3: Mind Your Own Business

When you go to work everyday, whose purpose are you fulfilling? It is the purpose of the company or organization you are working for. Irrespective of how big your salary is, the fact remains that your boss or the owner of the business will always make more money for the job work that you do! However, the situation gets more complex: many of us have been led into the belief that the organization's purpose is our own purpose. We whole-heartedly take up the cause of the organization as our own. Our thoughts and ideals slowly but surely come to be replaced by those of our workplace. We become the perfect employees. But what's wrong with that? Everything! According to Kiyosaki, financial struggle is often a direct result of people working all their lives for someone else and at the end of their working days, they have nothing left for themselves. Unfortunately, our education system hasn't helped in this regard. It has trained us to become what we study. If you study law, you become a lawyer, studying auto mechanics makes you a mechanic and studying cooking makes you a cook. The mistake in becoming what you study is that too many people forget to mind their own business. They spend their lives minding someone else's business and making that person rich. This employee mentality is what keeps most of us slaves to the economy and other people. Kiyosaki argues that the problem is that we focus too much on generating income instead of focusing on buying income generating assets. To become financially secure, you need to stop minding other people's business and start minding our own. At the very least you should do both, but do both well.

Let's say you have a salary of $48,000 per year. In other words, you are paid $4000 per month to mind your employer's business. But your monthly paycheck is for only $2500. The $1500 of withholding taxes is you minding Uncle Sam's business. Then you have to make your mortgage payment to the bank of $1500, which represents you minding the bank's business. Oh, and let's not forget that credit card balance that you let get away from you. That $400 payment is you working for the credit card company. Another $440 goes for living expenses. What are you left with? At the end of the month you are lucky to have $160 for investment, that's $1 per hour that you are earning working for others.

> *"Many people confuse their profession with their business. A highly paid slave is still a slave."*
>
> *—Robert Kiyosaki*

Keep your day job

The reality for most of us is we need to keep our daily jobs. Our corporate careers should be a means of being able to meet our basic needs whilst we work on our real purpose. Everything worthwhile takes time to build and become self-sustaining and profitable. During this building phase, we obviously need something to help us along. And don't forget, there could be a lot of value in working for someone else, only if you know why. It should not be, as most of us think, simply to be able to get a salary. Neither should that be our sole purpose in life. Corporate experience should instead be utilized as a way of developing ourselves and getting more knowledge and skills that we may need to be able to fulfill our own purpose. People, who work simply for the purpose of getting paid, are often not the most productive employees. It is those who realize the value addition from their jobs that perform better and are always ready to take up the next challenge. Mr. Narayana Murthy used his stint at Patni Computer Systems as a platform to gain all the experience and knowledge that he had to, before founding Infosys with six other software professionals.

Kiyosaki might have been working as a salesman at Xerox, but it was his own business investments that had him most engaged. He used his Xerox paychecks to purchase real estate. Within 3 years' time, his real estate income was far greater than his earnings at Xerox. He then left the company to mind his own business full time.

The value of changing Quadrants......instead of just changing jobs

In this section, Kiyosaki explains the significance of what he calls the "Cash Flow Quadrants". Each of us resides in at least one of these four quadrants. More than anything, it is the internal differences of our core values, strengths, weaknesses and aspirations that affect which quadrant we decide to generate our income from. Those who are motivated by security live on the E & S side of the Cashflow Quadrant, while those on the B & I side are inspired by freedom.

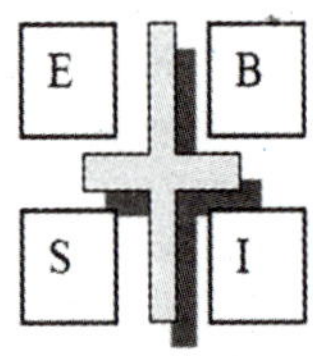

The letters in each quadrant represent:

E	for employee
S	for self-employed
B	for business owner
I	for investor

> *"Financial freedom happens when you have people working for you (B) and your money is working for you (I)."*
>
> *- Robert Kiyosaki*

Although Kiyosaki tells us that we can be successful regardless of which quadrant we are in, he recommends that we should try to move from being an employee to being an investor and a business owner so that we can have more free time to do what we really love. But remember that becoming an entrepreneur and building a B quadrant business is one of the toughest challenges a person can take on. The reason there are more people in the E and S quadrants is simply because those quadrants are less demanding than the B quadrant. As they say, "If it was easy, everyone would do it."

After a major business setback at the age of 37, Kiyosaki and his wife had to spend almost nine months homeless and dependent on the generosity of their friends. Even though Kiyosaki had the intelligence and technical knowledge to be successful, he lost faith in himself. It was the first time in his life he felt afraid to take risks. He finally understood why people with so much intelligence and knowledge fail to make it big in the real world. The reason is simple—fear. There is nothing wrong with being afraid to lose money. What is important is how you handle the fear. Indeed as human beings, making mistakes is how we are designed to learn. Just remember how you learnt to ride a bicycle. You probably still have that scar! It took an effort. It took a commitment. The bottom line, he writes, is that instead of giving up, get inspired by failure or the fear of failure. Another important personal skill required for any B quadrant business is leadership. There are many people in the S quadrant, the specialist or small business owners, who would like to expand, but they simply lack leadership skills. No one wants to follow them. The employees do not trust their leader or the leader does not inspire the employees to better themselves. The best way of facilitating this transition is to gain all the skills that are required in the B-I Quadrant, Kiyosaki adds.

> You can earn income in all the four quadrants irrespective of what you do professionally. A doctor can be employed by a hospital (E), have his own private practice (S), own a laboratory (B), and invest in share market & real estate (I).

To help overcome his own fears, Kiyosaki went back to the basics: setting a goal, writing a business plan, and letting nothing get in the way of his goals. When he finally got enough nerve to start another business, it took four years before he made his second million. However, he was hesitant to call himself a success until he discovered he would never have to work again for the rest of his life, what he calls true financial freedom.

Ask yourself, "Do I have what it takes? Am I willing to go beyond my comfort zones? Am I willing to be led and willing to learn to lead? Is there a very rich person inside of me, ready to come out?"

> *"The traditional corporate system really is a pyramid, because there are a few 'B's and 'I's near the top, and more 'E's and 'S's at the base."*
>
> *—Robert Kiyosaki*

Chapter 4: The History of Taxes and the Power of Corporations

Only two things in life are certain—Death & Taxes, Robert Kiyosaki tears this myth to shreds. If you look back into the history, it was the idea of "stealing from the rich to give to the poor" that eventually convinced the mass public to buy into the idea of income taxes. So, as the story goes, it was the rich who were targeted as the

Primary advantages of owning a corporation

1. **Tax Advantages**—A corporation earns, spends everything it can and then is taxed on anything that is left. Employees earn and get taxed and they try to live on what's left. By owning a corporation, all your major personal expenses can be disguised as company expenses like vacations as board meetings in Hawaii, car payments, health club memberships, etc.
2. **Lawsuit Protection**—Corporations and trusts protect a person's assets from creditors.

main source of additional tax revenue. However, as the size of the government increased, so did its expenditures and its need for more capital. The most natural thing for the government to do next was to bring the poor and middle classes into the tax bracket. What was initially a plan to tax only the rich eventually "trickled down" to the middle class and the poor, as the rich discovered a secret weapon to shelter them—corporation. It's one of the best kept secrets of the rich & wealthy and they have been using it for many generations now. There is a general misconception that corporations are only for big businesses with buildings, hundreds of employees, large operations, etc. However, anyone can create a corporation. It is relatively simple and would only require a little study on how to set one up. A corporation is simply a legal document in your attorney's file cabinet duly registered under a government state agency. But it can do so many things that an individual cannot, such as pay for expenses before it pays taxes and legally protect your wealth against lawsuits. Did you know that if you start a business from your home, everything you currently own and use for the corporation (tables, computers, chairs, etc.) can be considered a donation to the corporation, resulting in a write off on your individual tax return? You can even write off your rent if you operate from there! Kiyosaki recommends that one should do one's own research and find out what tax laws will bring the best advantages.

Since the rich shelter their wealth from taxes and the poor don't earn enough to be too concerned as they get far more back from the state than they give, it is really the middle class that pays the taxes and carry the burden stoically. That's not because they like paying taxes or feel that it is their moral obligation. It's because they don't know any different. They are not aware of tax loop-holes and they can't afford to pay a top-notch accountant or tax lawyer to help.

Playing by the Rules of the Rich

Kiyosaki bashes traditional financial advice, which tells us to ride out the waves of the stock market and continue investing in tax-deferred retirement accounts and mutual funds with strong track records. He goes on to say that moving your money makes more sense than parking it in cash, bonds, equities, or mutual funds—the strategy most financial advisors recommend. As an illustration, here's a real-life example which Kiyosaki has shared in one of his blogs:

2004: My wife, Kim, and I put $100,000 down to purchase 10 condominiums in Scottsdale, Ariz. The developer paid us $20,000 a year to use these 10 units as sales models. So, we received a 20 percent cash-on-cash return, on which we paid very little in taxes because the income was offset by the depreciation of the building and the furniture used in the models.

2005: Since the real estate market was so hot, the 380-unit condo project sold out early. Our 10 models were the last to go. We made approximately $100,000 in capital gains per unit. We put the $1 million into a 1031 tax-deferred exchange. We legally paid no taxes on our million dollars of capital gains.

2006: With that money, we purchased a 350-unit apartment house in Tucson, Ariz. The building was poorly managed and filled with bad tenants. It also needed repairs. We took out a construction loan and shut the building down, which moved the bad tenants out. Once the rehab was complete, we moved good tenants in and raised the rents.

2007: With the increased rents, the property was reappraised and we borrowed against our equity, which was about $1.2 million tax-free, because it was a loan—a loan which our new tenants will pay for. Even with the loan, the property still pays us approximately $100,000 a year in positive cash flow.

On the flip side, the poor and middle class toil away for their money, pay more in taxes the more they earn, and then park their earnings in savings and/or retirement accounts. In the meantime, they receive little or no cash flow on which to live while waiting for retirement—when they'll live on their meager savings. Doesn't it make more sense to do what the big daddies do, and earn more while paying less in taxes?

> *"Planning up to retirement is not enough. You need to plan beyond retirement age. In fact, if you intend to be rich, you should plan for at least three generations after you are gone. Most people do not even have enough to live on for three months if you take away their paychecks."*
>
> *—Robert Kiyosaki*

Chapter 5: The Rich Invent Money

The wealthy class use business as a vehicle to pursue their dreams and passions. After building their business, leading to a strong cash flow, they begin to invest in other assets that put more money in their pockets. Key among the behaviors of the rich is their ability to take calculated risks. They don't fear to make mistakes and this is the reason why they don't try to cover up unlike the poor and middle class who may lie, blame others, justify their mistake, quit or go into denial. The art of making a mistake in business is that you learn to take a risk, and pick yourself up and start a whole new venture, keeping in mind what went wrong during your first try. Also unlike their counterparts who crave for security, the rich measure worth of their investment plans in terms of the likely time that they would each take to give any meaningful returns. Poor people ride buses, which takes them longer to commute while the rich pay more to ride planes and buy more time to enjoy life. It may be an oversimplified example of how the rich value time over money, but it is very true. Another distinguishing factor for the affluent class is their ability to identify an opportunity everyone else has missed, while others just sit around waiting for the opportunity to happen. In the early 90's, the Phoenix economy was bad. Homes once valued at $100,000 sold for $75,000. Kiyosaki shopped at bankruptcy courts and bought the same houses at only $20,000. He resold these properties for $60,000 making a cool $40,000 profit. After six more transactions of the same manner, he made a total $190,000 in profit and it only took 30 hours of work time. The key to spotting such opportunities is learning to identify hidden freebies in business deals. For example, McDonald's may not make the best hamburgers in the world, but it owns the most valuable intersections and streets in America.

Self-confidence coupled with high financial IQ can certainly earn more for you than merely saving a little bit every month. Rich dad explains, there are two types of investors, each with a different mindset:

1. Buyers of Packaged Investments

This is when you call a real estate company, stockbroker or financial planner and put your money in ready made investments. It's a simple, clean way of investing.

2. The Professional Investors

The professional investors design their own investments. Assemble a deal and put together different components of an opportunity. Kiyosaki encourages this type of investment strategy, provided that you have mastered three main skills, which he believes are necessary to be able to do this, namely how to:

- Identify an opportunity everyone else has missed
- Raise capital
- Organize smart people

Chapter 6: Work to Learn, Don't Work for Money

"I often ask the classes I teach, 'How many of you can cook a better hamburger than McDonald's?' Almost all the students raise their hands. I then ask, 'So if most of you can cook a better hamburger, how come McDonald's makes more money than you?' The answer is obvious: McDonald's is excellent at business systems. The reason so many talented people are poor is because they focus on building a better hamburger and know little to nothing about business systems."

—Robert Kiyosaki

The rich "groom" the next generation by training their heir in all aspects of running the business. They are moved from department to department so that they learn how each one relates to the other. Specialization is not the key here, but picking up important lessons from each area and being able to see the business as a whole. Rich Dad groomed Kiyosaki and Mike in the same manner. Mike would later take over Rich Dad's empire, which included restaurants, convenience stores, and a construction company. Kiyosaki created his own empire with real estate, new products and educational materials.

Poor people have jobs, Rich and Successful people have careers

Kiyosaki makes the argument that during early days of your career, you should choose jobs based on what you can learn from them, not how much money you can make. Learn what it takes to get to the next step. It's important to know all aspects of running a business, i.e., how to manage cash flow, systems, and people. He puts equal emphasis on marketing & communication skills. He says there are many people who have the scientific bent and, hence, have a powerhouse of knowledge, but they fail miserably in communications. These are the people who are "one skill away from great wealth".

Kiyosaki's Odyssey:

After college graduation, Kiyosaki joined the Marine Corps. He learned to fly for the love of it. He also learned to lead troops, an important part of management training. His next move was to join Xerox, where he learned to overcome his fear of rejection. Initially, the very thought of knocking on doors and selling copiers terrified him. But soon he was among the top 5 salespeople at the company. For a couple of years, he was no 1. Having achieved his objective-overcoming his shyness and fear—he quit and began minding his own business.

Chapter 7: Overcoming Obstacles

Once people have studied and become financially literate, they may still face roadblocks to becoming financially independent. As per Kiyosaki, fear, cynicism, laziness, bad habits and arrogance are the main obstacles that come in our way to financial freedom.

- **Fear:** Robert cites fear as the core reason why people don't take risks and keep themselves just above the bread line. While it's normal to have fear, what matters is how one handles it. The mistake people make is they play it too safe because they are so afraid to lose. Instead of playing to win, they play not to lose. While most people avoid fear rather than seek it, Kiyosaki adheres to a different principle. "If I don't have butterflies in my stomach, there's no sense of working," he says. Getting into fear and confronting our greed, our weakness, our neediness is the way out. And the way out is through the mind, by choosing our thoughts.

- **Cynicism:** Don't give in to cynicism from yourself or others. Especially, don't take advice from someone who hasn't done what you want to do. Many people give advice on things they know nothing about. Mr. Colonel Sanders is a good example for this. His recipes for fried chicken were rejected 1009 times before he built up his multi-million dollar KFC empire. So, when you're in doubt and are afraid, just fry those noises surrounding you.

- **Laziness:** Greed is good and fights laziness. Think about the freedom and money you'll have and you will put in those extra work hours. Change your thinking. Instead of saying "I can't afford it", ask yourself "How can I afford it?" Challenge your mind to create solutions.

- **Bad Habits:** Spending habits should turn into saving and investing habits. Bear in mind, savings and investments are not necessarily functions of your earnings but rather functions of habits just like other habit-driven issues like smoking.
- **Arrogance:** Arrogance is ego + ignorance. Rich dad says what he knows makes him money but what he doesn't know loses him money. Every time you become arrogant, you lose money because when you are arrogant, you truly believe that what you don't know is not important. Never be complacent and think you know everything there is to know about money. Take investing for an example. It is a vast subject with many different people having as many different opinions. Two people can have different opinions on an investment and both have valid points. One investor's product may be another's pitfall. So, keep an open mind and listen to different points of view.

Chapter 8: Getting Started

"Pay more attention to your deep, silent thoughts- the things you do not say out loud; the inner voice that keeps telling you to become an investor so you can gain financial freedom by your forties. The worst thing you can do to yourself is run out of both time and money."

—Robert Kiyosaki

This chapter serves as a section on tips to create and build personal wealth. The author's first tip is to find a reason greater than reality, a big dream. Think of the freedom, the lifestyle, wherein you control your own time. Think of what you don't want, i.e., "I don't like being a corporate slave." The next tip is to feed the mind. By feeding the mind, the author suggests that people exercise their power of choice wisely. You can choose to watch MTV, or watch CNBC. It's how you choose to utilize your time and energy everyday that brings financial success in the long run. The author also advises people to pick friends carefully. Stay miles away from those who proclaim incessantly that the sky is falling and instead spend time with the educated few who enjoy talking about money because they may have valuable lessons to share. Further, the author observes that most people buy luxuries first, on credit. Wait for your asset base to grow first. Let the income from your growing assets afford you the new car. Another tip Kiyosaki gives is that of being generous. He thinks it makes a lot of sense to pay one's broker well as he's an ally, and "your eyes and ears to the market." After all, business is a team sport. You need to gather the best accountants, legal advisors, attorneys, brokers & bankers and you need to keep them happy. Finally, the author recommends finding oneself a hero. He believes heroes are indispensable in life because they not only inspire, they also make it seem so easy, "if George Soros can do it, why can't I?"

Chapter 9: Still Want More? Here Are Some To Do's

This chapter is sort of a supplement to the previous chapter. It gives readers additional tips to help them reach for financial rewards. First among them is to stop doing what you're doing—that is, if it's no longer working or viable.

> *"Insanity is do the same thing over and over again and expect a different result!"*
>
> *—Albert Einstein*

The author encourages readers to look for new ideas, to pick the brains of experienced individuals who have already done what one aspires to do. He advises on keeping the learning curve alive, taking courses, buying tapes and attending seminars. In looking for real estate investment opportunities in particular, the author recommends jogging around the neighborhood one is interested in. Finding a good business deal is a lot like dating. You must go to the market and talk to a lot of people, make offers, counteroffers, negotiate, accept and reject. The problem is many single people sit at home waiting for the phone to ring instead of going out and hitting the dating scene. Again most people believe that they need a huge amount of money for investing in real estate. But one can acquire real estate even if they don't have sufficient funds for the down payment. With a bit of cleverness, the author says people can make money even with a meager capital.

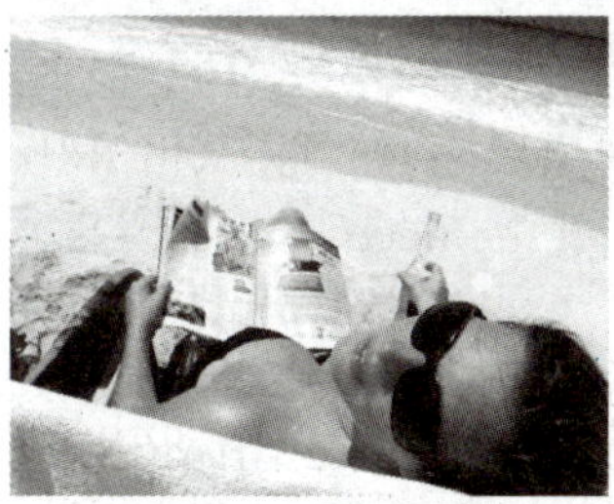

Is that you lying on the beach, listening to the waves lapping on the sand, your kids playing in the surf and no job to worry about going back to? It could be!

Getting out of rat race has nothing to do with your paycheck. Those with big incomes can get permanently caught up in the rat race. And those with moderate incomes can escape the rat race at remarkably early ages. The key is developing an understanding of how it works. But sadly, many people live in rat race without realizing it. To identify with this concept, let's trace the life-path of an average-educated, hard-working person. The chase of our financial dreams starts from the day we are sent to the school. During the next 14 years of our school education, we learn, excel, get fair to good grades, and are finally accepted into a college. After 3-4 years, we graduate, maybe go on to pursue a post-graduate degree and then do exactly as programmed: look for a safe, secure job or career. We find that job, maybe as a doctor, engineer, teacher or a lawyer or work for the government. But as soon as we begin to make money, our shopping begins, if it already hasn't. Having money to burn, we now go to places where other young people just like us hang out. We meet people, we date, and within a few years, get married. As our sources of income double, we feel successful, our future looks bright, and we decide to buy a house, a car, a television and take vacations. The demand for cash is enormous, so we mortgage ourselves up to the hilt. We realize that our careers are vitally important and begin to work harder, seeking promotions and raises. The raises come, and so do our children and the need for a bigger house. We work harder, become better employees, even more dedicated. We go back to school to get more specialized skills so we can earn more money. Maybe we take a second job. Our incomes go up, but so does the tax bracket we're in. As our children reach 5 or 6 years of age, we realize that we also need to save for their college funds. At 38 years of age, we are now trapped in the Rat Race which is only going to end after we retire. Employment becomes a necessary evil for most of us because deep down we would rather not be working for anyone else, but somehow we accept that it is the only way to get by. As, we work for the owners of our company, for the government paying taxes, and for the bank paying off a mortgage and credit cards, we continue to struggle and lie awake, worrying about how we are going to keep all these wheels spinning as interest rates increase. It's an endless, self-defeating or pointless pursuit of our financial dreams and we all are enduring it. If only our parents had learned from their experiences and not allowed the process to repeat into another hard-working generation.

Personal Money Allocation Made Easy

Ready! Set! But really how to? There is no denying the fact that RDPD is an inspirational life changing business classic, but as you would have discovered by now, it does fall a little short of expectation when it comes to describing the 'how to' specifics. So, I decided to include this extra section to make up for that.

The risk and reward balance strategy discussed below outlines three virtual buckets into which we need to allocate our monthly earnings (of course, after having paid for all the necessary expenses like food, electricity bills & child education). The 3 buckets are named as the "security bucket," the "momentum bucket," and the "buy and hold bucket." While the specific purposes of these buckets are different, overall the objective is to achieve a historically achievable return on investment while significantly reducing the likelihood of investment loss over the given time horizon. Here's a detailed description of each of them:

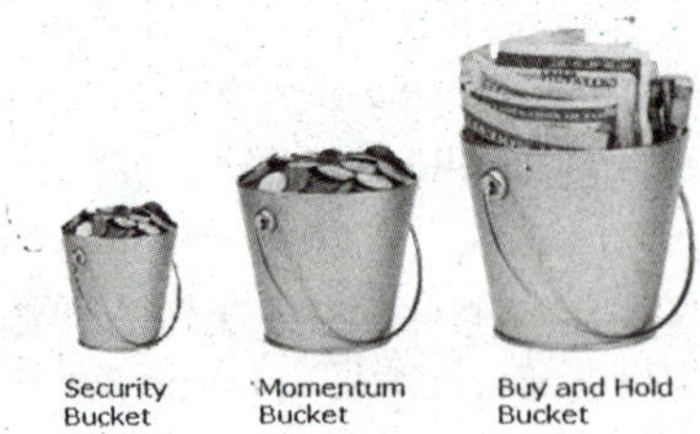

Why Money allocation is the best investment solution?

Because it is alone responsible for over 90% of variations in portfolio performance, while asset selection & timing explain just 4.6% & 1.8% of this variation. The rest is accounted by other factors.

- **The safety bucket:** This is where we put our money into conservatively safe and secure investments such as fixed deposits, dividend stocks, government bonds, insurances, etc. The safety bucket will not produce a good return, but then, that is not its purpose. Besides a risk-cover, we also need to ensure that we meet our ongoing financial commitments. So, within the safety bucket, we should always maintain at least 6 months' worth of our usual monthly income in liquid assets, in the event that we suddenly or unexpectedly lose our main income source. Depending on our age, risk tolerance and desired returns, the amount of capital we allocate to our safety bucket can vary, however, one should look to investing between 10% and 30% of one's capital. If we are nearing retirement, or financial independence, we may choose to increase that proportion, but when still acquiring assets, it's best to keep the safety bucket as small as possible, whilst still achieving its purpose of capital preservation.

- **The momentum bucket:** Filling this bucket would imply investing in short-term momentum investments, such as high beta stocks, futures & options, etc. They are relatively riskier but offer best returns in terms of time and value of money. They also demand huge commitment and must be tracked regularly. Needless to mention, investment newbies need to be careful and should avoid this bucket until they develop a sound technical knowledge base. Don't ever buy something because you hear about it on a news show, or because it's the thing to invest in right now, invest in it because you know and understand what you are investing in.
- **The buy and hold bucket:** The money you park in this bucket gets deployed into long-term wealth, building investments, such as retirement plans, blue chip shares, close-ended mutual funds, real estate properties or new business start-ups. Most successful investors adopt a 40-60 rule, in that they allocate 40% of their non-safety growth funds to momentum trades and 60% to long- term. Again the choice is yours, depending upon variety of factors, such as your tax bracket, level of investment knowledge, need for liquidity, tolerance for volatility & risk, current asset allocation, etc. The point is that you develop your plan and stick to it.

Any excess money, that spills over after you've successfully filled all your buckets, can be drawn upon periodically to splurge on luxury items, such as cars, boats, expensive clothes and jewellery, etc.

Most important investment advice: Choosing a portfolio management strategy is just the beginning. Tracking results, making necessary changes (guided by the discipline of selling winners & buying losers, not emotions) and keeping your strategy in line with a defined investment plan (maintaining consistency in the target asset mix throughout the investment period) are just as important, if not more.

TAKEAWAYS

Rich Dad's running theme is that you'll never get rich by chasing a higher salary. For an individual to be wealthy, he must aim to own the system or means of production, rather than work for another individual. Kiyosaki explains how the rich use their money to build investment vehicles which create an ever building passive income stream for them. The author also shares his understanding of the mechanisms employed by the government and the tax man and argues that it is the middle class that actually pay for the poor. The rich, on the other hand, are the ones who are hardly taxed because they have the knowledge to use tax legislation to their advantage. Most importantly, the book emphasizes on the message of not living below your means but to increase your means through financial literacy. Citing the example of his wife purchasing a Mercedes Benz, Kiyosaki claims that true luxuries are experienced when they are the outward manifestations of intelligent investing and asset building. "It was the car she liked, worked hard and, more importantly, made her money work harder to be able to purchase it", he adds.

Finally, Kiyosaki tells you things you don't want to hear. He is controversial. So is Donald Trump. Rich people are always controversial, but who are the people that make Kiyosaki and others controversial? Certainly it's not the wealthy. The wealthy agree with Kiyosaki because that is how they became rich. In fact, the advice he gives, resonates better today than ever before. Solely relying on a regular 40-hr-a week job, not only keeps you a financially broke corporate slave, but should anything ever happen to your company or the economy......well you get where I am going here.

❑❑❑

IMPORTANT NOTE

This summary culls the content of the book - "Rich Dad Poor Dad" down to its essence so that even an average reader can sensitize himself to it, sparing him with the time consuming details. In case you feel a need to further explore this topic, the author recommends reading the original work published by "Hachette Book Group USA".

A Snapshot of SIX THINKING HATS

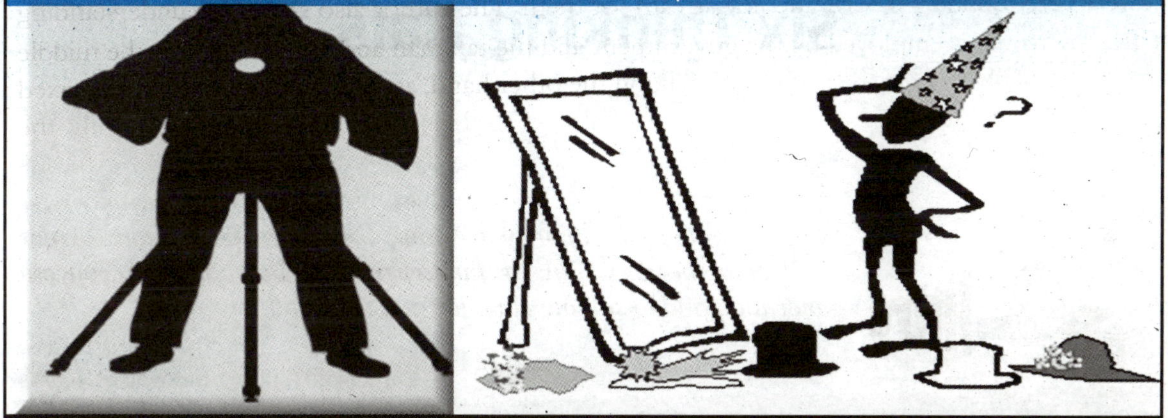

Have you ever attended a meeting that lasted longer than it needed to? Lacked focus or structure? Left you wondering why you, in particular, were invited? Or seemed totally unnecessary and produced no result? Most businesspeople would readily agree that meetings are the bane of their corporate existence, leading the list of top time wasters. I myself used to groan at the very thought of attending another meeting, but that was before I read the "Six Thinking Hats".

Six Thinking Hats

—Inspired by Edward de Bono

"Collaboration: A capacity to think and learn as a team across intellectual borders. This is fundamental to both original concept generation and to solving complex and uncertain problems."

—Chris Harris,
Author of Building Innovative Teams

At one time or another, everyone has felt frustrated by inefficient, wasteful meetings. Oftentimes, meetings are plagued by divisive arguments, side conversations, lack of preparation, and inaction. Imagine what might happen if you, your team, department, or entire organization learned specific thinking tools that would instantly eliminate these issues, opening the door to thorough decisions, better communication and easier problem resolution. To this end, six thinking hats provide a simple yet powerful method for improving communication, enhancing team productivity, promoting creativity and supporting organized decision-making. It helps you make better decisions by forcing you to move outside your habitual ways of thinking and break out of the 'thinking ruts'. A central principle to this framework is that 'thinking' entails a concoction of emotions, logic, experience and pattern recognition. Just as it would not be possible to design a golf club that was the best club for driving and, at the same time, the best club for putting, by the same token it is impossible to think rationally when in the grip of an emotive state. However, if these components could be identified and separated in the thought process, such that one field was addressed at a time, its overall quality would very likely be improved and simplified. So, the purpose of six thinking hats is to allow individuals, groups and teams to consciously untangle and unbundle their normal chaotic thinking process (that results from attempting to do too much all at once) and move towards the clarity of what de Bono calls, parallel thinking. As such, it helps you understand the full complexity of the decision, and spot issues and opportunities to which you might otherwise be blind. For example many successful people think from a very rational & positive viewpoint. This is part of the reason they are successful. Often, though, they may fail to look at a problem from an emotional, intuitive, creative or negative viewpoint. This can mean that they underestimate resistance to plans, fail to make creative leaps and do not make essential contingency plans. Similarly, pessimists may be excessively defensive; more emotional people may fail to look at decisions calmly and rationally.

Why do we need six hats?

Managers have long viewed meetings as a necessary evil. This attitude is understandable but unfortunate, as a good meeting should be an active forum in which colleagues exchange ideas, solve problems, and make decisions. The underlying problem is that group thinking often proceeds as drift and waffle and reaction to what turns up from moment to moment. There is a background sense of purpose, but this is never spelled out either as an overall objective or sub-objectives. Suggestions, criticism, information and plain emotion are all mixed together in a sort of thinking stew. It seems to be a matter of messing around until a thinker stumbles on some tried approach that seems to achieve what is desired. It is a haphazard exploration of experience strongly guided by negative criticism. The underlying assumption is that reasonably intelligent people provided with enough background information will, in the course of the discussion, list the action options and choose the most suitable.

Adversarial Thinking

Until recently, the argument or debate reigned supreme in group decision-making processes. We use the system in parliament. We use the system in the law courts. But as per the author, argument is an extremely crude, primitive and inefficient way of exploring a subject. de bono argues: "In a court of law, if the prosecuting lawyer thinks of a point which would help the defense case, is that lawyer going to put the point forward? Of course, not. If the defense lawyer thinks of a point that would help the prosecution, is that lawyer going to put forward the point? Of course, not. It is not a matter of 'exploring the subject' but of 'case making'."

A thinking system based on argument is excellent just as the front left wheel of a car is excellent. There is nothing wrong with it at all. But it's not sufficient. In argument, you have to start out with a position or point of view. You cannot argue without a position. In exploring a subject, you explore first and reach a position at the end, not at the beginning. Having a position at the beginning leads to selective perception and seeing only what we want to see. There is no effort to 'design' new possibilities. This limits the ways and extent to which each individual and, thus, the group as a whole can explore an issue.

A changing world

Imagine a situation where a doctor is treating a child with some rashes on his body. The doctor immediately thinks of some possible "boxes." Is it sunburn? Is it food allergy? Is it measles?

The doctor then examines the signs and symptoms and makes a judgment. Once the doctor has judged which box the condition of child fits into, he knows exactly what to do. This is traditional thinking at its best. From the past, we create standard situations. We judge into which "standard situation box" a new situation falls. Once we have made this judgment, our course of action is clear. Such a decision-making system works very well in a stable world. But in a changing world the standard situations may no longer apply. Instead of judging our way forward, we need to design our way forward and think about "what can be," not just about "what is." When a problem or issue needs to be thought through in detail, the brain needs to resist fixing on a pattern too quickly. This is notoriously difficult to achieve, even at an individual level. In a team brainstorming session, this problem worsens. Solutions can be quickly jumped to even while the problem is not fully understood, ideas can be shot down even before being fully developed and solutions can be pointed out as infeasible without the opportunity to consider them.

Congestion on the brain's highway

Getting stuck in a mental rut is a commonplace. You feel helpless and don't know how to dig any direction but down. Whether you can't decide on how to implement procedures, which career move is wisest, or if you should buy a low-maintenance goldfish or an attention-consuming puppy, everyone experiences "thinking log jams" at one time or another. Matters get worse when you're working in a group that is simultaneously throwing forth several unrelated ideas. Although everyone is working towards a solution in the company's best interest, tension and frustration mount as people get stuck on their perspectives and don't hear anyone else's. However, the Six Hats method, whether used individually or in a group, explores one thinking ingredient at a time, so that you can logically sort through information, feelings, caution, benefits, ideas, and process control. Juggling with six balls at the same time is rather difficult. Tossing up one ball at a time is much easier. Similarly, you cannot be sensitized in different directions at the same time. When we set out to do all aspects of thinking at the same moment, we are going to be suboptimal on all of them.

A Shift from Combative to Parallel Thinking

At a western-style argumentative meeting, the participants sit there with their points of view and, in many cases, the conclusion they wish to see agreed upon. The meeting then consists of arguing through these different points of view to see which survives the criticism and which attracts the most adherents. de Bono wants to get away from this judgmental, confrontational style towards a more open, positive, creative and playful way of discussing. Even with good courtesy and clear shared objectives in any collaborative thinking activity, there is a natural tendency for "spaghetti thinking" where one person is thinking about the benefits while another considers the facts and so on. The hats allow this to be avoided so that everyone together considers the problems, or the benefits, or the facts, reducing distractions and supporting cross pollination of thought. People learn best when they are playing, and the Six Hats approach clearly encourages a spirit of play. By giving each person a role (and each person eventually playing all of the roles), the method reduces the amount of personality-based conflict, encourages more participation, and gives validation to many different ways to present the question at hand. For example, if you do not like an idea, then you are not going to spend much time thinking of the benefits or good points of that idea. This is because if you uncovered sufficient good points for the idea to be accepted, then you would have "lost" the argument. With the Six Hats method, however, the thinker can be specifically asked to give a yellow hat "performance." This is a challenge to the thinker, who will not want to appear unable to perform this way. So, yellow hat thinking gets done even by someone who does not like the idea. In the course of this yellow hat thinking, ideas may turn up which cause the thinker to change his or her mind. It also can happen the other way around. An euphoric supporter can be asked to point out the downsides of a plan.

Here is how it works

Dr. de Bono identifies six distinct states in which the brain can be "sensitized". In each of these states, the brain will identify and bring into conscious thought certain aspects of issues being considered (example gut, instinct, pessimistic judgment, neutral facts). Hats are named for colours that are mnemonically descriptive of the perspective one adopts when wearing them. For example, the devil's advocacy is what one engages in when wearing the Black Thinking Hat.

Ingredients in thinking

Given below is a brief description of each of the hats and the thinking processes that they represent. Following which there is a discussion about various lateral thinking triggers that one can use. Then an illustration through an example from a typical commercial environment.

White Hat

This covers facts, figures, information, asking questions and defining information needs and gaps. With this thinking hat, you focus on the data available, look at the information you have, and see what you can learn from it. Watch out for gaps in your knowledge, and either try to fill them or take account of them. This is where you analyze past trends, and try to extrapolate from historical data. "I think we need some white hat thinking at this point......" means "let's drop the arguments and proposals and look at the database." It encourages the thinker to separate what is fact and what is interpretation. No one can push a particular point of view, but simply lay it out on the table. Overall, the objective is to facilitate a deeper understanding of the breadth and depth of the relevant issue with the neutral deposition of data.

All of us are familiar with meetings that begin with a creative proposal, which soon gets wounded up by comments about why it won't work and then left to die because a participant opines that there is not enough information to decide. The thought dies and is never explored sufficiently to determine what it has to offer or whether it can be adapted to address the obstacles raised by the critiques. Thus all the attendants must come prepared for the white hat thinking session by bringing with them data and information pertinent to the subject in hand. This avoids the need to break out of the session to get the data, or to move forward on the basis of an incomplete white hat thinking session or one wrongly based on opinion.

Red Hat

'Wearing' the red hat, you look at problems using intuition, gut reaction, and emotion. Emotions can be positive (happiness, joy, wonder, enthusiasm, hope, expectation), negative (anger, disappointment, mental-blocks, jealousy, cynicism) or neutral (intuition, curiosity). The objectives of the red hat are to lend credibility to "emotional" thinking, help feelings surface (rather than remain hidden and yet play an important role in the discussion) and free the participants from having to justify their intuitive thoughts. Intuition may be based on knowledge of the market, or past experience. "Putting on my red hat, I think this is a terrible proposal." It is important to be free from obligations to effectively wear the red hat. The purpose of the red hat is to express feelings, as they exist. It is not designed to force a judgment and is therefore applied more quickly than the other hats to ensure it is a gut reaction feeling that is recorded. At the end of the meeting you can sometimes be asked to put a red hat on and express how you feel about the outcome, and if you feel the group has done a good job.

In a normal business discussion, you are not supposed to allow your emotions to enter in. They enter in anyway – you merely disguise them as logic·

Black Hat

Black Hat thinking helps to make your plans 'tougher' and more resilient. It is a hat of judgment and caution. All constraints are noted down. The scope of the issue may be fine-tuned. Feasibility of ideas is evaluated. Pitfalls and shortcomings are identified. Problems and ideas are prioritized based on relevance or impact. Participants can play the "devil's advocate," discuss worst-case scenarios and identify bottlenecks and weak links. Black hat highlights the weak points in your plan and allows you to eliminate them, alter them, or prepare contingency plans to counter them. The objective of this hat is to critically evaluate & judge issues and converge on a specific problem or solution area.

A word of caution—overuse of the black hat may lead to an unhealthy cynicism, where people only seem to find fault with everything. Under the Black Hat, the speaker must give a logical reason for the risk or downside identified. It is not enough to say, "It won't work." Criticism should always be accompanied by an alternative option. No one likes to be blindsided, painted into a corner or caught in a trap, to use a couple of our figures of speech for situations where we have not Black Hatted to anticipate problems. However, unless shepherded, Black Hat thinking can impede and often prevent creative problem solving.

Yellow Hat

The one thing that all successful people share in common is their desire to make things happen. To this end, yellow hat thinking symbolizes brightness & optimism that keeps you going even when everything looks gloomy and difficult. It could be described as the "be positive" hat with the optimistic viewpoint that helps you to see all the benefits of the decision and the value in it.

The focus is on "value sensitivity" & "how-to-make-it-happen" rather than "how-this-may-not-work". It is a waste of time to set out trying to be creative, if you are not going to recognize a good idea. The yellow hat seeks value, so even unattractive ideas are given their due recognition.

Yellow hat thinking often requires a deliberate effort. Benefits are not always immediately obvious and we might have to search for them. Also, majority of us, being naturally wired to think with a black hat, love to pounce on any new idea and tear it to pieces, which is why the yellow hat is relatively harder to wear than the black hat. Now, there is such a thing as over-optimism, such as people who base their entire lives on the possibility of winning the lottery. That is sheer stupidity. The yellow hat instead calls for a reasonable amount of optimism. It doesn't simply assume like Pollyanna that good things will happen automatically.

Green Hat

This hat symbolizes a freewheeling way of thinking, in which there is little criticism of ideas. By removing judgment and feasibility analysis from the scope of the discussion, participants are free to generate crazy ideas that may not be immediately relevant or feasible. A whole range of creativity tools can help you here. Lateral thinking, or pattern switching, works when the thinker cuts across patterns instead of just following them, thus producing an Eureka effect. "PO" is another green hat device that allows one to think and use provocative operation. For example PO cars would have square wheels, PO planes would be able to land upside down. PO executives should be able to promote themselves. You'll be surprised when suddenly your team's "Devil's Advocate" is now showing off their ability to dream up wild solutions that just might work! (A detailed explanation of these methods is given in the section—Lateral Thinking Triggers)

The ideas generated under the green hat session are gathered and assessed under the yellow hat for constructive development, and then the black hat may be used. At any point, the white hat can be used for neutral facts or information to support or evaluate whether or not an idea will work. Red hat thinking is the last stage. Ask questions like: do we like the idea enough to proceed? Are we excited?

Blue Hat

The Blue Hat is responsible for summaries, overviews and conclusions. Like the conductor of an orchestra, it is worn by individuals who chair meetings and, thus, controls the overall flow of discussion—what hat to wear, when and for how long. This ensures that the agenda and timelines are adhered to and the rules of the game are followed. The blue hat is also used to arbitrate and re-focus. For example when the group discussion is going astray or gets stuck because ideas are running dry, the person wearing Blue hat may direct the group into Green Hat thinking; thereby designing a way forward.

It defines the problem, why we are meeting, what the objectives are & the results we want to achieve, keeps track of all of the ideas and issues that arise during the meeting and consequently harvests the most attractive ideas or solutions. Finally, towards the end of the meeting, the blue hat recapitulates what was achieved, the outcomes & conclusions.

With the Six Hats method, we try to do only one thing at a time. There is a time when we look for danger (black hat). There is a time when we seek new ideas (green hat). There is a time when we focus on information (white hat). We do not try to do everything at the same time. The thoughts are laid out in parallel. You do not respond to what the last person has said. You simply add another idea in parallel. In the end, the subject is fully explored quickly. Use of the Six Hats approach also provides a polite means to control the "Yes but"s and the doubters, that is, individuals who wake up and go through life wearing a black hat. They can be assured that time will be set aside to do Black Hat thinking and Black Hat comments made at other times can be welcomed and discouraged with a "Thank you for that comment, it will be helpful when we get to the Black Hat stage. We are doing Yellow Hat now, so share with us any benefits or advantages you can see." Individuals, who are comfortable only when all facts are known, get a reminder that information gathering is a White Hat activity and thinking under other hats can proceed without information concerns because those concerns will be addressed during the White Hat phase.

Because the participants are thinking in parallel, there is little to argue about. In the Yellow Hat mode, the stereotypical critique is called on to identify benefits of the challenged project while during the Black Hat mode, the proponent of the project must think in parallel with his stereotypical counterparts to identify risks and downsides of the project. Odds are, both will emerge with a better appreciation of his and the other's positions.

Lateral Thinking Triggers

One of the key impediments to thinking "out-of-the-box" is psychological inertia—the inertia of experience and core competence. It can be extremely difficult to break out of strong patterns that the brain is used to. Lateral thinking triggers like fractionation, reversal, analogies and random provocation are simple to apply and quite beneficial, especially while wearing the white and green hats.

Fractionation

The idea is to generate alternative ways to segment a specific issue or scenario; the segments do not have to make immediate sense. Fractions do not have to be mutually exclusive. Furthermore, each person can generate different fractions based on his/her perspective of the issue or scenario. Fractions generated in this manner can then be merged to bring out novel perspective on the discussion topic and generate new threads of thought.

Reversals

This technique is used to artificially invert or reverse the issue. It guarantees breaking out of rigid patterns. Often, the reversed scenario will be crazy, infeasible or comical. For example cat catches the mouse can be reversed as "mouse catches the cat" or "cat releases the mouse". After reversal, the new alternative scenarios are often potent in generating new radical ideas.

Analogies

Analogies are situations or scenarios similar to the topic of discussion in some way, but different enough to facilitate generation of new thoughts. For example, an analogy for a military crisis could be a pressure cooker or avalanche. Once suitable analogy is identified, the nuances of the analogy are described without looking back at the original problem. The scenario in the analogy is discussed in detail. Emerging thoughts are then applied to the topic of discussion to generate new perspectives and ideas.

Random Provocation

Sometimes, patterns are so rigid that even the use of fractionation, reversal or analogies results in the generation of same rigid patterns. In such cases, random provocation can provide the necessary jolt. It involves the use of random words as triggers to generate alternative patterns. Random words can be picked from dictionaries, newspapers and books or generated by participants themselves. With no apparent connection between the random word and the topic of discussion, participants are forced to think laterally to generate a new link or thought perspective.

Proven Simple Power

The six hats thinking is extremely simple and powerful. This powerful simplicity, together with the practical nature of the method, has led to its adoption by major corporations like Federal Express, IBM, NTT, Bell Canada & Rockwell International. The technique probably lends itself more to a group or business environment, but there is no doubt that it can also be usefully applied on an individual basis.

How to Think Through Your Hat

Hats should never be used to categorize individuals. In a meeting, someone has been chosen as the black hat thinker, someone else as the white hat thinker, and so on. The people then keep those roles for the whole meeting. That is exactly the opposite of how the system should be used. The whole point of parallel thinking is that the experience and intelligence of everyone should be used in each direction. It is true that some people may be permanently cautious and inclined to look for dangers. It is also true that some people might always be bubbling with ideas and others might be better at focusing on facts. People may prefer one mode to another. People might be better at one mode than another. Nevertheless, hats are not categories of people. The hats may be used one after another in any desired sequence. The sequence is set up at the beginning of the meeting under an initial blue hat. It is laid out in advance and followed. The correct sequencing is very important. For example, you should never use black hat thinking just before green hat thinking. Critical thinking used too early in a process kills creativity.

In practice, we refer to hats by color and never by their function:

"Take off your black hat for a moment".

"We do not have enough of white hat here."

"That's enough of the yellow hat thinking. Let's put on the white hat."

It is very important to note that the hats are directions and not descriptions of what has happened. It is not a matter of everyone saying what they like and then the hats being used to describe what has been said. It is a matter of setting out to think in that direction.

"Let's have some white hat thinking here" means a deliberate focus on information. Everyone now tries to think of information that is available, information that is needed, questions to be asked, other ways of getting information, and so on."I want your red hat on this" is a specific request for feelings, intuition and emotions on a particular issue.

Here's a theoretical example of a six thinking hats session: The directors of a property company are looking at whether they should construct a new office building. The economy is doing well, and the amount of vacant office space is reducing sharply. As part of their decision, they decide to use the 6 thinking hats technique during a planning meeting.

"AND NOW, GENTELMEN, THAT WE HAVE OUR THINKING CAPS ON, LET US CONTINUE."

Looking at the problem with **White Hat**, they analyze the data they have. They examine the trend in vacant office space, which shows a sharp reduction. They anticipate that by the time the office block would be completed; there will be a severe shortage of office space. Current government projections show steady economic growth for at least the construction period.

With **Red Hat** thinking, some of the directors think that the proposed building looks quite ugly. While it would be highly cost-effective, they worry that people would not like to work in it.

When they think with the **Black Hat**, they worry that government projections may be wrong. The economy may be about to enter a 'cyclical downturn', in which case the office building may be empty for a long time.

Putting on the **Yellow Hat**, they agree that if the economy holds up and their projections are correct, the company stands to make a great deal of money. If they are lucky, maybe they could sell the building before the next downturn, or rent to tenants on long-term leases that will last through any recession.

With **Green Hat** thinking, they consider whether they should change the design to make the building more pleasant. Perhaps they could build prestige offices that people would want to rent in any economic climate. Alternatively, maybe they should invest the money in the short term to buy up property at a low cost when a recession comes.

The **Blue Hat** is used by the meeting's Chair to move between the different thinking styles. He or she might have needed it to keep other members of the team from switching styles, or from criticizing other participant's points.

> Six thinking hats isn't a heavy handed approach. Instead, it's a subtle shift in strategy from free-for-all debate to focusing and coordinating your team's thinking power in a deliberate way. This lets everybody get heard as well as really bang on a problem from multiple angles in a teamwork sort of way.

Nothing More Than a Child's Play

Craig Elkins, manager of the Applied Thinking and Creativity Team at Boeing, Seattle, not only teaches Six Hats to Boeing employees, but also taught the method to his daughter, Chelsea, when she was only four years old. Now an eight-year-old Chelsea frequently uses Six Hats to solve dilemmas, for instance, whether to eat candy before dinner. Rather than pitching a temper tantrum, Chelsea will sift through all aspects of the problem to arrive at a sensible solution.

White Hat—"There's a grape lollipop in my backpack."

Blue Hat—"Should I have candy before dinner? I have to decide."

Red Hat—"I'm feeling like I'd love some candy."

Yellow Hat—"It tastes good."

Black Hat—"Candy could spoil my dinner and give me cavities."

Green Hat—"I could eat it after dinner."

After sorting all sides of the issue, Chelsea threw up her arms and said, "Never mind, no candy now!"

With color printing, each color is printed separately, one at a time, and in the end, the full color effect is obtained. It is the same with six hat thinking – we do one thing at a time and, in the end, the full picture emerges. But remember, just walking along the road will not make you a better tennis player or a better skier. Thinking like any other activity, needs deliberate practice in a framework that is set up for it.

TAKEAWAYS

The difference between brilliant and mediocre teams isn't so much in their combined mental capacity, but in how well they can tap into their collective wisdom and how well they function together. The six hats thinking neutralizes employee rank and allows participants to be creative without risk. It creates an awareness of multiple perspectives, sets up a clean method for switching gears, eliminates distraction, and improves overall communication. It also puts people who are quiet and reserved on an equal playing field with those who are more talkative and might otherwise monopolize a meeting. After your employees learn the skills behind the six thinking hats system, they'll show enthusiasm, creativity and courage to make every discussion, every decision come alive with new ideas. Consequently, your team meeting will witness the following desired results:

Power: With six hats method, at any given time, everyone is looking and working in the same direction. This is analogous to magnet. A magnet is powerful because all the particles are aligned in the same direction.

Time saving: When the six hats are used, meetings get dramatically shorter & take a third or a quarter of their usual time. Sometimes, as in the case of ABB, meetings take one-tenth of the time.

Removal of ego: Perhaps the biggest obstacle to quick and effective thinking is the ego. People tend to use thinking to parade their egos. Someone will choose to disagree on a point simply to show up the person who has made that point. If another person had made the same point, there would have been full agreement. With the six hats method, you exert your ego not in the confrontational and adversarial context but by performing well as a thinker under each of the hats.

My only suggestion is that you give this process a trial run with something unimportant before unleashing it on a big issue. Otherwise, you might be stalled by lack of understanding about how the process works. Keep practising until you are satisfied that it is working well.

❑❑❑

IMPORTANT NOTE

This summary culls the content of the book - "Six Thinking Hats" down to its essence so that even an average reader can sensitize himself to it, sparing him with the time consuming details. In case you feel a need to further explore this topic, the author recommends reading the original work published by "Penguin Books".

A Snapshot of
7 HABITS OF HIGHLY EFFECTIVE PEOPLE

"The 7 Habits of Highly Effective People" is unquestionably the best overall prescription for becoming effective. Its premise is that people deal with the problems in their life in a scattershot fashion which leads to disillusionment and disorder. To be a truly effective person, you need to learn to solve personal and professional problems with a integrated and principle centered approach – in other words, the decisions you make both personally and professionally should come from the same core set of values and ideas. The 7 habits are really about developing that core set of values to the point where it's easy to draw solutions to problems from them, making you a much more effective person in all aspects of life.

The Seven Habits of Highly Effective People

—Inspired by Stephen Covey

"Men's natures are alike; it is their habits that separate them."

—Confucius,
Great Thinker & Educator in Ancient China

Borrowing from the concepts of Quantum Mechanics, *The Seven Habits of Highly Effective People,* begins with an astute observation that people perceive the world differently, and because we view the world with our own unique 'lens,' it is difficult to separate the observation from the observer. Covey asserts that we all have our own paradigm, which is our own map of how we perceive the world and how we think the world should be in our ideal view. These paradigms are, in turn, the source of our attitudes and behaviours. We simply cannot act with integrity and maintain wholeness outside of them. So, to try to change outward attitudes and behaviours does very little good in the long run, if we fail to examine the basic paradigms from which those attitudes and behaviours flow.

Covey argues that our paradigms will affect how we interact with others, which understandably also affects how they interact with us. Thus, any effective self-help program must begin with an 'inside-out' approach, rather than looking at our problems as 'being out there'. We must start by examining our own characters, paradigms and motives. The inside-out approach says, 'If you want to have a happy marriage, be the kind of person who generates positive energy and sidesteps negative energy rather than empowering it. If you want to have a more pleasant, cooperative teenager, be a more understanding, empathic, consistent, loving parent. If you want to have more freedom, more latitude in your job, be a more responsible, a more helpful, a more contributing employee. If you want to be trusted, be trustworthy. If you want the secondary greatness of recognized talent, focus first on primary greatness of character.' Covey does not claim to have invented the seven habits, but rather to have discovered them and to have found a simple language for articulating them. He adds that habits are patterns of behaviour that involve three overlapping components: desire, knowledge and skill. Because these three components are learned rather than inherited, effective habits can be learned and, likewise, ineffective habits can be unlearned.

The first three habits (Be Proactive, Begin with the End in Mind, Put First Things First) are more about managing oneself and others in order to accomplish tasks and goals, but with habits four through six (Think Win/Win, Seek First to Understand, Then to Be Understood, Synergize). Covey provides 'Paradigms of Interdependence' which allows one to transform their relationship with others into a richer experience. The Seventh Habit (Sharpen the Saw) is about personal renewal, and how to spend a small amount of time daily to work towards continual improvement.

Habit No. 1: Be Proactive

There's a difference between knowing the path and walking the path

Covey contrasts being proactive or having a proactive mentality with being reactive. Reactive people, he says, are those who are resigned to the truth that whatever they do in the present can have no effect on their circumstances. And interestingly, for reactive people, it really is a truth, for whatever we believe in our heart affects our thoughts, words, and actions. If we really believe that we can do nothing about our unreasonable boss or the daily events in our lives, then we simply do not make the effort. Reactive people also tend to be out of touch with their core values. Instead of running their lives based on unchanging core principles, they pick up temporary values from others around them. If no special opportunities come their way, they'll stay at the same job year after year as long as it's semi-satisfying. If most of their friends exercise, they probably will too; otherwise, they probably won't. They go with the flow of the people and circumstances that surround them, but they don't direct the flow. Their lives are largely out of their direct conscious control; they tend to only exert their human endowments when they absolutely must, such as if they get laid off unexpectedly (and even then it's often to a minimal degree). But when things are pretty good, life is mostly on autopilot.......

If a reactive person were to captain a ship, the ship would flow with the currents. This person would be preoccupied with studying the currents, trying to predict where the ship will end up as a function of the currents. If the currents are good, this person is happy. If the currents are poor, this person feels stressed. On the occasion, this person might attempt to set a destination, and if the currents are good, the ship will arrive. But if the currents are poor, this person will bemoan them and give up the destination for an easier one.

On the other hand, proactive people are a different breed than most. While reactive persons are governed by social conditions, proactive people are driven by values and principles. Proactive people can control their feelings and are guided by internalized values and paradigms and their response to external stimuli is a value-based choice. They simply do not accept that there is nothing that can be done about the unreasonable boss or the events of daily life—they will point out that there are always choices. Even when things are pretty good, they're still making conscious choices. Sometimes that means maintaining the status quo, while other times, it means changing directions. Sometimes their values will align well with what's socially popular; other times, they won't. Proactive people will take actions that often seem mysterious to reactive people. They may suddenly quit their job to start a new business, even though everything seemed to be going well for them. They'll often start new projects or activities "out of the blue" when it seems like there's no externally motivated reason to do so. A proactive person will still pay attention to external events, but they'll pilot themselves to their desired destination regardless of those events.

If a proactive person were to captain a ship, the ship would go wherever the captain wanted it to go. This captain would still note the currents, but they'd merely be used for navigational purposes. Sometimes, the ship would flow with the currents; other times, it would steam against them. It matters little whether the currents are good or not; this captain will reach the intended destination regardless of the currents. The currents can only control the time of arrival and the exact path from starting point to final destination. But the currents have no power to dictate the final destination; that is entirely the captain's choice.

We all have concerns we can do little about. According to Covey, the problems, challenges, and opportunities we face fall into two areas—Circle of Concern and Circle of Influence. It is good to recognize that proactivity is mostly limited to our circle of influence. It's not likely that you can change the weather or personally broker world peace, so before you decide what values you are going to act on, recognize that you have a limited circle of influence. Proactive people work on the things they can do something about: health, children, problems at work. Reactive people focus their efforts in the Circle of Concern—things over which they have little or no control: the national debt, terrorism, the weather. Let's say, for example, that you're waiting for a very important phone call. Some people stress out waiting for the call—hat's a bad habit because you can't control when the phone call comes. On the other hand, others simply spend their time focusing on the things they can control- the phone call will eventually come, right?

How can we internalize the substance of first habit? Spend a day counting the number of times you spend focusing on stuff you can't alter the outcome of. Do you daydream about unachievable things? Do you worry about stuff you can't affect? Cast those efforts aside and spend your time on things that you can affect.

Metaphorically, this habit is like being a programmer for your life; the idea is that we are not some program being run. We may have no control over what life throws at us but we always have a choice about how we are to respond. Viktor Frankl, a Jewish prisoner, held in a concentration camp during World War II, explains this well: "We who lived in concentration camps can remember the men who walked throughout the huts comforting others, giving away their last piece of bread. They may have been few in number, but they offer sufficient proof that everything can be taken away from a man but one thing—the last of the human freedoms to choose one's attitude in any given set of circumstances, to choose one's own way."

The notion that having a particular attitude of mind (which is really where this habit begins) can make such a huge and positive difference to almost everything we experience in life is foreign to those who have already internalized the opposite habit as a part of their personalities. For such people, the glass is always half-empty and the feeling of melancholy is a pleasant reminder that something is indeed missing. For these people, this habit may seem like a bitter pill to swallow—but, says Covey, it is also completely liberating. So, take ownership, make the changes you know you need to make and become the transition figure your family, community or company needs.

Business Issue

We live in an era of strategic turmoil—of new business models, strategic combinations, globalization, and revolutions in technology. The rapid pace of change can cause organizations to suffocate from uncertainty, turn reactive and defensive. Fear and anxiety could set in. However, an organization can respond to change proactively and positively, seeking and seizing opportunity. Faltering organizations can turn around if they take a proactive stance.

- Greater focus on innovative ways to build value.
- Employees who take ownership for solving problems and adding value.
- Faster, more creative problem solving and decision making.

Habit No. 2: Begin with the End in Mind

The very essence of leadership is vision. You can't blow an uncertain trumpet.

> If your ladder is not leaning against the right wall, every step you take gets you to the wrong place faster.

This habit is based on the principle that all things are created twice. At first, there is a mental creation, and then the physical creation follows the mental, just as a building follows a blueprint. If you don't make a conscious effort to visualize who you are and what you want in life, then you empower other people and circumstances to shape you and your life by default. The problem is that many people climb the ladder of success only to find the ladder was leaning against the wrong wall. Being successful at their chosen career and committed to its progress, they come to realize that it does not bring any sense of real satisfaction. The reason for this ultimate dissatisfaction is that they did not begin with the end in mind. And it is not just that they did not begin with the end in mind; it goes a bit deeper—they did not ever get around to defining the end itself. So what does all this mean? Here is an example from the book: the end represents the purpose of your life. Imagine your funeral and what others are saying and thinking about you. What will your family say at your funeral? What will your coworkers say? What about your friends? What do you want them to say? The things that you want them to say are the real core values that you care about the most, and, thus, they should be the ones that you focus your life's work on, both personally and professionally.

One of the best ways to incorporate Habit No. 2 into your life is to develop a Personal Mission Statement. Personal mission statement can help add focus, direction and a sense of purpose to your daily decisions. In developing your personal mission statement, you can use your creative ability to imagine life milestones such as birthdays, anniversaries, retirement. What accomplishments would you like to celebrate? Visualize them in rich detail. An Olympic high jumper in one of his documentaries said that he trained the same amount of time visually as he did physically. This meant that half of his training was sitting in a chair envisioning every movement of the run up to the bar, then the jump, then the arched back, then the feet, and the successful fall down to the mat. He ran it in a slow motion, backwards, and forwards until it was smooth. Anytime there was a doubt, he stopped his visualization and checked where his feet were, where his hands were, and how high his knee was. Then when he practised physically, his body and mind had already "experienced" a successful jump and knew exactly what to do. This is the kind of visualization and affirmation that you need to do with principles in your mission statement. If one of your mission statements is to be an understanding mother, visualize your daughter coming home from the school and telling you that she failed a test. Visualize yourself being understanding in that situation.

Business Issue

The mission statement should be a clear and succinct representation of the enterprise's purpose for existence. It should incorporate socially meaningful and measurable criteria addressing concepts such as the moral/ethical position of the enterprise, public image, the target market, products/services, the geographic domain and expectations of growth and profitability. The intent of the Mission Statement should be the first consideration for any employee who is evaluating a strategic decision. One the biggest drivers of user contribution to Wikipedia is clear mission statement they have: "Create a comprehensive and accurate free encyclopedia in 10 years".

> *"That business mission is so rarely given adequate thought is perhaps the most important single cause of business frustration."*
>
> *– Peter Drucker*

We are in a time of strategic retrenchment when organizations are stripping away everything that isn't core and trying to find or renew their direction and focus.

- Core values and ideology enable more focused branding, better compatibility in hiring and partnering.
- Shared mission provides better sense of strategic direction.

Note: We need to have internalized the first two habits before we can benefit from the high leverage the next habit brings.

Habit No. 3: First Things First

The good is often the enemy of the best. In Goethe's words, "Things which matter most must never be at the mercy of things that matter least."

In Covey's view, we all strive to do the things that are important to us, but we're often distracted by things that are "pressing"—things that have to be done right now that aren't necessarily a part of the central values of our life. Furthermore, even if you discover an incredibly powerful method of personal productivity that enables you to get stuff done at a much faster rate, it doesn't always solve the problem of having lots of things to do. The real key is knowing how to seek out things that are really important to you and focusing on those, allowing the other things to simply fill in the remaining gaps in your life.

Consider the simple 2 x 2 matrix as shown. Quadrant II consists of activities which are both urgent and important—in other words, things to which you absolutely must attend. Why must you do these things? Because they are important—meaning that they contribute to your mission; and they are urgent—meaning that they have some sort of deadline associated with them.

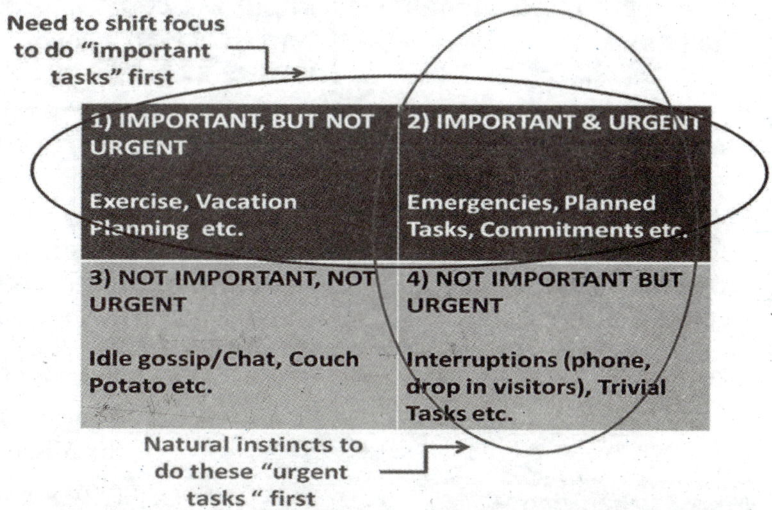

101

Quadrant I: stressed and burned out; forever focusing on crisis management.

Quadrant II: show vision, perspective, balance, discipline, control; suffer few crises.

Quadrant III: have shallow or broken relationships; suffer crisis management; "chameleon character"; see goals and plans as worthless.

Quadrant IV: depends on others or institutions for basic support; according to Covey, "leads irresponsible lives".

Choices about where to invest your time are really made in the other 3 categories; and most people driven by the concept of urgency—get drawn into Quadrant III; doing things that consume their time but do not contribute to their goals. But the key to true productivity is Quadrant I. This quadrant consists of all those things we know we should be doing but we put off anyway (like exercising, relationship-building, reading, improving our professional knowledge, praying, planning, etc.). Covey teaches that the key to being efficient and productive with our time is to take the time we are devoting to Quadrants III and IV and put it into Quadrant I. Once we begin to spend more time in Quadrant I, we discover that Quadrant II begins to shrink and there are fewer fires to put out in our lives.

So, as a tool for helping you prioritize your action items, start by identifying which part of the matrix each task belongs in, and then manage them as follows:

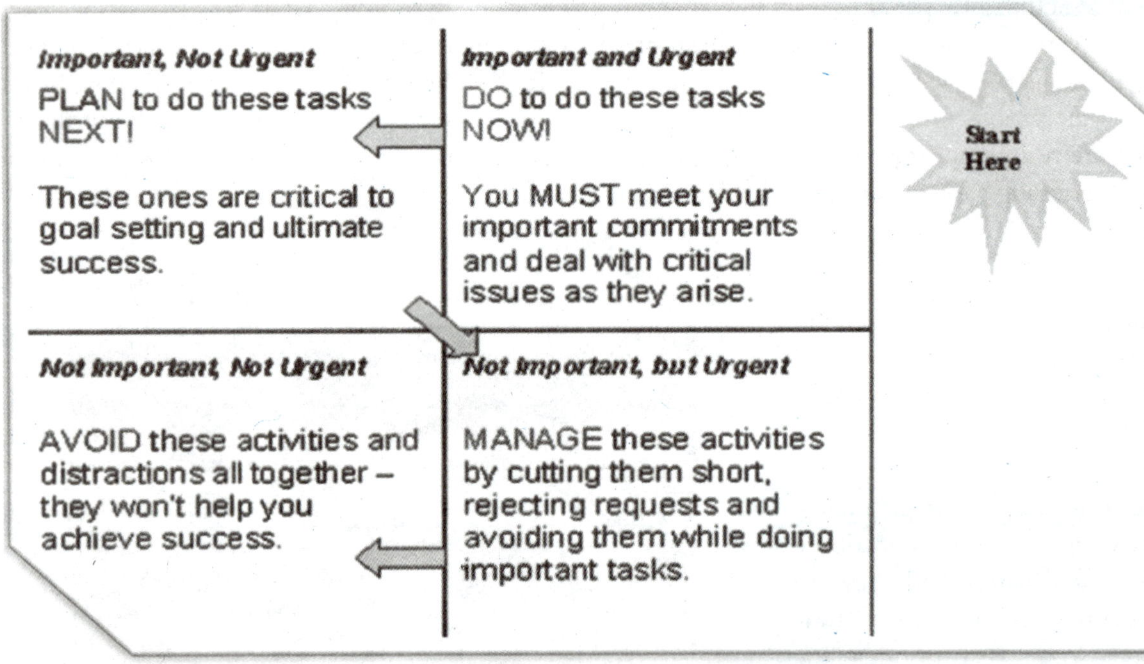

Weekly Organizing

If your week is broken down into 7 buckets, and you go into each bucket without planning ahead, and you fill it up with little pebbles and grains of sand and whatever other debris comes your way … soon there will be no room for the Big Rocks. Your buckets fill up faster than you know it, and once your buckets are full, you're done. You can't get bigger buckets. What you should do is put the Big Rocks in first, and fill in the pebbles and sand around them. The Big Rocks are the major things you want to get done this week- A report, going to the gym, spending time with your spouse and kids. These Big Rocks get pushed back from week to week because we never have time to do them. Our days fill up too quickly, and before we know it, weeks have passed and the Big Rocks are still sitting on the side, untouched.

Plan your week ahead of time, placing your Big Rocks first.

Here's how you do it (with the unavoidable list, of course!):

- **Make a list.** On Sunday evening or Monday morning write out the Big Rocks that you want to accomplish this week. These should be the important things—if you looked back on the week and said you did them, you would be proud of having done them. Be sure to include not only work stuff, but some of the tasks that will further along your life's goals and dreams.
- **Keep it short.** In the beginning, just have 4-6 … you don't need to try to do 10 or more Big Rocks, especially not at first. Later, you may get better at judging how many Big Rocks you can do in a week, but for now, shoot for about one per day.
- **Place the Rocks.** Look at your weekly schedule. If you don't have one, write out the days of the week with one-hour blocks (or print out a schedule from an online calendar). Write out pre-existing appointments. Now take your Big Rocks, and put them in the schedule. Try to put them in a spot where you know you'll get them done. Not a spot that's traditionally too busy to concentrate, and not in a little half-hour window between meetings.
- **Leave space for the incoming pebbles.** Don't fill in the rest of the schedule if possible. Every morning, look at your schedule and commit yourself to doing the Big Rock(s) for that day. If there are less important tasks, you can put them in the schedule, but don't put too much. A tight schedule tends to bump into itself, pushing things back when other things inevitably take too long.
- **Do it early.** If you can, place your Big Rocks first thing in the morning. Don't schedule them for later in the day if possible, because by that time, a few fires might come up, and the Big Rock will get pushed back as always. Do it first, and then you've got the rest of the day for the busy-work.
- **Be Proud.** When your week's done, look back on it—if you got any (or all!) of the Big Rocks done, be proud of yourself and happy. It feels good!

How does this simple method make you more productive? Well, productivity isn't about doing a lot of stuff. **It's about getting the important stuff done**. But if you're running around doing all the little stuff … sure, you did a lot and you were very busy, but how much did you really accomplish? Oftentimes we can look back on our week and say, "I didn't get a lot done, but I sure was stressed doing it!" This habit is a way of getting the important stuff done. Sure, you'll still have to worry about the little stuff. But at the end of the week, you can look back and say that you've been productive. It makes a world of difference.

Business Issue

Three-fourths of CEO failures are due to failure to execute. Somehow, they can't get their organizations focused on the things that matter most. Knowledge workers report being very busy, but spending less than half their time on key objectives. The issue is shared commitment to strategic objectives (alignment) and effective execution at all levels. "*First things first,*" as a habit facilitates:

- Tighter organizational alignment to strategy.
- Greatly improved cost-effectiveness of human resource.
- Faster, more precise execution of key objectives.

The remaining habits are the habits of Interdependence

The first 3 habits (Private Victory) precede the next 3 (Public Victory) just as algebra comes before calculus. Simply: if we want all the joys of outward success, first we must master ourselves.

Habit No. 4: Think Win-Win

The Law of Win/Win says – let's not do it your way or my way; let's do it the best way.

Most of us learn to base our self-worth on comparisons and competition. We think about succeeding in terms of someone else failing—that is, if I win, you lose; or if you win, I lose. Life becomes a zero-sum game. There is only so much pie to go around, and if you get a big piece, there is less for me; it's not fair, and I'm going to make sure you don't get anymore. We all play the game, but how much fun is it really?

Win-win sees life as a cooperative arena, not a competitive one. It is not based upon compromise—that is where most disputes naturally end. The win-win idea is about fostering an attitude that is committed to always finding solutions that will truly benefit both sides of a dispute. We both get to eat the pie, and it tastes pretty darn good! Win-win solutions do not, of course, exist in themselves; they must be created. And, even if we cannot see the solution to a particular problem, it does not mean that no such solution exists. To go for win-win, you not only have to be empathic, but you also have to be confident. You not only have to be considerate and sensitive, you also have to be brave. Achieving that balance between courage and consideration is the essence of real maturity and is fundamental to win-win. This attitude works well because it liberates the individuals concerned from the effort of trying to persuade the opposite party to shift ground or compromise. The effort is instead spend on trying to understand, which is where habit 5 comes in—you see, they are also sequential.

Think about your own relationships with your children. What can you do to create more win-win? Find a problem or issue you want to work on. Talk to your child about their needs or desires (their win). Explain what is a win for you. Then come up with ideas for meeting your child's needs in a way that will also meet your needs. Set up specific expectations, to-dos and outcomes. You even can put this down on paper and you both will sign it so you can always go back to it in case of questions. This also creates accountability.

Business Issue

Competition has its place against market competitors, last year's performance, or another location or individual where cooperation and interdependence aren't required. In a competitive situation where building a relationship isn't important, Win/Lose may be appropriate. But when relationships are paramount, Win/Win is the only viable alternative. So, in developing an organizational culture, be sure to reward win/win behavior among employees and avoid inadvertently rewarding win/lose behavior. Truly effective organizations develop strong networks up and down the value chain. They are trusted partners because they manage their relationships according to a widely known but little understood principle: Win-Win.

- Increased organizational buy-in to key objectives.
- More focus and alignment to real client needs without giving away the store.
- More productive relationships along the value chain.
- Fewer conflicts and confrontations.
- Increased incentive and empowerment of team members to execute.

Habit No. 5: Seek First to Understand

Diagnosis must precede prescription

> You spend years learning how to read and write, and years learning how to speak. But what about listening? What training have you had that enables you to listen so you really, deeply understand another human being? Probably none, right?

What most people do, naturally, when involved in some type of discussion, meeting or dialogue is exactly the reverse—they seek first to be understood. And in doing so, they ignore the other person completely, pretend that they're listening, selectively hear only certain parts of the conversation or attentively focus on only the words being said, but miss the meaning entirely. So why does this happen? Because most people listen with the intent to reply, not to understand. You listen to yourself as you prepare in your mind what you are going to say, the questions you are going to ask, etc. You filter everything you hear through your life experiences, your frame of reference. You check what you hear against your autobiography and see how it measures up. Consequently, you decide prematurely what the other person means before he/she finishes communicating. And, as Stephen Covey says, when both parties are trying to be understood, neither party is really listening; he calls such an interaction, 'the dialogue of the deaf'.

Do any of the following sound familiar? "Oh, I know just how you feel. I felt the same way." "I had that same thing happen to me." "Let me tell you what I did in a similar situation." Because you so often listen autobiographically, you ten to respond in one of four ways:

Evaluating: You judge and then either agree or disagree.
Probing: You ask questions from your own frame of reference.
Advising: You give counsel, advice, and solutions to problems.
Interpreting: You analyze others' motives and behaviors based on your own experiences.

You might be saying, "Hey, now wait a minute. I'm just trying to relate to the person by drawing on my own experiences. Is that so bad?" In some situations, autobiographical responses may be appropriate, such as when another person specifically asks for help from your point of view or when there is already a very high level of trust in the relationship. But effective listening is not simply echoing what the other person has said through the lens of one's own experience. Rather, it is putting oneself in the perspective of the other person, listening empathically for both feeling and meaning.

> Feelings (and perceptions) are interesting things - they are never "wrong". Even though you may not agree with someone's feelings or perceptions of an issue, their feelings are correct for them. As an empathic listener you must create for yourself the ability to understand the position that this person holds, in order to effectively communicate your own position.

If however we are prepared to invest the time and effort to really understand the other person's position, and to get into the habit of spending the first part of the discussion doing so, then, when it is felt by the other person that you do indeed understand the dynamic changes. People become more open, more teachable, more interested in what you may have to say and with the mutual understanding that flows from this habit, you are ready to practise habit 6; which concerns finding creative solutions.

Business Issue

Every interface with the client should add value to the relationship; that can only happen when different work groups and individuals within the organization develop the discipline of empathic communication. There is a principle in Neuro Linguistic Programming (NLP) which says, "the map is not the territory". What this means is that whatever our view of a situation is it can only be a representation of reality, just as a map is a representation of the terrain and, as such, it can never tell you the whole story of what is going on at any one time. In order to really understand, you need to get into the territory and start to make sense of the symbols on the map. One way to start this is to overlay your map with that of your client. By doing this first—and crucially this needs to be in an open and non-judgmental way—we build trust and rapport with our client and we do not obscure the detail with our own thoughts and beliefs about what is going on. This, in turn, leads to much more effective and open communication and by extension a significantly reduced potential for disagreement later on.

- More precise fulfilment of customer needs, better deals, more revenue.
- Improved, more enduring relationships along the value chain.
- Better organizational alignment through clearer communication.

Habit No. 6: Synergize

None of us is as smart as all of us

This habit involves you putting your head together with the other party or parties in order to creatively brainstorm a synergistic solution to a problem, i.e., to find a solution which contains win-win benefits. Synergy happens when two people with profoundly different ideas are able to listen to each other respectfully and with real empathy for the other person's position, enough to let go of their own preconceptions. When they do this, people become creative, rather than defensive. And this is when an elevated, third way, can be established that is better than what either party started with on their own. Synergy is not about compromise. It is about creating a whole that is greater than the sum of its parts, i.e., 1+1≠2 but 1+1=3 or more.

Do you truly value the mental, emotional, and psychological differences among people? Or do you wish everyone would just agree with you so you could all get along? Many people mistake uniformity for unity; sameness for oneness. But the person who is truly effective has the humility and reverence to recognize his own perceptual limitations and to appreciate the rich resources available through interaction with the hearts and minds of other human beings.

Putting habits 4, 5 and 6 together, you have a perfect model for human interaction. Put simply: first be mentally committed to the idea that a solution that will benefit all parties may be constructed; next invest the necessary time and effort to really understand the other party and do that first; finally creatively brainstorm a synergistic solution—a natural product of mutual understanding and respect.

As per Covey, many people have not really experienced even a moderate degree of synergy in their family life or in other interactions. They've been trained and scripted into defensive and protective communications or into believing that life and other people can't be trusted. This represents one of the great tragedies and wastes in life, because so much potential remains untapped—completely undeveloped and unused. Ineffective people live day after day with unused potential. They experience synergy only in small, peripheral ways in their lives.

Business Issue

Strategic combinations are becoming more important. Bigger and bigger bets are being made to achieve scale and global presence. However, most mergers fail: 83% fail to create value, over half destroy shareholder value. Merger and Acquisition's success is often hindered by territoriality, culture gaps, and incompatible systems. Clearly they fail to create synergies. On a smaller scale, alliances, supply-chain partnerships, even customer relationships are a form of "strategic combination" to create value. Often, they fail to do so. Alfred P. Sloan, who led General Motors to world dominance in the 1930's, once told a conference full of executives: "If we are all in agreement on the decision—then I propose we postpone further discussion of this matter until our next meeting, to give ourselves time to develop disagreement and perhaps gain some understanding of what the decision is all about."

By synergistically creating a mission statement, it becomes engraved in the hearts and minds of the participants. From the human resource context, synergy could mean recruiting people with varying skill-sets and from diverse backgrounds.

- Faster and more successful Merger and Acquisition integration.
- Increased leverage from diversity.

Habit No. 7: Sharpen the Saw

Even if you're on the right track, you'll eventually get run over if you stand still

"Sharpen the Saw" underscores the importance of setting time aside for personal renewal. It's about preserving and enhancing your most valuable asset—you. The rather odd title Dr. Covey assigned to this habit comes from the story of a woodcutter charged to cut a huge amount of timber, working hard from dawn to dusk at his task but never getting past the first tree. When asked by a passerby who observes the woodcutter wearing himself out with no apparent progress, "Why don't you sharpen the saw?" he replies with determination, "I can't—too busy sawing."

In this habit, you are the saw; and to sharpen the saw is to become better, keener and more effective. Dulled by use, the saw's serrated edge can no longer cut through wood. So, the solution is to periodically sharpen the saw. Without this renewal, the body becomes weak, the mind mechanical, the emotions raw, the spirit insensitive, and the person selfish. Not a pretty picture, is it?

In practice, most people fail to understand what sharpening the saw really means. If you're overworking yourself and your productivity begins to fall off, common wisdom says to take a break, maybe even go on vacation. However, that isn't sharpening the saw—that's putting the saw down. When you put down a dull blade for a while, the blade will still be dull when you pick it up again. Sharpening the saw is actually an activity, just as the analogy suggests. Think about what it would mean to sharpen the saw of your life. As per the author, sharpening the saw is to regularly engage in the exercise of the three dimensions which make up the human condition: body, mind and spirit. Covey also adds a fourth dimension—the social/emotional.

Physical Exercise

Too many of us still maintain unhealthy diets, do not exercise on a regular basis, and fail to take sufficient rest and true relaxation. This triad of diet, exercise and rest constitutes the pillars not only of physical health but also contributes to our well-being in the other three dimensions. It's one of those Quadrant I, high-leverage activities that most of us don't do consistently because it isn't urgent. And because we don't do it, sooner or later we find ourselves in Quadrant II, dealing with the health problems and crisis that come as a natural result of our neglect.

Mental Exercise

As soon as we leave the discipline of school, many of us let our minds atrophy. We don't do any more serious reading, we don't explore new subjects in any real depth outside our action fields, we don't think analytically, we don't write—at least not critically or in a way that tests our ability to express ourselves in distilled, clear, and concise language. Instead, we spend our spare time on casual dating, watching TV, or partying with friends. Ask yourself these questions. What am I doing to sharpen my mind? Am I engaged in a program of education or learning of some kind? What am I d oing to improve my professional knowledge? To begin with, it is vital that we find an area that excites and ignites our passion. Then everything flows and it is much easier to exercise.

Spiritual Exercise

This is the area which is perhaps the most misunderstood. The progress of our science, education and technology has leaded us to construct a view of the world and the universe that excludes the agency of God. We have, by and large, abandoned faith in the creator God, which has simultaneously abandoned the idea that life has any meaning or purpose; and it is purpose and direction in life that this habit refers to as spiritual exercise. Of course, if you are a religious person, then there will be a tie-up here with your personal faith; however, if you are not religious, don't also abandon the idea that life holds a special purpose for you. There are many approaches to discovering the meaning or inspiration in your life: spending time in nature; reading sacred or inspirational literature; listening to edifying music; meditation or prayer; rendering anonymous or charitable service; participation in the arts; religious observances; and other ways.

Social/Emotional

While the physical, spiritual, and mental dimensions are closely related to Habits 1, 2 and 3—centered on the principles of personal vision, leadership, and management; the social/emotional dimension focuses on Habits 4, 5 and 6—centered on the principles of interpersonal leadership, empathic communication, and creative cooperation. The social and the emotional dimension of our lives are tied together because our emotional life is primarily, but not exclusively, developed out of and manifested in our relationships with others. Renewing our social/emotional dimension does not take time in the same sense that renewing the other dimensions does. We can do it in our normal everyday interactions with other people. But it definitely requires exercise.

It's all up to you. You can renew yourself through relaxation or you can totally burn yourself out by overdoing everything. You can pamper yourself mentally and spiritually. Or you can go through life oblivious to your well-being. You can experience vibrant energy. Or you can procrastinate and miss out on the benefits of good health and exercise. You can revitalize yourself and face a new day in peace and harmony. Or you can wake up in the morning full of apathy because your get-up-and-go has got-up-and-gone. Just remember that every day provides a new opportunity for renewal—a new opportunity to recharge yourself instead of hitting the wall. All it takes is desire and commitment.

How are your various blades doing? Are they all sharp & effective? Which ones are dull, and what can you do to sharpen them?

Business Issue

Everyone believes in the principle of continuous improvement. Nevertheless, because of the dysfunctional habits of many organizations—and their people—getting better at what they do is often pushed to the back of the priority list. As a result, ineffective organizations eventually die as their competitors overtake them in product and service quality and market share.

- Greater focus on increasing productive capacity
- Ever-increasing quality in products and services
- Ever-improving relationships with internal /external clients

Balancing your act between P & PC

Covey says the very essence of effectiveness is encapsulated in the P—PC balance. P stands for production of desired results and PC stands for production capability. As an example of this, someone might want a pay rise and work very long hours to achieve it but in doing so neglect and seclude himself from his family. It's just a matter of time and soon this would start showing up in the form of household conflicts and put his production capability on a downward spiral. Covey uses Aesop's tale of the goose and the golden eggs as another example. The Goose and the Golden Egg is the story of a poor farmer, who one day finds a glittering, golden egg in the nest of his goose. Every morning, thereafter, the farmer gathers one golden egg from the nest of his goose. He soon becomes fabulously wealthy. As he grows rich, however, he also grows greedy and impatient with only one golden egg a day. Attempting to seize all the gold in the goose at once, he slaughters it, only to find nothing. The moral of this fable has both personal and professional application. Like the foolish farmer, we often push production (golden eggs) at the expense of what makes us capable to produce (the goose). In attempts to be efficient, we overlook effectiveness and destroy our capability for getting results. Put into a nutshell: don't overburden the goose that lays the golden eggs. Do not push the envelope to the max, but invest just as much time into the maintenance of the production capability of your assets—a Quadrant I activity.

As illustrated, the Seven Habits are interrelated, interdependent, and sequential. Using the habits, individuals work on the Private Victory (or self-mastery with Habits 1, 2 and 3) before moving to the Public Victory (building relationships with Habits 4, 5 and 6). The seventh habit is the habit of renewal; it sustains physical, social/emotional, mental and spiritual growth.

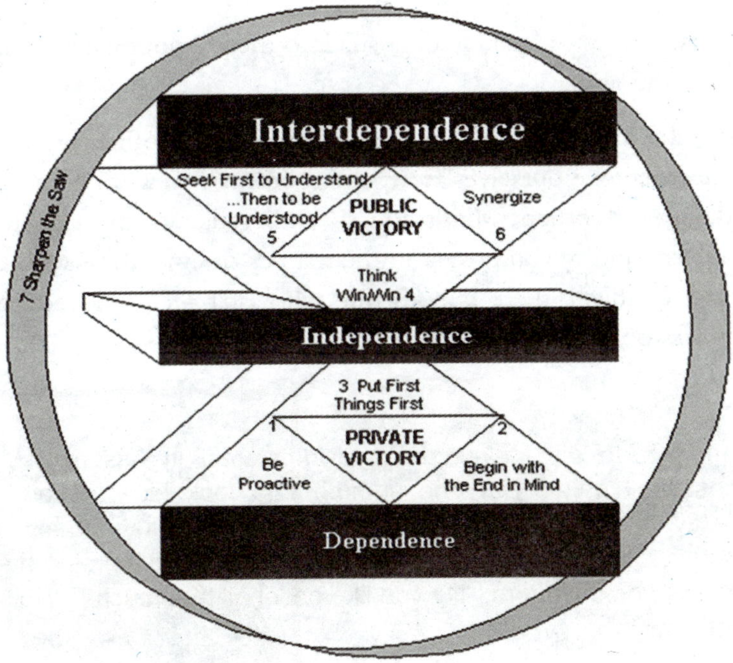

The Concept of Emotional Bank Account

Imagine that each person with whom you have a relationship of some kind, whether it be your coworkers, family or friends, has an emotional bank account with you. This account begins on a neutral balance. And just as with any bank account, you can make deposits and withdrawals. A deposit would be when you pick up a couple of skateboard magazines for your son on your way home. When you compromise or give up what you wanted, so your spouse could have something she wanted. Deposits are made when you share intimacy and sincere affection and appreciation. A withdrawal would be when you make a promise to come watch your son's baseball game, but you do not show up when you fail to call your wife or when you make fun of her in public. You make withdrawals, when you fail to show acceptance, or consideration, or when you disregard your partner's needs and interests.

When we make emotional deposits into someone's bank account, their fondness, trust, and confidence in us grows. And, as a result, our relationship develops and grows. If we can keep a positive reserve in our relationships, by making regular deposits, there will be greater tolerance for our mistakes and we'll enjoy open communication with that person. On the contrary, when we make withdrawals and our balance becomes low or even overdrawn, bitterness, mistrust and discord develop. If we are to salvage the relationship, we must make a conscious effort to make regular deposits.

Covey discusses six major ways of making deposits into these emotional bank accounts and how we can avoid making withdrawals:

1. **Understanding the individual**—Truly understanding what others are feeling is not always that easy. We must remove ourselves from our egocentric viewpoint and put ourselves into the minds and shoes of others. Minds and shoes because we must try to first understand the thought patterns and, second, walk in their shoes or empathize with them. Remember, underneath most conflicts, there is someone who isn't feeling loved enough, respected, appreciated, understood, or listened to.

> From Covey:
>
> "I have a friend whose son developedan avid interest in baseball. My friend wasn't interested in baseball at all. But one summer, he took his son to see every major league team play one game. The trip took over six weeks and coast a great deal of money, but it became a powerful bonding experience in their relationship. My friend was asked on his return, "Do you like baseball that much?" "No," he replied, "but I like my son that much."

2. **Attending to little things**—Negative comments, coming home late, or not asking for your partner's input regarding an important decision may seem like small things but can certainly disintegrate the peace and start a battle when your emotional bank account is low. On the other hand, little courtesies, kind words & warm smiles are at the heart of the little things that can brighten up any relationship.

3. **Keeping commitments**—Certainly when we break our promises to others, we make major withdrawals from their emotional bank accounts. However, keeping commitments is not just relegated to promises. It also includes things such as arriving to work and appointments on time, fulfilling our duties, and living up to every word that comes out of our mouth.

4. **Clarifying expectations**—There is nothing more frustrating in a relationship than not understanding what is expected of you. Although many of us wish we could be, we are not mind readers. And because each of us sees life differently and has different backgrounds and life experiences, expecting someone to just "know" is not only unfair but completely unrealistic. It's important that the person with whom you are dealing with, knows exactly what is expected of them. Doing this will keep them out of the dark and allow them to relate to you confidently, knowing that what they are doing is in line with your expectations.

5. **Showing personal integrity**—Nothing is probably more damaging to a relationship, then a lack of integrity. Being that the emotional bank account is based upon trust, you could essentially be doing all of the previous things, but without trust, it is to no avail.

6. **Apologizing sincerely when you make a withdrawal**—Granted, we are all mortal. We make mistakes. That's part of life and learning. Knowing when you are wrong and admitting your mistakes prevents the wounds that you've caused in others from festering and allows them to heal. When appropriate, sincere apology will keep your relationships accounts in the positive, allowing you to maintain the balance that has been created in your application of all of the previous steps.

It's not about keeping a ledger but to strive for more and more daily deposits. Avoid making excuses or rationalizing inconsiderate or hostile actions by telling yourself you can afford a few withdrawals. Remember, there's no real way of reaching a safe balance. You don't become a billionaire to where your relationship can withstand any withdrawal. Things like adultery or abuse can wipe out years of savings and leave your emotional account bankrupt.

Think of your own crisis you may be dealing with—perhaps a broken trust at work or at home or with a friend—and think of how you can restore trust in the relationship. Examine your emotional bank account with this person; it's most likely strained because of withdrawals. Make a commitment to start making deposits that matter most to that person, and do it little by little. Even with small deposits, you will find that the account will grow. It may take time. But slowly, depending on the severity of the broken trust, you can find trust being re-built and restored, and new relationship will be born. Of course, this also depends on the other person, but you can choose to do your part regardless of the other person—to focus on your circle of influence. And you will find some peace, knowing that you've done your part. It is a challenging path and a time consuming one, but trust can be re-built and restored. All is never lost.

P Problems are PC Opportunities

Effective people are not problem-minded; they're opportunity-minded. They feed opportunities and starve problems. The flat tire on your way to an important meeting is still a flat tire, but the situation becomes an opportunity to show your resolve to act in a crisis situation. Or take the example of William Least Heat Moon, author of the book *Blue Highways*: in a period of three months back in the 70s, his wife divorced him and his college fired him. So, he put all the money he had in a shoebox, packed up his van and drove around America on all the blue (smallest) highways writing a book about his travels through small town American culture. Today the book is a classic. Similarly, all relationship problems should be treated as chances to build up emotional bank accounts.

> From Covey:
>
> "When parents see their children's problems as opportunities to build the relationship instead of as negative, burdensome irritations, it totally changes the nature of parent-child interaction. Parents become more willing, even excited, about deeply understanding and helping their children. When a child comes to them with a problem, instead of thinking, "Oh, no! Not another problem!" their paradigm is, "Here is a great opportunity for me to really help my child and to invest in our relationship." Many interactions change from transactional to transformational, and strong bonds of love and trust are created as children sense the value parents give to their problems and to them as individuals."

Rather than tackling specific problems or making external changes to processes, systems and so on, Covey's approach helps you focus on developing yourself personally and your relationships with others. It's a paradigm shift away from the Personality Ethic (success attributed to personality traits, skills, techniques, maintaining a positive attitude, etc.) and towards the Character Ethic (success attributed to underlying characteristics such as integrity, courage, justice, patience, etc). As you learn and apply these habits, you will increase your power, influence, and unity with others. For starters, the Self-scoring Seven Habits Profile shown below can help you evaluate your current level of effectiveness.

Self-scoring Seven Habits Profile

Instruction: Read each statement and, using your best judgement, circle the number that indicates how well you perform in the following categories:

Category 1 Emotional Bank Account		Very Poor	Poor	Fair	Good	Very Good	Out-stading
1	I show kindness and consideration towards people.	1	2	3	4	5	6
2	I keep promises and honour commitments.	1	2	3	4	5	6
3	I do not speak negatively of others when they are not present.	1	2	3	4	5	6
						Category Total →	( )

Category 2 Life Balance		Very Poor	Poor	Fair	Good	Very Good	Out-stading
4	I am able to maintain an appropriate balance among various aspects of my life-work, family, friends & so forth.	1	2	3	4	5	6
5	While working on task, I also keep in mind the concerns and needs of those I am working for.	1	2	3	4	5	6
6	I work hard at the things I do, but not in a manner that causes burnout.	1	2	3	4	5	6
						Category Total →	( )

Category 3 Be Proactive		Very Poor	Poor	Fair	Good	Very Good	Out-stading
7	I am in control of my life.	1	2	3	4	5	6
8	I focus my efforts on things I can do something about rather than on things beyond my control.	1	2	3	4	5	6
9	I take responsibility for my mood and actions rather than blame others and circumstances.	1	2	3	4	5	6
						Category Total →	( )

Category 4 Begin with the Mind		Very Poor	Poor	Fair	Good	Very Good	Out-stading
10	I know what I want to accomplish in life.	1	2	3	4	5	6
11	I organize and prepare in a way that reduces having to work in a crisis mode.	1	2	3	4	5	6
12	I begin each week with a clear plan of what I desire to accomplish.	1	2	3	4	5	6
						Category Total →	( )

Category 5 Put First Things First		Very Poor	Poor	Fair	Good	Very Good	Out-stading
13	I am disciplined in carrying out plans (avoiding procrastinatiion, timewasters & so forth).	1	2	3	4	5	6
14	I do not allow the truly important activities of my life to get lost in the busy activities of my day.	1	2	3	4	5	6
15	The things I do everyday are meaningful and contribute to my overall goals in life.	1	2	3	4	5	6
						Category Total →	( )

Category 6 Think Win/Win		Very Poor	Poor	Fair	Good	Very Good	Out-stading
16	I care about the success of others as well as my own.	1	2	3	4	5	6
17	I cooperate with others.	1	2	3	4	5	6
18	While solving conflicts, I strive to find solutions that benefit all.	1	2	3	4	5	6
						Category Total →	( )

Category 7 Seek First to Understand		Very Poor	Poor	Fair	Good	Very Good	Out-stading
19	I am sensitive to the feelings of others.	1	2	3	4	5	6
20	I seek to understand the viewpoints of others.	1	2	3	4	5	6
21	When listening, I try to see things from the other person's point of view, not just my own.	1	2	3	4	5	6
						Category Total →	( )

Category 8 Synergize		Very Poor	Poor	Fair	Good	Very Good	Out-stading
22	I value and seek out the insights of others.	1	2	3	4	5	6
23	I am creative in searching for new and better ideas and solutions.	1	2	3	4	5	6
24	I encourage others to express their opinions.	1	2	3	4	5	6
						Category Total →	( )

	Category 9 Sharpen the Saw	Very Poor	Poor	Fair	Good	Very Good	Out-stading
25	I care for my physical health and well being.	1	2	3	4	5	6
26	I strive to build and improve relationships with others.	1	2	3	4	5	6
27	I take to find meaning and enjoyment in life.	1	2	3	4	5	6
						Category Total →	( )

CHARTING YOUR SEVEN HABITS EFFECTIVENESS: Total your points for each category in the category total cell. There are 9 categories; the first two are the foundation habits of the seven habits and the last seven are the seven habits. The higher you score, the more closely you are aligned with the seven habits principles. Where your score is lower than you would like, refer to the corresponding chapters to better understand how to increase your effectiveness in those habits.

❑❑❑

IMPORTANT NOTE

This summary culls the content of the book - "The Seven Habits of Highly Effective People" down to its essence so that even an average reader can sensitize himself to it, sparing him with the time consuming details. In case you feel a need to further explore this topic, the author recommends reading the original work published by "Simon & Schuster".

A Snapshot of
WHO MOVED MY CHEESE?

Thanks to the economic slowdown, this book has gained a lot of popularity in the recent times. The contextual message being - while the recession is a time for caution, don't be so resistant of change that you are left asking "dude, who moved my cheese?" Even if change finds you through a layoff, seize the opportunity to discover your new piece of cheese. It just may turn out that you prefer Brie to cheddar.

Who Moved My Cheese?

—Inspired by Dr. Spencer Johnson

"The greatest danger in times of turbulence is not the turbulence; it is to act with yesterday's logic."

—Peter Drucker,
Globally Renowned Management Guru

"Who Moved My Cheese?" provides inspirational guidance to those suffering job loss, downsizing, divorce, or altered life situations. It is a story about change that takes place in a Maze where four amusing characters look for "Cheese"- cheese being a metaphor for what you want in life— whether it is a good job, a loving relationship, money, or spiritual peace of mind. Cheese is what we think will make us happy, and when circumstances take it away, different people deal with change in different ways. The "Maze" in the story represents where you spend time looking for what you want. It can be the organization you work for, the community you live in, or the relationships you have in your life. On a more general note, it can be a manifestation for anything in your life where you constantly reach dead ends and are challenged in finding the path you want or can take to get you to where you need to be.

The premise of this alarmingly forthright parable is that change happens— our cheese will be moved sooner or later whether we like it or not. Dr. Johnson contends that change is the nature of life, and we do better when we prepare for it. Henceforth, we need to smell our cheese on a regular basis so that we can have a sense for when the cheese is getting old. And when our cheese gets old, we've got to let it go and move on. What it means is we must be willing to go to new places and embrace new ways of doing things. When change requires new learning, as it often does, some people don't think they will be able to master the new skills, so for them it is easier to simply renounce the changes than adapt. The problem is that these are the people who are left in the dust. It is a paradox of life that while our children change rapidly, we as adults try to put the brakes on the speed of change. We fool ourselves believing that we are in control of our life by holding on to what we're used to, until it's too late. My advice to all my readers is that after reading this book summary, reflect on areas of your life where your own cheese had been moved and you have just been in denial and paralyzed about it. Hope the learnings presented here will inspire you to jump-start afresh.

A Gathering

The book starts off with a group of friends (Angela, Nathan, Carlos, Jessica and Michael) meeting up after their high school reunion. They wanted to hear more about what was happening in each other's lives. After a good deal of kidding, and scrumptious meal, they settled into an interesting conversation. The topic came around to change, and how each person experienced it. Everyone was trying to cope with the unexpected changes in their lives and most admitted that they did not know a good way to handle them. Michael, whose life changed tremendously after reading an amazing book about change, narrates its story to his other batch mates.

A still from the movie – *Who moved my cheese?*

The cast of characters in the story— (Hem, Haw, Sniff & Scurry) represent parts of ourselves whenever we are confronted with change. They live in a maze and spend their days scurrying about in the eternal pursuit of cheese; however, each of the four personality types have their own unique approach to this hunt. Sniff is extremely good at sniffing out cheese, while Scurry specializes in scurrying after newly discovered cheese. Hem and Haw are not so single-minded in their cheese pursuit, but rather spend more time philosophizing about the hunt. By providing four easily-relatable characters, Johnson helps the reader to characterize his or her own reactions to change in terms of one of these characters and evaluate the long-term consequences of those actions. The tale begins with Sniff, Scurry, Hem and Haw in their daily jog to the maze in search of cheese, only to discover one day that their cheese has disappeared. The reaction of the characters lends itself to comparisons with our own family's and/or co-workers' reactions when experiencing change. We may be like Sniff, who anticipates change early by sniffing it out, or Scurry, who quickly scurries into action and adapts. Maybe we are more like Hem, who is hemmed into his situation and denies change out of fear, or Haw, who learns to adapt in time when he sees something better— even if reluctantly driven to do so. Whichever character we choose to play, we all share the common need to find our way in the maze of life and succeed in changing times.

The Story

A still from the movie – *Who moved my cheese?*

Everyday Hem, Haw, Sniff and Scurry went about their business collecting and eating cheese. Every morning, the mice and little men put on their jogging suits and running shoes, left their homes, and raced around the maze looking for their favorite cheese. One day, the four stumble onto a piece of cheese (Cheese Station C) so large that Hem and Haw declare that they shall never again need to search for cheese. "This is great," Hem said. "There's enough cheese here to last us forever." The littlepeople felt happy and successful, and thought they were secure. Every night Hem & Haw would waddle home, full of cheese, and every morning they would confidently return for more. They became accustomed to this constant source of cheese and pushed aside any thought of ever having to find another piece. The littlepeople eventually moved their homes closer to it, and built a social life around it.

The two mice, however, never stopped exploring their surroundings and kept themselves constantly attuned to change in their environment. They arrived early each morning and sniffed and scratched and scurried around Cheese Station C, inspecting the area to see if there had been any changes from the day before. Then they would sit down to nibble on the cheese. This went on for quite some time. Meanwhile, the supply of cheese slowly dwindles and one day the chunk of cheese is finally exhausted and the four are left with nothing. Sniff and Scurry are able to take this new development in stride and scamper off in search of a new cheese source. The mice did not overanalyze things, they knew it was coming, so they simply untied their running shoes from their necks and put them on. To the mice, the problem and the answer were both simple. The situation at Cheese Station C had changed. So, Sniff and Scurry decided to change. They both looked out into the maze. Then Sniff lifted his nose, sniffed, and nodded to Scurry, who took off running through the maze, while Sniff followed as fast as he could.

A still from the movie – *Who moved my cheese?*

On the contrary, Hem and Haw were completely bowled over, as they've come to think they were entitled to the cheese at the Cheese Station C. Having taken their cheese for granted, they were unprepared for what they found. "What! No cheese?" Hem yelled. He continued yelling, "No cheese? No cheese?" as though if he shouted loud enough, someone would put it back. "Who moved my Cheese?" he hollered. Finally, he put his hands on his hips, his face turned red, and he screamed at the top of his voice, "It's not fair!" Haw just shook his head in disbelief. He stood there for a long time, frozen with shock. He was just not ready for this. "What will happen if the cheese is not there tomorrow, I have made plans based on this cheese", he said. The little people's behavior was not very productive but it was understandable. After verifying that the cheese is indeed gone and ranting at the unfairness of the situation, both head home hungry & discouraged. But before they left, Haw wrote on the wall:

A still from the movie – *Who moved my cheese?*

Next day, Hem & Haw returned to the Cheese Station C. But situation hadn't changed. The littlepeople didn't know what to do. Haw didn't want to know that the cheese supply had gradually been getting smaller. He believed it had been moved all of a sudden. Hem tried to analyze the situation over & over but eventually his complicated brain with its huge belief system took over. "Why did they do this to me?" he demanded. "What's really going on here?" Finally, Haw opened his eyes, looked around and said, "By the way, where are Sniff and Scurry? Do you think they know something we don't?" Hem scoffed, "what would they know? They're just simple mice. They just respond to what happens. We're smarter." All the while, Sniff & Scurry went farther into the maze until they bump into Cheese Station N. They finally found what they had been looking for the whole time— a great supply of new cheese. It was the biggest store of cheese the mice had ever seen.

Back at Cheese Station C, bamboozled by the new sate of affairs, Hem and Haw blame each other for their predicament. After much whining, Haw suggested, "Maybe we should stop analyzing the situation so much and just get going & find some new cheese." But Hem, dead set in his victimized mindset, nixes the proposal. "Oh no," Hem argued. "I'm going to get to the bottom of this." So everyday, the littlepeople continued to do what they had done before. They went to Cheese Station C, found no Cheese, and returned home, carrying their worries and frustrations with them. Sometimes, Haw thought about his mice buddies, Sniff and Scurry, and wondered if they had found any cheese yet. He believed they might be having a hard time, as running through the maze usually involved some uncertainty. But he also knew that it was likely to only last for a while. Haw would at times imagine Sniff and Scurry finding new cheese and enjoying it. He thought about how good it would be for him to be out on an adventure in the maze, and to find fresh new cheese. He could almost taste it. The more clearly Haw saw the image of himself finding and enjoying the new cheese, the more he saw himself leaving Cheese Station C. It wasn't long before Haw knew what to do. One day, overcoming his debilitating fear, Haw decides to follow Sniff and Scurry's lead of wandering off into the maze in search of new cheese. While Hem remains behind, laboring under the delusion that somehow, someway, his old cheese will someday be replaced. Haw announced, "It's MAZE time!" and wrote:

As he started out into the maze, Haw looked back to where he had come from and felt its comfort. He could feel himself being drawn back into familiar territory— even though he hadn't found cheese there for some time. He became more anxious & wondered if he really wanted to go out into the Maze. He wrote a saying on the wall ahead of him & stared at it for some time:

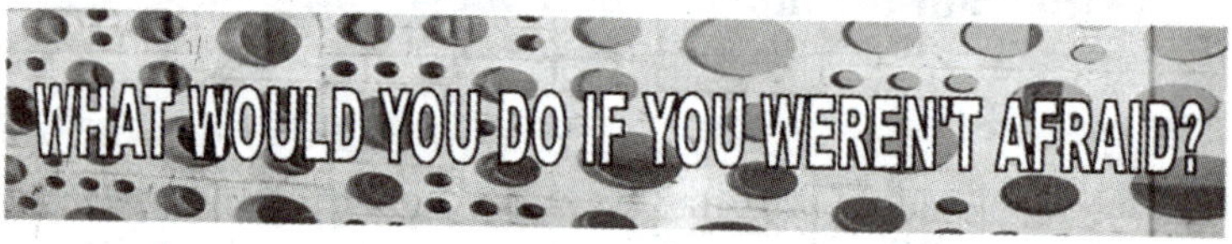

During the next several days, Haw found a little cheese here and there, but nothing that lasted very long. Things seemed to have changed since the last time he was out here. Just when he thought he was getting ahead, he would get lost in the corridors. It was a challenge, but he had to admit that being back in the maze, hunting for cheese wasn't nearly as bad as he feared it might be. He realized that the fear you let build up in your mind is worse than the situation that actually exists. Change probably would not have taken him by surprise if he had been watching what was happening all along. He stopped for some rest & wrote on the wall of the Maze:

Starting re-energized, he lets go of all his fears & begins trusting what lay ahead for him, even though he did not know exactly what it was. To his surprise, Haw starts to enjoy himself more & more. To make things even better, Haw paints a picture in his mind where he imagines himself in great realistic detail, sitting in the middle of a pile of all his favorite cheeses— from Cheddar to Brie! The more clearly he saw the image of himself enjoying new cheese, the more real & believable it became. He stopped to write again on the wall:

He found a cheese station but it was empty as someone had already been there. He realized that if he had moved sooner, he would have very likely found a good deal of new cheese here. So he wrote on the wall:

Haw wondered if Hem had moved on, or if he was still paralyzed by his own fears. He went back to the cheeseless station to offer Hem some bits of cheese he had picked up along the way. But uncompromising Hem turns the offer down because he wanted only the old cheese that he was used to. Haw shook his head in disappointment and went back into the maze. He smiled as he realized:

Haw begins to appreciate that his new beliefs were encouraging him to behave in a positive way. He was taking control, rather than simply letting things happen to him. It all depends on what you choose to believe, he paused to write on the wall:

By now, Haw had kissed goodbye to his past and was adapting to the future. He continued to run through the Maze with greater strength & speed. And then it happened. Eventually, after much trial and error, Haw catches up with Sniff and Scurry and the new piece of cheese they had discovered. He didn't recognize all that he saw, as some of the cheese was new to him. He also realizes that Sniff and Scurry had been enjoying the new cheese for quite a

A still from the movie – *Who moved my cheese?*

while. As he reflects on what he had learned, Haw vowed that next time he would change faster. He knew that it would be easy for him to slip back to his old ways if he got too comfortable. So, each day Haw inspected cheese station N to stay in touch with what was happening around him. While he still enjoyed a great supply of cheese, he often went out and explored new areas. He knew that it was safer to be aware of his real choices than to isolate himself in the comfort zone.

The moral of the story: Change is constant and inevitable. Look at nature's cycles. Trees bud in the spring and by summer they are full of delicious fruit. In the autumn, leaves fall to the ground and when winter arrives, the trees are barren and the cycle begins anew. You know for certain there's intelligence in nature's way of doing things. You can bring this change about yourself or it can come in ways that give you little choice about its what, when and how. Like the characters in this story, some of us will never let ourselves become satisfied with the status quo and instead will constantly be on the lookout for change so that we could make necessary adjustments before it comes. Others will allow themselves to become blinded to the world around them while they focus on the gluttony of the familiar and comfortable. They will not notice the downward spiral of the source of their comfort until it is all gone and nothing remains. Then some will reluctantly move on, driven by necessity, in search of something new, while others will remain behind in the fruitless hope that their comfort will somehow be restored. The ones who move on will have a chance to find a new source of comfort, while those that remain behind are doomed to failure. So, there is no point dwelling upon random misfortune as it only leads to more madness than enlightenment. Bear in mind, there is always new cheese out there and that you are rewarded with it when you go past your fear and savor the adventure.

A Discussion

The group of former classmates gathered at a hotel lounge later that evening for drinks. Each one could identify with one of the characters in the story.

- Nathan's retail business suffered from unanticipated change. Their chain of small stores had to compete with mega-stores. These retail giants had huge inventory and low prices, forcing Nathan to close down some of the stores in their chain.
- Jessica's encyclopedia company resisted change when someone suggested they sell their product in disk format. The idea was that disks would be cheaper to update and produce, and would sell for a fraction of the cost of actual hardbound encyclopedias. Jessica's company didn't change but their competitor did. Sales fell badly, and her job security became threatened. She may need to go out into the maze and look for new cheese.
- Michael applied the story to his work, asking each person in his organization who they thought they were: Sniff, Scurry, Hem or Haw. He recognized each character type had to be treated differently.

- ➢ Sniffs could sniff out changes in the marketplace, and update the corporate vision. They identified possible new products and services consumers would want.
- ➢ The Scurrys liked to get things done, so they took action based on the new corporate vision. They only needed to be monitored so they didn't scurry off in the wrong direction.
- ➢ The Hems wanted to work in a place that was safe and where the changes made sense to them, turning them into Haws. If they didn't change, they were eventually fired. The Haws were hesitant at first, but were open-minded enough to learn something new, and adapted.

- Richard realized how his children had been acting like Hem lately. They were angry and didn't want to accept the change in their family, since Richard had recently separated from his wife.
- Jessica and Cory each recognized it was time for new cheese in their personal relationships, which could mean getting out of a bad relationship, or adapting new behaviors to save the relationship.
- Richard also thought perhaps new cheese could mean changing the way he behaved on the job rather than completely changing jobs.

Michael concluded that the cheese parable works best when everyone in the organization knows about it, because an organization can only change when enough people in it change. He added that passing the story on to people they wanted to do business with had proved profitable. They promoted themselves as that client's new cheese, which led to new business.

No Cheese?

- Reflect on the different reactions of the mice and the little people.
- Block nay-sayers: Folks with fear and negative thoughts who only want to HEM you in.
- As you proceed, you'll find morsels of the new cheese along the way— a promise of what lies ahead! Visualize success: *"it's the cheesiest!"*

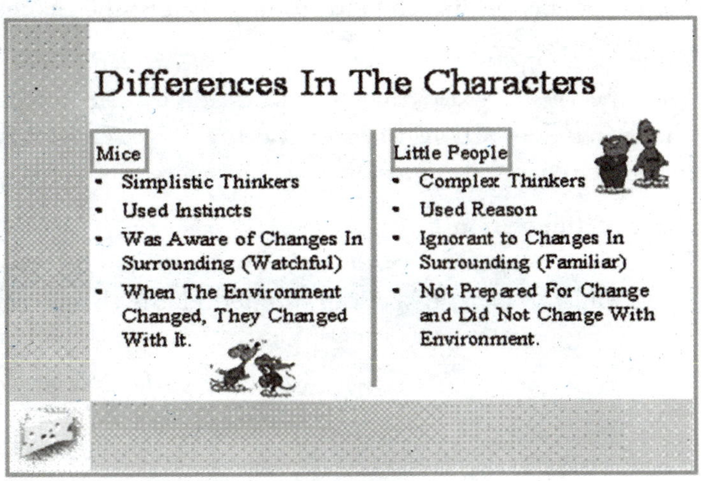

Change follows a predictable pattern both for companies and for individuals. The model given below helps you diagnose where you are and what you should be doing to get the most out of whatever changes you are dealing with.

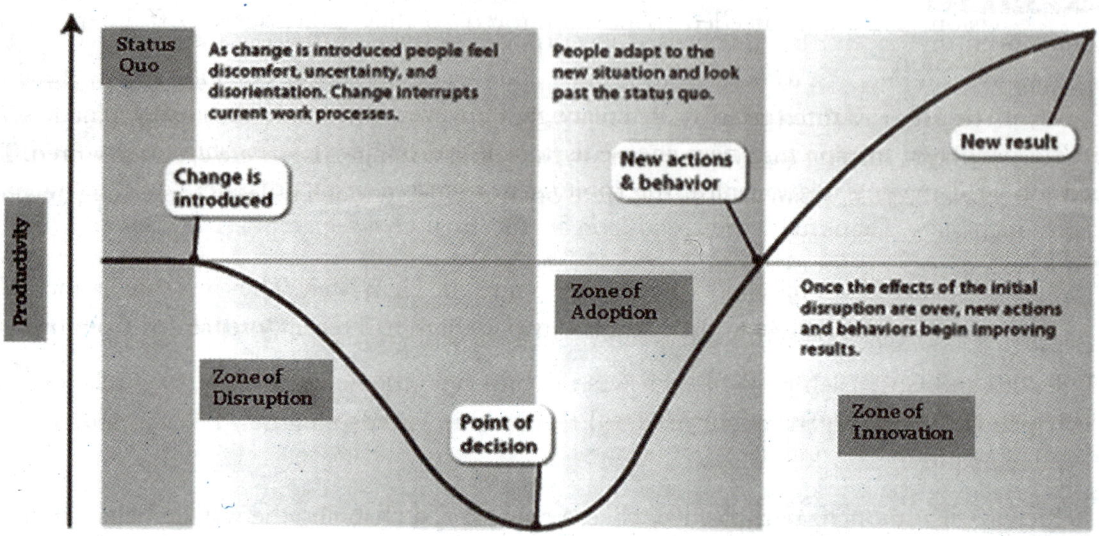

Change is Introduced: Whether change is introduced by choice or by outside forces, the key to success is being prepared to handle the consequences as quickly as possible.

The Zone of Disruption: When change happens, it causes a downturn in productivity in some way or another. The bigger the change, the more severe the disruption.

Point of Decision

Disruption continues until people decide to adapt to the change instead of fighting against it. Sometimes people will continue to fight against the change indefinitely.

Zone of Adoption

Once people have decided to adapt to the change, a period of adoption begins and they make changes to their actions to accommodate for it. This leads to a point of productivity that existed before the change was introduced. The change continues to cost until this break-even point is met.

Zone of Innovation

Finally, when people begin taking advantage of the change and doing new things, there is an opportunity to benefit. Without this period, the change will always cost more than it gained.

TAKEAWAYS

"Who moved my cheese?" is much used in corporate settings. Employees are ordered to read the book, to write reports, to break into groups and discuss the book. Such iconic has the book become; its principles are referred to in meetings. However, as I read the book, I realized that there's a danger in interpreting new cheese as a new job or new relationship (as a solution to a bad job or damaging relationship). Interpreting new cheese in this manner could result in an escapist mentality. Thankfully, the discussion in the final chapter emphasizes that new cheese often means new behavior or attitude rather than a new situation. In relationships especially, a new relationship rarely solves the problem and is a convenient escapist excuse. This occurs because we tend to carry over our old baggage and bad attitudes into the new relationship. After that relationship fails, we then lament that we can't find our soul mate when the real problem actually lies in ourselves. Instead, one should explore creating a new relationship with the same person. This often also applies to employment because our bad work attitudes are carried over to the next job. By changing the work one does at a certain job or even changing one's attitude towards the job, far more positive results can be generated.

IMPORTANT NOTE

This summary culls the content of the book - "Who Moved My Cheese" down to its essence so that even an average reader can sensitize himself to it, sparing him with the time consuming details. In case you feel a need to further explore this topic, the author recommends reading the original work published by "Ebury Publishing".

A Snapshot of
22 IMMUTABLE LAWS OF MARKETING

"22 Immutable Laws of Marketing" is a timeless classic that spells out the basic tenets of brand development and positioning and while you can read the most detailed marketing texts in the world, if you read this book summary you would know most of what you need to know. It is a must read for everyone who owns and works with brands, be that a major corporation or a corner mom & pop store.

The 22 Immutable Laws of Marketing

—Inspired by Al Ries & Jack Trout

"Half the money I spend on advertising is wasted, and the problem is I do not know which half."

—Lord Leverhulme,
British Founder of Unilever

After years of working on marketing principles and problems, Al Ries and Jack Trout distilled their findings into the basic laws that as per them govern success and failure of a brand in the marketplace. The authors argue that the market position of a product or service in the perception of the customer is everything, and offer twenty-two "immutable" laws of marketing that to them demonstrate this fundamental point. As you read along, don't expect an excruciating marketing treatise with elaborate case studies and What-If scenarios. Expect instead 22 capsules of business wisdom, or 'laws' of common sense marketing with some brilliant examples from the real world to prove them.

The Law of Leadership

Many people believe that the basic issue in marketing is convincing prospects that you have a better product or service which is not true. The basic issue in marketing is creating a category you can be first in. Let's say you didn't know the name of the first college founded in America. You can always make a good guess by substituting leading for first. So what's the name of the leading college in America? Most people will probably say Harvard, which is also the name of the first college founded in America. One reason the first brand tends to maintain its leadership is that the name often becomes generic. Xerox, the first plain-paper copier, became the name for all plain-paper copiers. People will stand in front of a Ricoh or a Sharp or a Kodak machine and say, "How do I make a Xerox copy?" So if you're introducing the first brand in a new category, you should always try to select a name that can work generically. Lawyers advise the opposite, but what do they know about the laws of marketing?

You can demonstrate the law of leadership by asking yourself two questions:

1. What's the name of the first person to fly the Atlantic Ocean solo? Charles Lindbergh, right?
2. What's the name of the second person to fly the Atlantic Ocean solo? Not so easy to answer, is it?

The second person to fly the Atlantic Ocean solo was Bert Hinkler. Bert was a better pilot than Charlie— he flew faster, he consumed less fuel. Yet who has ever heard of Bert Hinkler?

In spite of the evident superiority of the Lindbergh approach, most companies go the Bert Hinkler route. They wait until a market develops. Then they jump in with a better product, often with their corporate name attached. In today's competitive environment, a me-too product with a line extension name has little hope of becoming a big, profitable brand, even though it is functionally better.

Heineken was the first imported beer in USA and still is No. 1 imported beer. Same for Miller Lite, first domestic light beer. Hewlett-Packard was first in laser printers. Gillette was the first safety razor. Tide was the first laundry detergent. The law of leadership also applies to magazines which is why Time leads Newsweek, People leads US and Playboy leads Penthouse.

Not every first is going to become successful, however. Some firsts are just bad ideas that will never go anywhere. Frosty Paws, the first ice-cream for dogs, is unlikely to make it. The dogs love it, but the owners are the ones who buy the groceries, and they think that dogs don't need an ice-cream of their own. They should be happy just to lick the plates.

The Law of Category

A large market is really just a cluster of small markets. Tackle the large market and you will probably lose. Tackle a small market and you might just win. Don't think of MacOS as the number two desktop computing platform. Instead, think of them as the number one desktop computer in the graphic design category. Microsoft may be number one in a category which is many times the size of the category in which Apple is number one. But finding a category in which Apple is number one is not an effort to claim equality. Rather, it simply explains who buys Macintosh and what differentiator is important to them. So, the point of creating a category is to make sure you and your customers understand what your key differentiation is. What makes you different? To whom does that difference matter? In the minds of those people, you are number one. To this end, a new category doesn't have to be radically different, e.g., if there's dominant player in imported beer, one can become the first to import light beer. If one can't be the first to fly over Atlantic, one can still be the first woman to fly over Atlantic. This is counter to classic marketing thinking, which is brand-oriented: how do I get people to prefer my brand? Forget the brand. Think categories. Charles Schwab didn't open a better brokerage firm. He opened the first discount broker.

Starbucks dominates the high-end coffee category. Google dominates the search category. The Body Shop dominates the natural-cosmetics category. Whole Foods dominates the organic-food category. BlackBerry dominates the wireless-email category. Does it surprise you that all of these relatively recent brand successes (Red Bull, Starbucks, Google, The Body Shop, Whole Foods and BlackBerry) were started by entrepreneurs, not by established companies? It shouldn't. Big companies are busy burnishing their brands while entrepreneurs are looking for ways to dominate new categories. Big companies think of brands whereas entrepreneurs think categories.

The brand is only a marker for the category itself. If you want an energy drink, you reach for a Red Bull. If you want soy milk, you buy Silk. Rental DVDs by mail? Netflix. Creating a new category and then branding that category in such a way that your brand is perceived as the innovator and category leader (in both senses of the word) is the essence of marketing today. To create a new category, however, you have to think different, not better. Pepsi-Cola tastes better than Coca-Cola, but it's not different and, therefore, can never become a market leader.

The Law of Mind

It's better to be first in the mind than to be first in the marketplace

Being first in the market place is important only to the extent that it allows you to get in the mind first. The world's first personal computer was the MITS Altair 8800. The law of leadership would suggest that the MITS Altair 8800 (an unfortunate choice of names) ought to be first in personal computer brand.

Surprisingly, the product is no longer with us. On the other hand, Apple's problem in getting into its prospect's minds was helped by its simple and easy to remember name.

Problems in Measuring Mindshare

We underestimate the value of mindshare when we try to change the minds of people. Ries and Trout say that "The single most wasteful thing you can do in marketing is to change a mind." At times, we tend to overestimate the value of mindshare as well. During the dotcom bubble, venture capitalists sacrificed several billion dollars on the altar of this Law. Mindshare was sought and purchased at unbelievable premiums. In hindsight, it seems apparent that mindshare, which was quickly gained, can be quickly lost.

The problem here is that we talk about customer minds without reminding ourselves that not all of those minds think the same way. Remember the marketing bell curves Changing the mind of an early adopter is cheap and easy. Changing the mind of a conservative or a laggard is expensive and hard. These differences cause us to either overestimate or underestimate the value of mindshare:

- If most of your mindshare inventory is in early adopters, you are in trouble. Early adopters don't stay anywhere very long. Eventually, you will lose most of them.
- Your valuable mindshare is among conservatives. It will be very expensive for anyone who wants to take these people away from you.
- If you are a new player trying to gain mindshare, don't be afraid to steal early adopters from your competitor. It's easier than you think. Just remember that the next guy is going to steal them from you.

This is why some companies, despite being first in their category and having enormous mindshare, end up in the same place as the dotcoms, at the bottom of the chasm. They build their mindshare among the early adopters, but never really make it into the mainstream markets of the pragmatists and conservatives.

The Law of Perception

> ***People are seldom, if ever wrong; at least in their own minds***

Marketing is not about products (their features or quality) but about perceptions (how people perceive products). Reality doesn't exist, what we call 'reality' is just a perception of reality that we create in our minds. With a modicum of experience in a product category, a consumer assumes that he or she is right. A perception that exists in the mind is often interpreted as a universal truth. Honda is a leading Japanese car manufacturer in the USA but only third in Japan (after Toyota and Nissan). So what's the difference between Honda in Japan and Honda in the USA? The products are the same, same quality, the same styling, the same horsepower and roughly the same prices hold true for Japan as they do for the USA, but the perceptions in customers' minds are different. If you told friends in New York you bought a Honda, they might ask you, 'What kind of car did you get? A Civic, an Accord?' If you told friends in Tokyo you bought a Honda, they might ask you, 'What kind of motorcycle did you buy?' In Japan, Honda got into customers' minds as a manufacturer of motorcycles, and apparently most people don't want to buy a car from a motorcycle company.

"What makes the battle even more difficult is that customers frequently make buying decisions based on second-hand perceptions. Instead of using their own perceptions, they base their buying decisions on someone else's perception. This is the 'everybody knows' principle. Everybody knows

Japanese make higher-quality cars than Americans. So people make buying decisions based on the fact that everybody knows the Japanese make higher-quality cars. When you ask shoppers whether they have had any personal experience with a product, most often they say they haven't. More often than not, their own experience is twisted to conform to their perceptions. So if you have had a bad experience with a Japanese car, you've just been unlucky, because everybody knows the Japanese make high-quality cars. Conversely, if you have had a good experience with an American car, you've just been lucky, because everybody knows that American cars are not as well made.

> **Subjectivity**
>
> The real issue here is that the words "better" and "best" are subjective terms. People have different requirements and preferences upon which they form very different opinions. There are very few absolutes. One could credibly argue that OS/2 was "better" than Windows 3.x. The 68k chip was better in some ways than the x 86 line. But those are perceptions and opinions. In hindsight, we can simply say that more people perceived Windows and the Intel chip to be better.

Your Author's Take – Reality Still Matters

My only gripe with this law is that it sometimes tries to convince me that perception and reality are entirely disjoint. They're not. Quite frequently, perception is merely an exaggeration of reality. And as long as I'm giving unsolicited advice to marketing legends, let's not just give up on our desire to make our products better choosing instead to spend all our resources on the management of customer perception. The Law of Perception can help us understand when things don't seem to make sense, but it's not so powerful that product excellence doesn't matter.

The Law of Focus

The most powerful concept in marketing is owing a word in the prospect's mind

'We need an IBM machine.'. Is there any doubt that a computer is being requested? By the same token, if the given words are copier, chocolate bar and cola, the three words most associated to them will be Xerox, Hershey's and Coke. You burn your way into the prospect's mind by narrowing the focus to a single word or concept. It's the ultimate marketing sacrifice. Once you have a word, you have to go out of the way to protect it in the marketplace. The case of BMW illustrates it very well. For years, BMW was the ultimate driving machine. Then the company tried to imitate Mercedes-Benz with large, 700-series sedans. The problem is, how can a living room on wheels also be the ultimate driving machine? As a result, things started downhill for BMW. Luckily, they have regained their focus. For another example, take a look at two of the major wireless phone providers in the United States today. Each of them has carefully chosen just one concept as their message.

- For Sprint, the concept is Clarity. Ten times a week we hear their spokesman clearing up some goofy misunderstanding caused by the unclear calls of one of their competitors.

- For Verizon Wireless, the concept is Coverage. Twenty times a week we hear their spokesman saying, 'Can you hear me now? Good!'

Each of these two companies has plenty of other benefits they could be talking about. They could tell us about their great selection of phones. They could brag about their pricing. They could talk about safety issues. Instead, they each have focused their marketing message around just one idea.

Count Your Words

During the dotcom bubble, venture capitalists taught us one useful concept: The elevator pitch. The idea is that you have to explain your product and its benefits in the amount of time you spend in an elevator. In other words, you've got well under a minute and there is no time for product love poetry. One step further, the Law of Focus would claim that even an elevator ride is far too long. The Law of Focus insists that a 25- word description is about 24 words, too many. The wire between your marketing efforts and your customer's mind is an extremely low bandwidth connection. Less is more.

The Law of Exclusivity

When a competitor owns a word in the prospect's mind, it is futile to attempt to own the same word. It is obvious that we should all eat better and exercise more, but we don't. Similarly, marketers do routinely find a way to violate this law. They do a smart thing by following the Law of Focus and choosing one key benefit around which they build their product message. Then do a dumb thing by choosing the same benefit as somebody else. Almost invariably, they end up beating their head against the wall in futility. It is irrefutable that we should not try to beat somebody else at their own game. And yet, we often try. McDonald's was perceived to be the fastest hamburger chain in the country. Undaunted by this fact, Burger King launched its campaign with the slogan 'best food for fast times'. The program quickly became a disaster. Many people have paid the price of violating the law of exclusivity. You can't change people's mind once they are made up. In fact, what you often do is reinforce your competitor's position by making its concept more important.

What marketers can learn from Obama's campaign

Obama was a relatively unknown man. Younger than all of his opponents. Black. With a bad-sounding name. Consider his first opponent: the best-known woman in America, connected to one of the most successful politicians in history. Then consider his second opponent: a well-known war hero with a long, distinguished record as a US senator. It didn't matter. Barack Obama had a better marketing strategy than either of them. "Change."

What word did Hillary Clinton own? First, she tried 'experience'. When she saw the progress Mr Obama was making, she shifted to 'Countdown to change'. Then when the critics pointed out her me-too approach, she shifted to 'Solutions for America'. Then there's John McCain. An October 26 cover story in The New York Times Magazine was titled 'The Making (and Remaking and Remaking) of the Candidate'. The visual listed some of the labels the candidate was associated with: 'Conservative. Maverick. Hero. Straight talker. Commander. Bipartisan conciliator. Experienced leader. Patriot.' Subhead: 'When a Campaign Can't Settle on a Central Narrative, Does It Imperil Its Protagonist?' Actually, Mr McCain did settle on a slogan, 'Country first,' but it was way too late in the campaign and it was a slogan that had little relevance to the average voter. Tactically, both Ms Clinton and Mr McCain focused their messages on 'I can do change better than my opponent can do change.' 'Better' never work in marketing. The only thing that works in marketing is 'different.' When you're different, you can pre-empt the concept in consumers' minds so your competitors can never take it away from you.

The Law of Ladder

The strategy to use depends on which rung you occupy on the ladder

This law underscores the fact that mind is selective. Prospects use their ladders in deciding which information to accept and which to reject. In general, a mind accepts only that data which is consistent with its product ladder in that category. Everything else is ignored. Take the car rental category. Hertz got into the mind first and wound up on the top rung. Avis came second. For years, Avis advertised the high quality of its rent-a-car service. 'Finest in rent-a-cars' was one of its campaigns. The reader looked at the ad and wondered how could they have the finest rent-a-car service when they're not on the top rung of my ladder? For 13 years in a row, Avis had lost money. Then, when it admitted to being No. 2, 'Avis is only No. 2 in rent-a-cars. So why go with us? We try harder'; it started to make money, lots of money.

The Hierarchy of Categories

In our discussion of the previous laws, authors had emphasized the importance of finding a sub-category in which you can be #1. However, when you pop the stack frame up one level to the enclosing category, you find that you are ranked on a ladder among the other players. The consumer's mind can only remember a few rungs. Research indicates a maximum of about seven, and a more practical limit of about two or three. How many brands of toothpaste can you name? How many brands of cola? How many brands of automobiles? Some categories have more rungs than others. The best strategy for you depends entirely on your ranking on the ladder. The right strategy for the #1 player is probably wrong for the #2 player, and vice-versa. The Avis rent-a-car example has been very much discussed in the ten years since the book was written, but it still rings with a bell of wisdom. Avis showed a lot of self-awareness and its customers respected that.

In the long run, every market becomes a two-horse race

The Law of Duality

Young markets are highly fragmented and have many rungs on their ladder. Gradually, as the market matures, less competent players disappear and the market settles on exactly two primary players. In batteries, it's Eveready and Duracell. In photographic film, it's Kodak and Fuji, in hamburgers, it's McDonald's and Burger King, in sneakers, it's Nike and Reebok. It's the kind of thinking that built companies like P&G into the powerhouses that they are. In 32 of its 44 product categories in the USA, P&G commands the No. 1 or No. 2 brands.

It often takes a long time for things to settle down, but in the end, markets usually give people what they want, which is two strong choices. Buyers don't like choosing between ten or twenty players. It's too stressful. A big reason for this effect is that most people don't make their own buying decisions. People tend to buy what somebody else is buying. Pragmatists buy something only after they see the Early Adopters buying it. Conservatives buy it only after the pragmatists are buying it. Laggards buy it only when the peer pressure and ridicule is so severe that they look like absurd for not buying it. Market share begets market share, and the rich get richer.

Even as the market gets very mature, it will continue to tolerate the presence of more than two players. However, the top two will have the lion's share of the market. All other players are essentially in the niche segments. Once a market reaches this state, it will generally not allow #1 and #2 to move around. For example, the market will never allow the top two players to change positions. Burger King will never be #1. Furthermore, the market will not allow #1 to get too far ahead. Just as markets hate having a ten-horse race, they also hate having a one-horse race. When #1 gets too far ahead of #2, the market will usually correct the problem.

The Software Industry

Everything we discussed above makes virtually no sense at all when we look at the software industry. We don't have two strong choices. Most software market segments are a one-horse race. In many cases, Microsoft is so utterly dominant that there is no clear #2.

- There is no strong #2 desktop operating system
- There is no strong #2 office suit
- There is no strong #2 developer IDE

Why do these markets not follow the Law of Duality?

The popular notion today is that Microsoft is an illegal monopoly. But whether or not Microsoft is a violator of government law, it is clearly a violator of the law of duality. The market should have ensured the presence of a strong #2, but it has not. Even more strange here is the fact that software is still a rather young industry. At its tender age of perhaps three decades, we should expect to still have very high fragmentation. But we don't. It is quite clear that the federal government is no match for Microsoft. But the market itself still has a lot of power. The Law of Duality may yet show up.

The Law of Opposite

If you're shooting for second place, your strategy is determined by the leader

Much like a wrestler uses his opponent's strength against him, you should leverage the leader's strength into weakness. If you want to establish a firm foothold on the second rung of the ladder, study the firm above you. Where is it strong? And how do you turn that strength into a weakness? Don't try to be better than the leader, try to be opposite. How come Pepsi solidified its position as the second most dominant player in the cola market? It marketed itself as a "choice for the new generation" when faced with Coca-cola's "old and established" brand.

Be the opposite, is a marketing strategy that can work for any brand in any product category. How did Lowe's, for example, manage to make substantial progress against market leader Home Depot? Home Depot is the leading home improvement warehouse chain. But Home Depot is also a messy place originally designed that way in part to attract men. So Lowe's made a special effort to be neat and clean with wide aisles and brighter lighting. A place that was particularly attractive to women and, in the process, became the fastest-growing home improvement chain.

Wal-Mart is the world's largest retailer with extremely low prices and a slightly downscale clientele. So Target went slightly upscale with a focus on good design. The theme: 'Cheap chic'. Trapped in the mushy middle was Kmart, a company that went bankrupt. Notice what Kmart tried to do. First they went after Wal-Mart by cutting prices, but that didn't work. Then they went after Target by doing a deal with Martha Stewart and other designers. Neither strategy was likely to work because the strategies were based on a "better than" approach rather than a "be the opposite" approach.

Dell Computer became the world's largest seller of personal computers by choosing a distribution channel (direct by phone) that was the opposite of the computer retail stores channel used by its competitors.

Montblanc marketed "fat" pens when its major competitor (Cross) was focused on selling "thin" pens.

Prince became the leading tennis racquet company by marketing "over-size" racquets when its major competitors were selling regular-size tennis racquets. And so it goes……..

The Law of Division

Over time, a category will divide and become two or more categories. This effect is an obvious and natural consequence of other laws. Each company will try to set up a new category in which it can be #1. Not all of these categories will end up becoming real, but some will. For example, computers started as a single category but broke up into mainframes, workstations, personal computers, laptops, etc. Like the computer, the automobile started off as a single category but divided into luxury cars, sport cars, RVs, minivans, etc. Instead of understanding this concept of division, many corporate leaders hold the naive belief that categories are combining. “Convergence”, “synergy” and its kissing cousin, “the corporate alliance” are the buzzwords in the boardrooms. Companies make a mistake when they try to take a well-known brand name in one category and use the same brand name in another category. A classic example is the fate that befell Volkswagen, the company that introduced the small-car category to America. Its Beetle was a big winner that grabbed 67% of the imported-car market in the USA at its peak. Volkswagen was so successful that it began to think it could be like GM and sell bigger, faster and sportier cars. So it swept up whatever models it was making in Germany and shipped them all to the USA. But unlike GM, it used the same brand, Volkswagen, for all its models. Needless to say, the only thing that kept selling was the “small” thing, the Beetle. Well, Volkswagen found a way to fix that. It stopped selling the Beetle in the USA and started selling a new family of big, fast, expensive Volkswagens. Now, you had the Sirocco, the Jetta, the Golf GL and the Cabriolet. It even built a plant in Pennsylvania to build these wondrous new cars. Unfortunately for Volkswagen, the small-car category continued to expand. And since people couldn’t buy a long-lasting, economical VW, they shifted to Toyota, Honda and Nissan. Today, Volkswagen’s 67% share has shrunk to less than 6%. Eventually, VW brought back the Beetle, but the damage had been done.

What keeps leaders from launching a different brand to cover a new category is the fear of what will happen to their existing brands. GM was slow to react to the super-premium category that Mercedes-Benz and BMW established. One reason was that a new brand on top of Cadillac would enrage GM’s Cadillac dealers. Eventually, GM tried to take Cadillac up-market with the $54,000 Allante. It bombed. Why would people spend that kind of money on a so-called Cadillac, since their neighbours would probably think they paid only $30,000 or so? No prestige. A better strategy for GM might have been to put a new brand into the Mercedes market. It might have brought back the classic LaSalle brand.

The way for the leader to maintain its dominance is to address each emerging category with a different brand name. For example, when Honda wanted to go up-market, it created a new brand, Acura.

The Law of Perspective

Marketing effects take place over an extended period of time. It's a mistake to sacrifice long-term planning with actions to improve short-term balance sheet

Is alcohol a stimulant or a depressant? Chemically, alcohol is a strong depressant. But in the short-term, by depressing a person's inhibitions, alcohol acts like a stimulant. Many marketing moves exhibit the same phenomenon. For example, sales increase short-term profits but in a long-term, it also educates customers not to buy for regular price. Almost all the companies that go for sales, find the need of a quarterly dose of couponing to keep their business on an even keel. In other words, you keep those coupons rolling out not to increase sales but to keep sales from falling off. Couponing is a drug. You continue to do it because the withdrawal symptoms are just too painful.

Patience is the key here

It is generally understood that public companies are forced into a three-month planning horizon. Earnings must be reported to the public every quarter. If the stockholders are not happy with those earnings, they will sell the stock and its price will go down. In other words, the public is short-sighted, so publicly-owned companies must, therefore, find a way to be short-sighted as well. Defeats all management logic! Long-term plans must be well thought out marketing plans, not to be forgone for shortlived financial gains.

The Law of Line Extension

Line extension suffers from the hockey stick effect: Short term up, then long term down

Why does top management believe that line extensions work, in spite of the overwhelming evidence to the contrary? One reason is that while line extension is a loser in the long-term, it can be a winner in the short-run. Why else will Pepsi Co have introduced crystal Pepsi inspite of the past failures of Pepsi light and Pepsi AM? General Motors is into anything and everything on wheels, sedans, sports cars, cheap cars, expensive cars, trucks, minivans, even electric cars. Today, it stands for everything, which means it stands for nothing. The antidote of line extension is corporate courage, a commodity in short supply.

You hurt the ones you love

You think that the power of the brand will help sell the new product. Instead, the brand itself is tarnished as line extension often destroys what a brand stands for. Budweiser used to be The King of Beers. Coors was the beer brewed with Rocky Mountain spring water. And Miller was the brand you drank after a hard day's work. "It's Miller time." Today, these three brand positions are mostly meaningless, buried under an avalanche of line extensions.

The mathematics of line extension

Every company wants to increase sales. So the logical approach is to "broaden the line." If we appeal to a larger segment of the market, goes the thinking, we can't help but move more merchandise. But if you analyze the market mathematically, what seems obvious in theory is not true for the market as a whole. Take a typical example, beer. Years ago, three major brands dominated the American market: Budweiser, Miller and Coors. Today, each of the three major brands has metamorphosed into a family of brands, as each brewery broadened its line to appeal to a larger segment of the market. So now we have regular, light, dry, draft, reserve and a number of other variations on each of the basic brands. Why the raft of beer line extensions? To increase sales, of course. What might be true for one brewery is obviously not true for the beer industry as a whole. No matter, how many line extensions each brewery introduces, the average market share of the average brewery will remain exactly the same. The only difference (and it's a big difference) are the extra expenses of all those additional brands. Advertising, packaging, sales promotion, etc. Line extensions also increase the costs of distribution without providing any increases in overall sales of the category. They also increase the possibility of a given "flavor" being out of stock. In this respect, line extensions can actually reduce sales of a given category. Whether line extension is good for one particular brewery or not might be a matter of discussion. But what isn't a matter of discussion is that line extension is mathematically bad for the beer industry as a whole. The case could be made that line extensions broaden the entire beer market. More people drink more beer because they now have more choices. It's not true of the beer business, of course, because per-capita beer consumption has been essentially flat for the last 25 years. Metaphorically speaking, it's like casino gambling in Los Vegas. Sure, there might be some winners, but on average, the average player is a loser. Even if line extension in total is a loser, maybe the "first mover" can gain an advantage. Research shows just the opposite. It's usually the "last mover" that wins a line extension war. Miller was the first line-extension mover in the beer wars. (Miller Lite, an enormous initial success, started the industry down the line extension path.) Yet Miller Brewing has been hurt the most in recent years. It was Budweiser, the last mover in the beer line-extension war that has increased its market share dramatically.

The Law of Sacrifice

It's all about saying "no" to any and every opportunity that comes to your doorsteps

Saying "No"

When people hear about the Law of Focus, the first reaction is to say, "Yes, yes, focus is good." People seem to forget that the word "focus" implies a decision about what you are not going to do. With the word "sacrifice", that particular implication is much clearer. This skill is incredibly difficult to learn. The only way to learn to say "no" is to experience the pain of saying "yes" too often.

Where is it written that you have to appeal to everyone? If line extensions and diversification were effective marketing strategies, you'd expect to see the generalists riding high. But they're not. Most of them are in trouble. When clothing chain with the name of banana republic can be successful, you know we live in the age of specialists. Take the cola field. Coca-cola got into the prospect's mind first and built a powerful position. In late fifties, for example, Coke outsold Pepsi by more than five to one. What could Pepsi cola have done to compete against Coke's powerful position? In the early sixties, Pepsicola finally developed a strategy on the concept of sacrifice. The company sacrificed everything except the teenage market. Even though Pepsicola's target was teenager, the market was for everybody. For a 50 year-old-guy who wants to think he is 29 will also drink Pepsi. Today Pepsi is only 10% behind coke in the US Market. In supermarts, it actually outsells Coca-cola.

The Law of Attributes

For every attribute there is an opposite, effective attribute

Too often a company attempts to emulate the leader. "They must know what works," goes the rationale, "so let's do something similar." Not an intelligent marketing thinking. Burger King was unsuccessful when it tried to take the attribute "fast" from McDonald's. What should Burger King have done? A single trip to any McDonald's should be enough to find another attribute that it owns: "kids". If McDonald's owns kids, then Burger King has the opportunity to position itself for the older crowd, which includes any kid who doesn't want to be perceived as a kid. That generally works out to be everyone above the age of 10. Not a bad market! To make the concept work. Burger King would have to invoke the law of sacrifice and give all the little kids to McDonald's.

The Law of Candor

When you admit a negative, the prospect will give you a positive

It may come as a surprise to you that one of the most effective ways to get into a prospect's mind is to first admit a negative and then twist it into a positive. Every negative statement that you make about yourself is instantly accepted as truth. Positive statements, on the other hand, are looked as dubious at best. Have a look at this advertisement: "Joy-- The most expensive perfume in the world." What it tells you as a customer is that if people are willing to pay $ 375 an ounce then Joy must be a sensational perfume.

Being Genuine

Conventional wisdom says that absolutely everything in your marketing message must be positive. In fact, a primary function of the marcomm team is to sanitize all public statements ensuring that the company never says anything it does not want to say. But the fact of the matter is that consumers today are being bombarded with so much advertising that traditional marketing is less effective than ever before. Sanitized press releases are out. Transparency is in.

- Listerine did it when they acknowledged that their mouthwash tastes terrible.
- Avis did it when they acknowledged that they are #2.
- Volkswagen did it when they acknowledged that the "bug" is ugly.

Ignoring the Law of Candor can kill your credibility. Whatever your negative issue is, everybody already knows about it anyway. If you don't talk about it, then it will become "the elephant in the room". When you issue yet another sanitized press release, your customers eagerly read it, hoping to see some evidence that you have any self-awareness at all. They ask themselves, "Don't these people realize how awful their mouthwash tastes?" Drowning in a sea of marketing mumbo jumbo, people admire companies that choose to be genuine.

The Law of Singularity

There is only one place where the competitor is weak and that place should be the focus of entire marketing invading force

Successful generals study the battlefield and look for that one bold stroke that is least expected by the enemy. Finding one is difficult. Finding more than one is usually impossible. Part of the problem here is the assumptions we make about the total result we will get from a list of marketing ideas. We make our list in Excel and for each item, we calculate the results that item will generate for us. And then, at the bottom, we enter SUM(B2:B11). This is our mistake. The proper estimate for the total result should instead be MAX(B2:B11). In recent years, there have been two strong moves against GM. Both were flanking moves around the GM Maginot Line. The Japanese came at the lower end with cars like Toyota. The Germans came at the high end with super-premium cars like Mercedes and BMW.

Remember Peter's law: the unexpected always happens

The Law of Unpredictability

Research does best at measuring the past. Radically, new ideas and concepts are almost impossible to measure. The classic example to this is the research conducted before Xerox introduced its photo-copiers. What came back was the conclusion that no one will pay five cents for the plain paper copy when they can get a thermofax copy for a cent and a half. Xerox ignored the research and the rest is history. One good way to cope with the unpredictable is to build an enormous amount of flexibility into your system in order to fight out any uncalled competitive move. Kodak has been a culprit of this law; it was too slow to respond to Sony's pioneering move in digital photography and lost its No. 1 spot in the process.

You should be focused on all the long-term plans for your brand but with the ability to be flexible in your approach.

The Law of Success

Success often leads to arrogance and arrogance to failure

Arrogance blurs vision and often leads to wrong turns. Tom Monaghan of Domino's Pizza is one of the few executives who have recognized how ego can lead you astray. He once said and I quote, "You start thinking you can do anything. I got into frozen Pizzas for a while and that was a disaster. If I hadn't messed around with frozen pizzas for the better part of the year trying to sell them in bars and restaurants, Domino's probably would have a lot more stores by now." Many small companies have great customer understanding and pay close attention to keeping the customers happy; but when they grow due to their good customer insights, they become cocky and lose touch with those same customers and go on a path of failure. GM was successful into the 70s but continued to lose share througt the 90s, and all that time, they assumed they knew what consumers wanted.

The Law of Failure

Failure is to be expected and accepted

We need to give ourselves the freedom to take risks and try a lot of different things. But the obvious corollary here is that not all of those risks will work out. It's always better to drop things that don't work instead of trying to fix them. Ford almost lost the company on the Edsel in the 50's. Launched September 4, 1957 after years of hype and hoopla, the Edsel enjoyed more showroom traffic on introduction day ("E" Day) than any other vehicle in history. But the much awaited Edsel quickly lost favor as the new model failed to live up to the hype. The styling, while unique and interesting, was not widely accepted by the masses, and the car quickly became the butt of jokes. The top comedians of the day seized every opportunity to throw barbs at the Edsel's unique front grille. Roy Brown, Ford's head stylist in charge of the Edsel program, had designed a grille harkening back to the glory days of luxury cars of the 1930's to create a car "that could be instantly recognized from a block away." But the "horsecollar" shape was derided frequently on national television by comedian Bob Hope and others, relating the style to an "Olds sucking a lemon" and even worse as a very discreet part of the female anatomy! Ford attempted in vain to give the Edsel a fresh look over the next two model years, but the damage was irreparable. In November 1959, Ford Motor Company discontinued the Edsel and all remaining Edsel dealerships were either shuttered or converted to sell Ford's other brands. The unloved Edsel was history. The lesson to be learned— when you realize you've made a mistake, cut your losses. Denial or persistence will only make things worse.

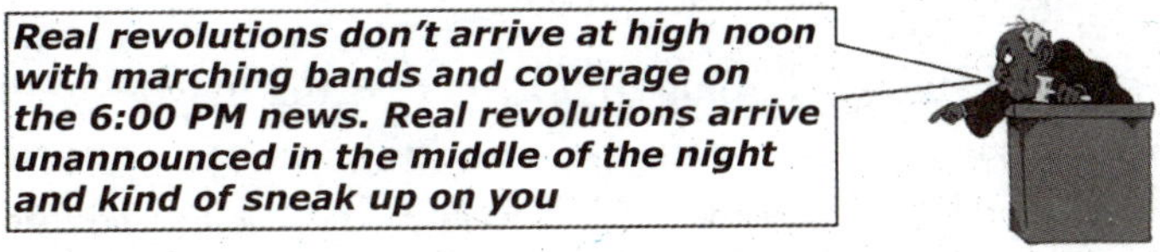

The Law of Hype

This law talks primarily about new things which claim to make existing things obsolete. Such products tend to become darlings in the press, because the notion of breakthrough innovation is very attractive to readers. People love to read stories about things like the personal helicopter which was supposed to make cars obsolete several decades ago. So the press jumps on the bandwagon, stories get written, newspapers get sold, and people get excited. And they still drive their cars to work everyday. Relate this to the other overhyped things of the last ten years. The truth is that fundamental change doesn't occur so easily. Even when the innovation is quite real, people are not quick to give up existing mainstream products and services.

The author argues that when things are going well, companies don't need the hype. In fact, the situation is often opposite of the way it appears to be in the press. When you need the hype, it usually means you are in trouble. History is filled with market failures that were successful in the press. So, forget the front page. If you are looking for cues to the future, look in the back of the paper for those innocuous stories.

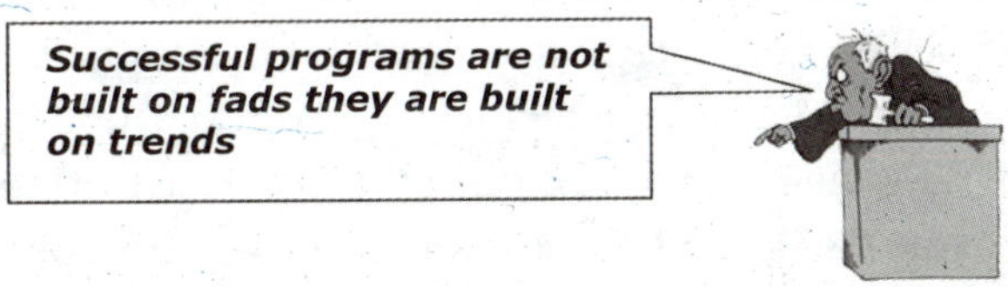

The Law of Acceleration

Drawing their examples from mainstream consumer products, the authors observe the tendency for companies to blindly set sail for anything big and hot, spending a lot of money doing so. They restructure, invest in new equipment, irrespective of whether it is their core competency. In most cases, they fail to make it big, and the company usually goes into a deep financial shock. What happened to Atari is very typical in this aspect. Back in 1984, it was a computer game behemoth. But then it gave in to the temptation of jumping into the new & potentially more profitable computer market. The PC and Macintosh were still in diapers, Bill Gates was a paltry multimillionaire, and Commodore's Amiga was considered one of the best computers in the market. There was a chance that Atari could be the big name in personal computers. But Atari's serious aspirations could never materialize in the ever evolving computer market while Apple- and IBM-based computers, thanks to their focus and good understanding of the user needs began to capture the broader consumer market. Macintosh sewed up the educational computing category and with its slick advertising campaigns, became a household word. IBM's name recognition, along with its "open architecture" allowed its machines to be cloned by other companies such as Compaq, thereby ensuring its ubiquity. But here is the saddest part of the Atari fiasco— Nintendo kicked Atari's ass as they took the game market away completely because of Atari's failure to read the market that they once ruled.

Another important thing to note here is that if you are faced with rapidly rising business with all the characteristics of fad, the best thing you can do is to dampen the fad. By dampening the fad, you stretch the fad out and it becomes more like a trend. Elvis Presley's manager, Colonel Parker, made a deliberate attempt to restrict the number of appearances and records that the king made. As a result, every time Elvis appeared, it was an event of enormous impact. Ninja Turtles, on the contrary, could have been the next Barbie dolls if the market hadn't been flooded, and if the makers had tried to turn the fad into a trend.

The Law of Resources

Without adequate funding, no idea can get off the ground. No matter how good it looks on the paper. You need money to get into the prospect's mind. And you need even more money to stay in its mind once you get there. Mindshare costs a heckuva lot of money. You can't save your way to success.

A word of caution, chapter 22 is likely to serve as ammunition for the marcomm guy who is always trying to convince you to spend more money. He will quote chapter 22 as if it were scripture, trying to make you feel guilty for underfunding your marcomm efforts. But the real problem is in taking chapter 22 out of the context of the rest of the book. This chapter is the last one in the book, and for a good reason— it depends on the other 21. Marketing has two phases, strategy and communications. No matter how much money you have, don't spend money in the communications phase until your strategy stuff is done and solid.

Sheepish Confession of a Marketing Geek

"The 22 Immutable Laws of Marketing" is one of my favorites. It had a significant impact on my life, probably more than the authors know. But I couldn't help mentioning that the word "immutable" in the title, is a gross exaggeration. We literalists will have to endure the authors' word choice. Also, some of these laws seem to have more punch than others. For example, I find the Law of Focus to be a concept with a lot of impact. It's very counter-intuitive, and yet very powerful. But I can't really defend the authors when they say, "for every attribute, there is an opposite, effective attribute". If you think of the attribute that crest owns in the toothpaste market, it makes you wonder how can there be an attribute which is the opposite of "cavity prevention" and is equally effective. But do not dismiss the laws for some of their imprecision. This book is not a crock! Incidentally, guys, this is the reason why our girlfriends or wifes don't like going to watch movies with us. Nobody wants to watch a film with some anal-retentive dork who is ready and waiting to discard the entire film because the producers made a minor mistake in science or technology. We need to sensitize ourselves to the fact that Marketing books are written for big-picture thinkers. They contain broad sweeping generalizations which are only true most of the time. Guys like Ries and Trout don't feel the need for a lot of precision. I wish marketing was as logical and precise as Six Sigma. But it's not.

This tidbit of marketing advice is provided at no extra charge. 

The basic notion behind this book is that people project themselves on the outside world to cope with the terrifying reality of being alone in the universe. They "live" in the arena of books, movies, television, newspapers and magazines. They "belong" to clubs, organizations, institutions. These outside representations of the world seem more real than the reality inside their own minds. People cling firmly to the belief that reality is the world outside of the mind and that the individual is one small speck on a global spaceship. Actually, it's the opposite. The only reality you can be sure about is that exists in your own perceptions. If the universe exists, it exists inside your own mind and, of course, in the minds of others. That's the reality that marketing programs must deal with.

The laws presented here can best be used as a 'diagnostic check' of your company's marketing plan. Instead of just chalking up every failure to the fault of "bad marketing", you can review each decision and figure out the need to undertake qualitative research, such as focus groups and in-depth interviews to better understand and define this perception.

This book also acts as a good reminder of the importance of the perception of your service or product in the mind of your customer and underscores the consequent.

❒❒❒

IMPORTANT NOTE

This summary culls the content of the book - "The 22 Immutable Laws of Marketing" down to its essence so that even an average reader can sensitize himself to it, sparing him with the time consuming details. In case you feel a need to further explore this topic, the author recommends reading the original work published by "Harper Collins".

A Snapshot of FISH!

"Fish" is a fable that draws lessons aimed at combating dysfunctional workplaces from the happy fishmongers at Seattle's Pike Place Market. The few simple ideas presented here can transform your daily grind of a nine to five workday into an enriching, easy and yes, even a fun time at the office!

Fish!

—*Inspired by Stephen C. Lundin Ph.D., Harry Paul & John Christensen*

"A business has to be involving, it has to be fun, and it has to exercise your creative instincts."

—Richard Branson,
British Industrialist, best known for his Virgin brand

They say inspiration can come from anywhere, who would think that such an ordinary thing as a fish market on a busy day could inspire an entire management philosophy. Renowned for its bustling atmosphere and great customer service, and largely thanks to its committed and satisfied staff, the pike place fish market is an outstanding example of how a traditionally difficult work environment can be positively transformed. The Fish Philosophy isn't just another bland teaching tool for the ho-hum workplace; it's an eye opener for those of us who grew up with notions like: "Work is serious, let's have no fooling around!" Why can't the mantra of workers be: 'Thank God it's Monday'? You can accomplish this if you live the Fish! Manifesto.This book summary is, thus, a must read for anyone attempting to "catch the energy and release the potential" of themselves and those around them.

The lessons are couched in a fable about Mary Jane Ramirez, who works at First Guarantee Financial, a fictional company in Seattle. A widow with children, Mary Jane is offered a promotion and raise to manage "the third floor employees," a group that authors deșcribe as a "toxic energy dump." Mary Jane reluctantly accepts the position for the increased pay and benefits. She has to now face the daunting task of turning the department around or having it downsized. Overwhelmed with fear of losing her job, Mary Jane soon loses hope and retreats to her own private world every lunch hour as she walks the downtown Seattle streets. Serendipitously, during one of her lunch breaks, she discovers a fish market that does not fit preconceptions for that environment most of us would have, i.e., hard, tedious work under unpleasant, uncomfortable conditions. What she does experience is a group of people who are totally involved with their customers, having a lot of fun, and selling lots of fish! She asks one of the fishmongers (Lonnie) about how they do this. And so begins the odyssey that uncovers the key lessons that she later on applies to turn her department around.

Flinging Fish for Fun and Profit

The situation looked grim for Johnny Yokoyama. The seafood market, where he had once been an employee but was now the owner, was more than $300,000 in debt and sinking deeper fast. In fact, employee morale was at an all-time low, and the business was almost as dead as the fish that no one was buying.

Now fast-forward to today and imagine yourself in Seattle's lively landmark, the Pike Place Market, overlooking Puget Sound and the snow-capped Olympic Mountains beyond. As you walk closer to the crowd gathered near the open-air center of this sprawling bazaar, you can't help wondering what all that laughter and shrieking are about ...... until you see a hefty two-foot long salmon flying over the gathering and into the waiting arms of the young man behind the counter and the crowd goes wild!

Someone asks another rubber-aproned fellow for two pounds of halibut. "Two Pounds of Halibut!" the order-taker calls out. "Two Pounds of Halibut!" comes the reply, in unison, from everyone else on the fish market crew. The worker behind the counter makes an unbelievable one-handed catch, and then bows his head to the people applauding his skill.

Tourists are snapping photos like crazy, even handing their giggling toddlers up to pose with fish bigger than they are. And every so often, someone leans in for a closer look at that giant monkfish the one there on the lower shelf, that prehistoric-looking fish with a mouth as big as a saucer. But that someone doesn't stay there long because one little tug on the string that's tied to the fish's tail and hidden under the ice makes that fish move and makes the curiosity-seeker straighten up fast! The place is wild! This is certainly like no fish market you've ever seen before. Then you notice that in addition to all the silliness and good-natured clowning, something else is happening here... People aren't just laughing, they're buying fish. A lot of fish!

Oh, you see those two dozen executive-looking types over there, giggling like little kids? The ones wearing the matching jackets emblazoned with their famous corporate logo? They're here as part of a seminar on how to revitalize their customer service teams. Turns out the fish flingers have stumbled upon some "secrets" that big corporations spend millions looking for.

What turned a dark, dingy, dying seafood store into the star attraction of a famous city's famous landmark? Amazingly, the fishmongers didn't focus on the obvious question, "how can we sell more fish"? Instead, they imagined a thriving market filled with happy customers and happy employees. And then they realized that if visitors were to enjoy the experience, first they had to change their own thinking and behavior. Consequently, the staff at pike place fish market employed four main tenets to achieve this change.

"When you look for the worst you will find it everywhere"

There is always a choice about the way you do your work, even if there is no choice about the work itself. Each day when we come to work, we bring our attitude along. We can bring a moody attitude and have a depressing day. We can bring a grouchy attitude and irritate our coworkers and customers. Or we can bring a sunny, playful, cheerful attitude and have a great day. We can choose the kind of day we will have. As long as we are going to be at work, we might as well have the best day we can have. Think of small children who simply decide to be grumpy. Whatever goes on around them, they force a frown. Then suddenly they decide to be silly. At that point, they can't suppress their smiles and everything becomes a game.

Discuss as a Group

1. Do you know people who control their attitude?
   - ➢ Do you have control over your attitude? Think of a time you had to control your attitude.
2. Are you being the kind of person you want to be around?
   - ➢ What do you think about your day when you get out of bed?
   - ➢ Do you get through the day with as little effort as possible?
3. Are you going to be at work in body only or with your whole self?

Answer Individually

4. I usually brace myself for a difficult situation when ___________
   - ➢ I might create a different outcome if I __________________

Part of cherry-picking your attitude is choosing never to behave like a victim. Work-wise we are not victims of specific technologies or clients or managers or team members. We are people with the ability to choose our own attitudes independently of all those things. This means that our attitudes don't need to mirror others. If someone else is becoming uptight or aggressive, there's no need to respond in kind. At the Pike Place Fish Market, a character named Wolf was the best example of choosing an attitude. He was once on the road to a career as a professional race-car driver when he had a serious accident. He wallowed in self-pity for a while, but when his girlfriend left him and friends stopped calling, he realized he had an important choice to make. He could choose to live fully, or he could let life slip away in a series of missed opportunities. Wolf's story shows us how we can choose our attitude everyday and choose it well. Furthermore, it also teaches us that life is too precious to be passing through to retirement.

"An all-business approach has a human cost: It's not inspiring. We shut down emotionally and many who might make creative contributions keep that part of themselves at home."

Playing at work is usually frowned on. It's considered counter-productive, unhelpful, and silly-a-time-waster. But play is not about goofing off or acting irresponsibly. In the livable workplace, it is about finding ways to have more fun accomplishing serious goals. We learn the same way we did as children: by playing with ideas. In fact— anywhere creativity flourishes, play is happening. Just like the shock absorbers on a car, which keep rough roads from shaking the car apart, humor can keep the challenges of a livelihood from rattling us into a quivering mass of protoplasm.

Buying fish at the Pike's Street Market is more than just commerce— the hand-written placards placed all over the stall, the "flying fish" antics of the fishmongers and the shout-fest gives the place a joyful carnival atmosphere. The fish salesmen in their big hip-waders and rubber aprons are always laughing with the customers, joking with each other, yelling out the orders, and throwing fish through the air to the "ooh's and ahh's" of the assembled audience. The guys treat their place as an 'entertainment center'. Every minute when the stall is open for business, it's "showtime" and the teams put on their best performance to entertain, make friends and bring laughter to the spectators, and the constant ka-ching of the cash register tells us their 'play' philosophy is working.

If fishmongers can find a way to make their difficult & smelly job a fun, anyone can

Some businesses are already discovering that fun at work isn't simply a catch-phrase; it is a way to empower people and to boost revenue. An example to this is Southwest Airlines, where fun is indeed taken very seriously. In fact, the company's recruiting and hiring practices are built upon an idea that humor can help people thrive during change, remain creative under pressure, work more effectively, play more enthusiastically, and stay healthier and more positive in the process. As per an article in USA Today, flight attendant Larry Edwards made this announcement when he saw a few passengers uptight about a rough take off: "The captain can get the plane off the ground all by himself, so those of you gripping the armrest can stop lifting now." Smooth, but does this fun stuff boost the bottom-line? Thanks to its fun-driven work environment, Southwest Airlines has turned a profit every year since its launch, they are an industry leader in on-time departures and arrivals, and have the fewest customer complaints.

It's time to loosen up & lift the lid on play and freedom. But bear in mind that initially, playing might require some serious practice. You can try to duplicate what the fishmongers do on the surface but if you don't have the shared commitment and trust that make playfulness possible at work, it may not happen. You need to learn how to use the positive power of humor to enhance cooperation and teamwork, to improve communication, to eliminate conflicts, to supercharge creativity, to boost morale, to take responsibility, to improve relationships, and to build self-esteem through recognition and celebration. Not to mention, if implemented by the book, it will increase the laugh lines on your face as you make your way to the bank. See you are already smiling just thinking about it.

"Making someone's day is not about being a brown-noser who uses compliments to manipulate people into doing whatever he or she wants."

At the pike place fish market, fish mongers don't say they're selling fish. They say they're making the world a better place, one engagement at a time. Mary Jane observed this in the way her son Brad was allowed to help out in the fish storage, doing 'big guy' stuff. This principle helps in personal life too! Start by observing others closely, waiting to catch them doing something— or being someone— you can sincerely admire. Then, be willing to "expose" your observations to that person. The best way to give a compliment is to be sure you always back it up with evidence. Here's an example: "You are so great with kids!" (Now most people would stop there, but you need to give some evidence.) "They are so well behaved whenever you are in charge. I think it's because they can tell how much you care about them— and I loved the game you taught them to help them wait patiently in line. You are so creative and fun. No wonder kids love you."

From the context of a workplace, the best thing to do every time is to give credit where credit is due. Some managers refrain from giving praise for good ideas or a job well done, simply because they are jealous. Give a worker high praise and the next thing you know, they're jumping over you on the corporate ladder— that's how they feel. This type of thinking is self-defeating. Recognize good work and you give an employee the will to do better work. Don't recognize it and you feed one of the biggest gripes employees have— lack of recognition.

Because of our modern-day busy lifestyles, it's easy to forget that we live alongside others who have needs just like we do. We start treating people like props set up behind an orchestra, which solely exist to play the background tunes to our lives. If we paid a little more attention to the needs of other people around us, our lives could be much happier and more fulfilling.

Here are a few examples you should ponder and act on:

1. Write a thank you note to your child's teacher for no apparent reason. It will make her/his day, and it would also reap benefits for your child.
2. Buy a ticket to a movie and send it to someone who's been working very hard lately.

3. Send a funny card with a loving message to your partner's office. It will put a smile on their faces and remind them that you still love them, and that you still enjoy fun in your relationship just as you did in the beginning. You could also include a picture of you two taken on your honeymoon or first holiday.

4. Seek out a manager to compliment an employee. You could be out clothes shopping and appreciate the extra help in finding the pants that you were looking for. Or maybe you are at the bank and you want to give recognition to the teller that always remembers your name. Express to the manger what an asset this person is to the company.

5. Once in a while, get a hot drink for the beggar/homeless/busker you pass in the street on your way to work in the mornings. Ask him his name and on your pay day, get him a sandwich as well. It will cost you next to nothing but to him, it would mean the world.

6. If you know that a friend is due home after a long time away, leave milk, bread, juice, some cakes and a paper or magazine at his/her home.

7. Make a new person feel welcome. Maybe you have a new employee at work, or a new person in the neighborhood, or a new member in your networking group— whatever the case, walk over and give them a warm welcome. Let them know you are there if they have any questions or if they would like to get together for a cup of coffee.

8. Fill up a box of stuff that you and/or your kids don't want, take it into a slum or an orphanage and invite your soon-to-be well-wishers to help themselves.

Just do not wait too long. The sooner you spread the love to someone, the sooner that person can spread the love to someone else.

"Be Present"

"Remember when we were in school and the teacher was up in front of the room taking attendance? Each of us responded with the monotone 'here' but most of the class wasn't really there. The same can be true for us in the workplace."

Being present for your customers says it all. How many times have you been kept waiting at a store counter for someone to attend to you, while the clerk finished his phone call or conversation with another salesperson? What it tells you is that we need to be continuously tuned in to opportunities to be there for our customers and fellow staff. The antidote to burnout is not necessarily rest— it is wholeheartedness. It's the halfhearted things we do while juggling other things that wear us out. When advanced team members interact, they are not just physically present, they are wholeheartedly present. It is uplifting and, instead of draining our energy, actually replenishes it.

We need to examine if we are just going through the motions without really focusing on the moment. Here's an example from the field of nursing that beautifully illustrates this point: When one nurse said she was so overwhelmed with work already, she didn't have time for fish philosophy, another nurse re-explained what Lundin had been saying about the concept of "being there". She said, "Martha, I don't think what Tuna is suggesting is that we add another thing to our to-do-list. Sometimes, I go into a patient's room and I catch myself thinking about something outside the room and I look at the patient and I see that reflected in their face".

Being truly present also means suspending judgment while you're listening. Too often we listen like we are in a debate. Our minds are focused only on gathering information for the brilliant comeback we are determined to make. But, it's difficult to hear what another person is saying if our minds are stuck on what we want to hear. What's more, given all of life's distractions (Cell phones ringing, e-mails coming in, many people vying for your attention); to "be there" can be a real challenge.

Consequences of not being fully present are fatal: You may be physically alive, but become emotionally dead. Relationships start to feel empty and people seem like temporary stops on your way to some unknown destination.

Find Ways to Let Your Staff Discover the Fish Philosophy for Themselves

Mary Jane realized it wouldn't work to simply tell her staff about the Pike market, they had to see it for themselves. After a field trip to the market at lunch, she assigned her staff the task to think how they would translate fish philosophy to their third floor department. How could they create more fun and energy? How could they engage customers in ways that makes their day? What can the fishmongers teach us about being present for each other and our customers?

Things won't get better until we choose to make things better

The third floor then flew into action. Each team would make presentations on one of the four key ingredients of Fish philosophy. Every presentation was to have action items for implementation, and respective teams would be responsible for setting and facilitating their own meetings.

The Play Team designed a game using a path of circles cut from colored paper and arranged on the floor so you could step from one circle to the next as the music played. Each circle had written on it a key point from their report. When the music stopped, the person standing on a specific circle would be asked to read the text on it. One group of items was a list of benefits, the other group, a list of implementation ideas.

Benefits of play:

- Happy people treat others well.
- Fun leads to creativity.

- Having a good time is healthy.
- Work becomes a reward and not just a way to rewards.

Implementing play on the third floor

- Post signs saying, "This is a playground. Watch out for adult children."
- Start a joke-of-the-month contest with its own bulletin board.
- Add more color and make the environment more interesting.
- Add more life with plants and an aquarium.
- Organize special events such as a lunchtime comedian.
- Have a designated creativity area called the Sand Box.
- Form an ongoing play committee to keep the ideas flowing.

The Make Their Day Team presented results of the third floor's customer survey:

- Our customers dread working with us. They call us "the sleepwalkers".
- We often treat customers as if they are interrupting us.
- We frequently pass our customers around from one person to another without ever conveying an interest in solving the problem. We appear to be attempting to avoid responsibility.
- Our customers joke about our response, or lack thereof, to a problem that arises after 4. They laugh about the stampede to the elevator at 4.30.
- Our customers question our very commitment to the enterprise.
- Discussions have started concerning the possibility of replacing our department with an outside contractor.

Benefits of Make Their Day

- It is good for business.
- Serving our customers well will give us the satisfaction that comes to those who serve others. It will focus our attention away from our own problems onto how we can make a positive difference in others' life.

Implementing Make Their Day

- Stagger our hours so there is coverage from 7 am to 6 pm. This will be good for our customers and may also be helpful to some of us, who need different start times.
- Pull together some focus groups to study ways we can be of service to our customers. Should we have specialty groups, for instance, focusing on specific customer categories?

- Have a monthly and an annual award for service, based on the recommendation of our customers who said their day had been made.
- Implement a 360-degree feedback process.
- Appoint a special task force dedicated to surprising and delighting our customers.

The Present Moment Team related personal stories on the importance of being present for people. John spoke of how he passed up many opportunities to take his daughter to the park because he was too busy, Janet described how she was not able to help a co-worker in a past job, resulting in a lost client and the loss of her own job. Everyone confirmed their commitment to be fully present for one another and their customers. There would never again be unfocused behavior such as answering e-mails or reading while speaking on the phone with a colleague or customer.

The Choose Your Attitude Team presented a brief report, listing the benefits of choosing one's attitude:

- By accepting that you choose your attitude, you will demonstrate a level of personal accountability and proactivity that would fill the third floor with energy, all by itself.
- We may not be able to do exactly what we love at the present time, but any of us can choose to love what we do. We can bring our best qualities to our work. It is our choice. If we can accomplish this one thing, our work area will become an oasis of energy, flexibility, and creativity.

Implementing Choosing Your Attitude

- The group distributed copies of "Personal Accountability: The Path To A Rewarding Work Life" to everyone with the intent of conducting discussion groups on the book. Other titles for discussion were Raving Fans, The 7 Habits of Highly Effective People, Gung Ho!, and The Road Less Traveled.
- The group prepared an Attitude Menu. On one side it said, "Angry, disinterested, bitter" and, on the other, "Energetic, caring, vital, supportive, creative". At the top of the menu was written: The Choice Is Yours.

One Year Later

Lonnie and Mary Jane are engaged. Mary Jane receives the Chairwoman's Award for her work on the third floor, which she shares with members of the Pike Market, her staff, and with Lonnie.

Literally, dozens of organizations have used the Pike Place Fish Market as an inspiration to make their work fun—Southwest Airlines, Milwaukee Public Schools, Blue Shield, Sprint PCS, University of Florida, Nordstrom, and St. Jude Children's Hospital are just a few examples that show that implementing Fish philosophy is not as slippery and slimy as it sounds.

Stumbling Blocks

Although he hasn't seen any all-out Fish flops, Paul (Co-Author of FISH!) admits implementation can be difficult because of a 2-way resistance from both employees and management. Play can be the biggest stumbling block. It's the most fun, but too many managers have trouble letting go especially when it comes to trusting their employees with the Fish! philosophy. "What they need to do is define a safe place for their employees to play", says Paul. Workers, on the other hand, usually will buy into the program sooner, but may have trouble believing it for real.

Understandably, before employees can dive head first into the pool of fishy job satisfaction they need to get to know each other on a level that extends beyond emails and phone calls. If the workers at Pike's Place were not in tune with one another, there would be a very smelly disaster—fish all over the place! To this end, there are loads of options to suit each individual workplace and its unique dynamics. Corporate team building camps with activities like Scavenger Hunts, Nature Walks and Survival Training offer a good chance to bridge the gaps and instill a greater sense of team spirit amongst the staff. You may even wish to lead your employees down a more active path where they can bond over a rush of adrenalin while they tackle White Water rapids, Fast Bikes or the High Seas.

Who are You Being?

One of the most insightful statements in the book comes when a fishmonger says, "It's all about who you're being while you're doing what you're doing." "Doing" is necessary, but it's just the mechanical side of our lives. It's easy to get wrapped up in our doings, especially with all the tasks we have to complete. When that happens, we get stuck on autopilot and react without thinking. We feel rushed & impatient. Sometimes, it feels like we are human doings rather than human beings. On the other hand, when we focus on being who we want to be, it influences everything we are doing. We are better equipped to deal with difficult people and situations more calmly. We are able to notice when we are not being who we want to be. The principles of FISH! may seem like actions you do but they're really ways of being. When we are being lighthearted, no one has to tell us how to play. Ways to play just show up. When we are in a make-their-day state of being, we find opportunities everywhere to create special moments and make people smile.

While you're doing?

WHO ARE YOU BEING	WHAT ARE YOU DOING
RESENTFUL	Doing yard work with your spouse and grumbling
HELPFUL	Doing yard work with your spouse and making work easier
MANIPULATIVE	Coaching someone to make them do it "your way
SUPPORTIVE	Coaching someone to help them meet their goals
INCONSIDERATE	Listening and having side conversations in staff meetings
ENGAGED	Listening and contributing in staff meetings
FEARFUL	Hearing feedback and becoming defensive
GRATEFUL	Hearing feedback and accepting it
IMPATIENT	Rushing through customer interactions
EFFECTIVE	Being with customer fully during each interaction
LIVING WHOLE HEARTEDLY	Living FISH! In all parts of your life

Where Does Your Workplace Fall on the "Fish" Scale?

A good starting point would be rating your workstation on the 4 pillars of Fish philosophy, basis the 5 point scales as given below.

Play

1	2	3	4	5

1 being – "This place is so uptight that play is nothing more than a four-letter word."
5 being – "The atmosphere is lighthearted and playful. It brings a smile to my face just thinking about it."

Make Their Day

1	2	3	4	5

1 being – "Students and colleagues are treated with indifference or as an interruption."
5 being – "Students and colleagues are treated in a way that leaves them feeling special."

Be there

1	2	3	4	5

1 being – "People here seem so distracted, it is hard to know if they are listening."
5 being – "You are the sole focus of attention when talking with someone here."

Choose Your Attitude

1	2	3	4	5

1 being – "Workers demonstrate the mental maturity of a two-year-old having a bad day."

5 being – "There is a high level of accountability and everyone knows she or he chooses her or his attitude."

And what next....
Pick the principle whose rating you would like to improve and write a statement about it. Set a goal and make a commitment to move that category in a positive direction.

Living the Fish Philosophy

Why not make it your objective to become "world famous?" To find ways to bring the same "sunny, playful, cheerful attitude" to your job or business and to begin to revel in the delight of seeing the very same kind of results, including the ones you can take to the bank. If the fishmongers can do it, so can you! In fact, when you think about it, though your workplace may more closely resemble an office decked out with new carpet, air-conditioning and all of the latest technology, it is really not too far off from the working environment of the spirited folk at Pikes Place Fish Market.

□□□

IMPORTANT NOTE

This summary culls the content of the book - "Fish!" down to its essence so that even an average reader can sensitize himself to it, sparing him with the time consuming details. In case you feel a need to further explore this topic, the author recommends reading the original work published by "Hodder & Stoughton".

A Snapshot of
BLUE OCEAN STRATEGY

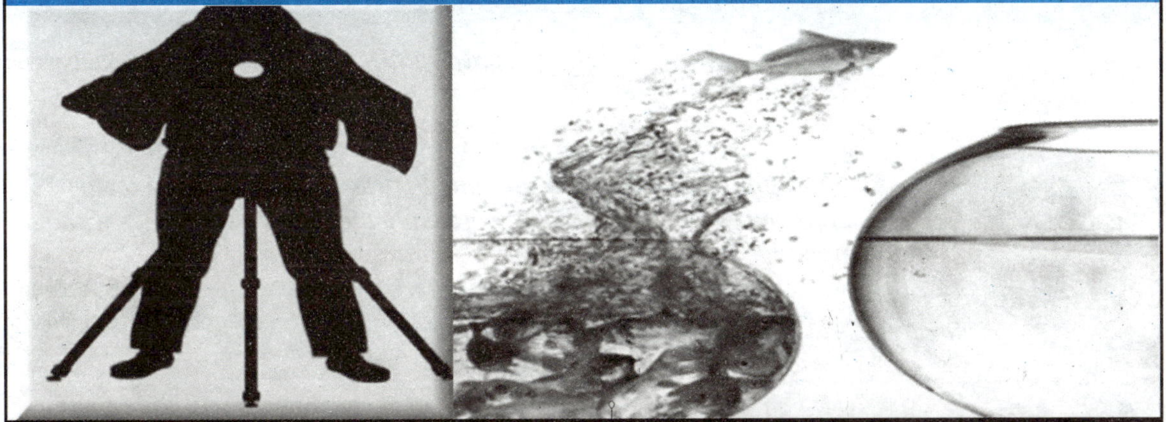

While a heavily MBA'ish read, the message in "Blue Ocean Strategy" is simple—Stop battling with competitors, make them irrelevant! Upending traditional thinking about strategy, this landmark book charts a bold new path to winning the future with notable examples of companies which have implemented strategies that separated them from the competitive pack. If you like marketing, clever and witty ideas or the kind of thrill that comes from playing chess then this book summary will definitely interest you.

Blue Ocean Strategy

—Inspired by W. Chan Kim and Renee Mauborgne

"To fight and conquer in all your battles is not supreme excellence; supreme excellence consists in breaking the enemy's resistance without fighting."

—Master Sun Tzu,
Author of 'Art of War'

Companies have long engaged in head-to-head competition in search of sustained, profitable growth. They have fought for competitive advantage, battled over market share, and struggled for differentiation. Yet in today's overcrowded industries, competing head on results is nothing but a bloody "red ocean" of rivals fighting over a shrinking profit pool. In a book that challenges everything you thought you knew about the requisites of strategic success, W. Chan Kim and Renée Mauborgne contend that while most companies compete within such red oceans, this strategy is increasingly unlikely to create a higher profitable growth in the future. Tomorrow's leading companies will succeed not by battling competitors, but by creating "blue oceans" of uncontested market space ripe for demand creation, thereby seizing new profit and growth opportunities. The term "blue oceans" is an analogy for all the industries not in existence today, untainted by competition, where the rules of the game are waiting to be set. Red oceans, in contrast, are the known market space in which the industry boundaries are defined and accepted, and the competitive rules of the game are known. Companies operating in the red ocean try to outperform their rivals to grab a greater share of existing demand. As the market space gets crowded, prospects for profits and growth are reduced. Products become commodities, and cutthroat competition turns the red ocean bloody. To sustain themselves in the marketplace, red ocean strategists focus on building advantages over the competition, usually by assessing what competitors do and striving to do it better. Here, grabbing a bigger share of a finite market is seen as a zero-sum game in which one company's gain is achieved at another company's loss. Blue ocean strategists on the other hand do not let existing market structures limit their thinking. To them, extra demand is out there, largely untapped and there is scarcely an attractive or unattractive industry per se. As market structure is changed by breaking the value/cost tradeoff, so are the rules of the game. Blue ocean strategy therefore allows firms to largely play a non-zero-sum game, with high payoff possibilities.

Why red oceans continue to dominate companies' strategic agenda?

Blue and red oceans have always coexisted and always will. But with supply exceeding demand in more industries, competing for a share of contracting markets, while necessary, will not be sufficient to sustain high performance. At present, however, competing in red oceans dominates the field of strategy in theory and in practice. Part of the reason traces back to the historical foundation of business strategy—war, where territory is defined and limited and opponents compete to protect and enlarge their share of limited and existing terrain. This focus on beating the competition in existing market space was exasperated by the meteoric rise of the Japanese in the 1970s and 1980s. Faced with mounting competition in the global marketplace as, for virtually the first time in corporate history, customers were deserting Western companies in droves, the center of strategic thinking gravitated further towards the competition. A slew of competition-based strategies emerged, which argued that competition is at the core of the success and failure of firms, and that competition determines the appropriateness of a firm's activities that can contribute to its performance. The result has been a fairly good understanding of how to compete skilfully in red waters, from analyzing the underlying economic structure of an existing industry, to choosing a strategic position of low cost or differentiation or focus, to benchmarking the competition. Yet, although some discussions around blue oceans exist, little practical guidance exists to create and capture them. This largely explains why CEOs mostly remain focused on red oceans even as the business imperative for navigating blue oceans takes on new urgency— it's the ocean they are familiar with and feel equipped to compete in.

Creating Blue Oceans—Lessons from the circus

As a run-up to the principles and frameworks of the blue ocean strategy, let's first dig into the thought-provoking tale of a vivid blue ocean success—the Canadian entertainment company, Cirque du Soleil. It took less than 20 years to exceed the revenue achieved by Ringling Bros. and Barnum & Bailey circus in 100 years of circus performance worldwide by introducing an entirely new form of live entertainment. What makes its rapid growth all the more remarkable is that it was charted in a declining industry in which traditional strategic analysis pointed to limited potential for growth. Supplier power on the part of star performers was decreasing audiences and, in turn, declining revenue and profits. There was also increasing sentiment against the use of animals in circuses by animal rights groups. Ringling Bros. and Barnum & Bailey set the standard, and competing smaller circuses essentially followed with scaled-down versions.

Another compelling aspect of Cirque du Soleil's success is that it did not win by taking customers from the already shrinking circus industry, which historically catered to children. Cirque du Soleil did not compete with Ringling Bros. and Barnum & Bailey. Instead, it appealed to a whole new group of customers—adults and corporate clients prepared to pay a price several times as great as traditional circuses for an unprecedented entertainment experience. To achieve this, it took the following four steps:

- Whereas other circuses focused on offering animal shows, hiring star performers, presenting multiple show arenas in the form of three rings, and pushing aisle concession sales, Cirque du Soleil did away with all these high cost components carrying little sway with customers.
- It kept clowns but shifted their humor from slapstick to a more enchanting, sophisticated style. Acrobats and other thrilling acts were also retained but their roles were reduced and made more elegant by the addition of artistic flair and intellectual wonder to the acts.
- Unlike traditional circus shows having a series of unrelated acts, each Cirque du Soleil creation had a theme and story line, somewhat resembling a theater performance. Each show had an original score and assorted music, which drove the visual performance, lighting and timing of the acts rather than the other way around.
- Cirque du Soleil strategically priced its tickets against those of the theater, lifting the price point of the circus industry by several multiples while still pricing its productions to capture the mass of adult customers, who were used to theater prices.

Cirque du Soleil succeeded by entirely redefining its corporate function, audience and market. This approach directly contrasts with the concept of the environmental determinism mandating that business in any given industry must accept their existing realities and compete within industry boundaries. That kind of thinking produces red ocean situation where companies compete on price and minor product differentiation. Compare that to the accomplishment of Cirque du Soleil that recreated an entirely new business and defied traditional classification.

Formulating & Executing the Blue Ocean Strategy

Without analytical frameworks to create blue oceans and principles to effectively manage risks, navigating blue oceans has remained a wishful thinking that is seen too risky for managers to pursue as a strategy. Explained below are the principles behind the successful creation of blue oceans and the risks that they each attenuate. The first four principles address blue ocean strategy formulation:

Blue Ocean Strategy: Principle No. 1: Reconstruct Market Boundaries

Companies cannot afford to be riverboat gamblers betting their strategy on taken for granted industry assumptions, intuition or on a random drawing. The challenge is to successfully identify, out of the haystack of possibilities that exist, commercially compelling blue ocean opportunities. Companies must break out of the accepted boundaries that define how they compete. Instead of looking within these boundaries, companies need to look systematically across them. They need to look across alternative industries, across strategic groups, across buyer groups, across complementary product and service offerings, across the functional-emotional orientation of an industry, and even across time. This gives companies keen insight into how to reconstruct market realities to open up blue oceans.

Revaluate the premises that form your industry assumptions and shake your company's business model. In the case of the U.S. wine industry, by thinking in terms of the current industry logic and looking across alternatives and non-customers, Casella Wines created a wine [yellow tail], whose strategic profile broke from the competition and created a blue ocean. Instead of offering wine as wine, Casella created a social drink accessible to everyone: beer drinkers, cocktail drinkers, and other drinkers of non-wine beverages. To achieve this, Casella streamlined its wine's taste making it fruitier and sweeter. It reached out to beer and cocktail drinkers by promoting its wine as fun. Breaking all marketing habits, Casella completely changed wine's traditional appeal based on complex taste and ageing. Instead it built the brand with the targeted differentiated intriguing blue ocean strategy. In the space of two years, the fun, social drink [yellow tail] emerged as the fastest growing brand in the histories of both the Australian and the U.S. wine industries and the number one imported wine into the United States, surpassing the wines of France and Italy. Today the brand swims in the clear blue water of new market space. Similarly, in 1984, Chrysler unveiled the minivan that broke the boundary between car and van, creating a blue ocean in the auto industry. Smaller than the traditional van and yet more spacious than the station wagon, the minivan was exactly what the nuclear family needed to hold the entire family plus its bikes, groceries, and other necessities. And the minivan was easier to drive than a truck or van. Built on the Chrysler K car chassis, the minivan drove like a car but provided more interior room and could still fit in the family garage.

Blue Ocean Strategy: Principle No. 2: Focus on the Big Picture, Not the Numbers

Traditional numbers-driven strategic planning is usually a data cemetery exercise that involves preparation of large, complicated spreadsheet documents. However, a closer look reveals that most of these "strategic" plans don't contain a strategy at all but rather amount to a loose collection of tactics that individually make sense, but lack a compelling collective logic. Each team member manages his section quite well, but with only a limited knowledge of the big picture. Taken as a whole, they don't provide a unified, clear, distinctive direction that sets a company apart from its rivals—let alone make the competition irrelevant. Kim and Mauborgne suggest a four-step process providing a remedy for this problem:

The first step is **visual awakening**. By discursively trying to design a *strategy canvas* of one's own company and the competitors, it becomes possible to agree on a common status quo and building on this to identify a common need for change.

Next, the **visual discovery** phase involves going into the field to explore the six paths to creating blue oceans. In the conversation with lost and potential customers, new customers as well as customers of the competition, existing impressions can be analyzed, new knowledge gained as well as the advantages of alternative products considered. The company is now in a position to decide which factors should be eliminated, created or changed.

In the third step, a **visual strategy fair** is organized. Many new value curves are drawn expressing a wide variety of choices for a new company strategy. The strategy walls drawn up from the knowledge gained in the second step, which show a possible target state, are then presented to the interlocutors of step 2. Their feedback is now included into the construction of the optimized target strategy.

In the last step 'visual communication', the strategy is communicated company-wide so that it is easily comprehensible to each employee. The best method of communicating a new strategy is by distributing before-and-after strategic profiles on one page for easy comparison.

* *Strategy canvas is the central diagnostic and action framework for building a compelling blue ocean strategy. The horizontal axis captures the range of factors that the industry competes on and invests in, and the vertical axis captures the offering level that buyers receive across all these key competing factors. A detailed explanation to be found in the BOS tools section.*

Blue Ocean Strategy Principle No. 3: Reach Beyond Existing Demand

The natural strategic orientation of many companies is towards retaining and expanding existing customers. This often leads to finer segmentation and greater tailoring of offerings to better meet customer preferences. The more intense the competition is, the greater, on an average, is the resulting customization of offerings. As companies compete to embrace customer preferences through finer segmentation, they often risk creating too small target markets. Although this might be a good way to gain a focused competitive advantage and increase share of the existing market space, it is not likely to produce a blue ocean that expands the market and creates new demand. To maximize the scale of their blue oceans, companies need to take a reverse course. Instead of concentrating on customers, they need to look at their non-customer base. And instead of focusing on customer differences, they need to build on powerful commonalities in what buyers value. Although the universe of non-customers typically offers big blue ocean opportunities, few companies have keen insight into who their non-customers are and how to unlock them. To this end, there are three tiers of non-customers that can be transformed into thriving new customers. They differ in their relative distance from your market.

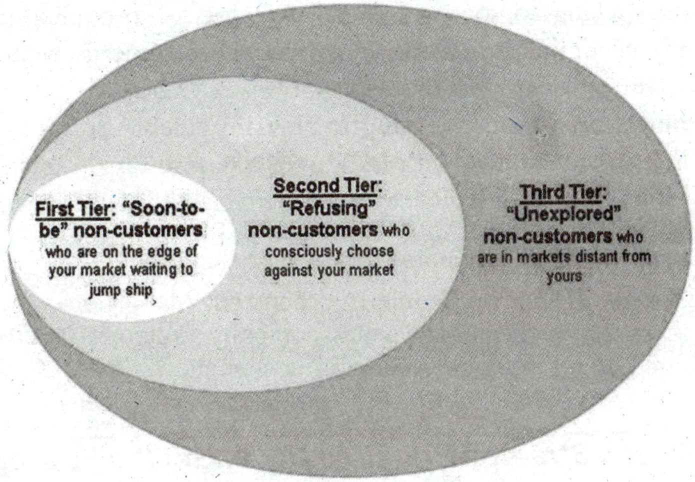

The *first tier of non-customers* is closest to your market. They are buyers who minimally purchase an industry's offering out of necessity but are mentally non-customers of the industry. They are waiting to jump ship and leave the industry as soon as the opportunity presents itself. However, if offered a leap in value, not only would they stay, but also their frequency of purchases would multiply, unlocking enormous latent demand.

The *second tier of non-customers* is people who refuse to use your industry's offerings. These are buyers who have seen your industry's offerings as an option to fulfill their needs but have voted against them.

The *third tier of non-customers* is farthest from your market. They are non-customers who have never thought of your market's offerings as an option.

Will you lose existing customers by focusing on non-customers? It can happen. But often this is not the case as existing customers gain new benefits from the non-customer offering—Cirque du Soleil is popular with both existing circus customers (families) as it is with a whole new ocean of once non-customers. The problem is that when you ask existing customers, 'what would you like us to give to you?' their insights tend towards the familiar 'offer me more for less.' That is why, customer-based strategy tends be less likely to yield insight into how to create blue oceans. Consider how JCDecaux, a vendor of French outdoor advertising space, pulled the mass of refusing non-customers into its market. Lack of stationary downtown locations was the key reason the industry remained unpopular and small. In searching for a solution, JCDecaux found that municipalities could offer stationary downtown locations, such as bus stops, where people tended to wait a few minutes and, hence, had time to read and be influenced by advertisements. JCDecaux reasoned that if it could secure these locations to use for outdoor advertising, it could convert second-tier non-customers into customers. This gave it the idea to provide street furniture, including maintenance and upkeep, free to municipalities. JCDecaux figured that as long as the revenue generated from selling ad space exceeded the costs of providing and maintaining the furniture at an attractive profit margin, the company would be on a trajectory of strong, profitable growth. In return for free products and services, JCDecaux gained the exclusive right to display advertisements on the street furniture located in the prominent downtown areas. By making clutter-free ads available in city centers with increased exposure time, the company significantly improved the recall for its featured advertisements. The increase in exposure time also permitted richer contents and more complex messages. Moreover, as the maintainer of the urban furniture, JCDecaux could help advertisers roll out their campaigns in two to three days, as opposed to fifteen days of rollout time for traditional billboard campaigns. Today, the firm operates in 33 countries and profitably dominates this specialized advertising sector.

Blue Ocean Strategy Principle No. 4: Get the Strategic Sequence Right

This principle discusses the strategic sequence of fleshing out and validating blue ocean ideas to ensure their commercial viability. With an understanding of the right strategic sequence and of how to assess blue ocean ideas along the key criteria in that sequence, you dramatically reduce business model risk. All such sequencing of potential strategic moves should be guided first by getting buyer utility right, then moving progressively to getting the balance between price and cost structure, and ultimately gaining wide user adoption. At each step, there are only two options: a "yes" answer, in which case the idea may pass to the next step, or "no". If an idea receives a "no" at any point, the company can either park the idea or rethink it until you get a "yes".

The sequence of questions to be answered is:

Q1. Why should anyone buy your product? Does it have exceptional utility? A quick "no", for example, can indicate a purely technology-driven innovation, market pioneering or futuristic design that may shoot beyond what buyers are ready to accept and pay for. The tool suggested by Kim and Mauborgne for the identification of the buyer utility is a 6x6 matrix where the six utility drivers namely-customer productivity, simplicity, convenience, risk, fun, environment friendliness are listed vertically while six stages of the buyer experience cycle (purchase, delivery, use, supplements, maintenance and disposal) are listed horizontally. In combination, there are 36 hot spots to unlock buyer utility— A detailed explanation of this is given in the BOS tools section.

Q2. Is your product really priced to appeal to a large audience? In setting a price, all companies look first at the products and services that most closely resemble their idea in terms of form. Typically, they look at other products and services within their industries. That's still a necessary exercise, of course, but it is not sufficient to attract new customers.

The main challenge in determining a strategic price is to understand the price sensitivities of those people who will be comparing the new product or service with a host of very different-looking products and services offered outside the group of traditional competitors. A good way to look outside industry boundaries is to list products and services that fall into two categories: those that take different forms but perform the same function (Ford's Model T vs. the horse-drawn carriage), and those that take different forms and functions but share the same over-arching objective (Cirque du Soleil vs. restaurant/bar). This approach provides a straightforward way to identify where the mass of target buyers is and what prices these buyers are prepared to pay for the products and services they currently use. The price bandwidth that captures the largest groups of target buyers is the price corridor of the mass. Next, determine how high or low the strategic price should be set within the corridor without inviting imitation from competition.

- If the product of the company is patented, has exclusive properties or has production capacities such as expensive factories that cannot easily be copied, then the product can be priced at a high level. Dyson, a British electrical white goods company, for example, has been able to charge a high unit price for its bagless vacuum cleaner since the product's launch in 1995, thanks to both strong patents and hard-to-imitate service capabilities. Many other companies have used upper-boundary strategic pricing to attract the mass of target buyers. Examples include DuPont with its Lycra brand in specialty chemicals, Philips' ALTO in the professional lighting industry, SAP in the business application software industry, and Bloomberg in the financial software industry.
- If the product has however high fixed and marginal variable costs, if its attractiveness is based on network externalities and the cost structure benefits from steep scale yields, it should be priced at a low level.
- Should the product not belong to either group, a mid-price level needs to be chosen.

Q3. Can you create your offering at the right cost to earn a healthy profit margin? To maximize profit potential, a company should start with Strategic Price, then deduct desired profit margin from the price to arrive at Target Cost. Price minus costing, and not cost plus pricing, is essential if you are to arrive at a cost structure that is both profitable and hard for potential followers to match. It's easy to start with market need and then quickly jump to adoption hurdles, cost things out, and go with a cost-plus pricing strategy. In particular, pricing first, then costing second, is both more market-focused (what will people pay?) and more innovative (how can I think creatively to work within the constraint of that price point?). To hit the cost target, companies have three principal levers. The first involves streamlining operations and introducing cost innovations from manufacturing to distribution. Can the product's or service's raw materials be replaced by unconventional, less expensive ones such as switching from metal to plastic or shifting a call center from the U.K. to Bangalore? Can high-cost, low-value-added activities in your value chain be significantly eliminated, reduced, or outsourced? Can the physical location of your product or service be shifted from prime real estate locations to lower-cost locations, as The Home Depot, IKEA, and Wal-Mart have done in retail or Southwest Airlines has done by shifting from major to secondary airports? Can you truncate the number of parts or steps used in production by shifting the way things are made, as Ford did by introducing the assembly line? Can you digitize activities to reduce costs?

By probing questions such as these, the Swiss watch company, Swatch, for example, was able to arrive at a cost structure some 30 percent lower than any other watch company in the world. At the start, Nicolas Hayek, chairman of Swatch, set up a project team to determine the strategic price for the Swatch. At that time, cheap (about US$ 75), high precision quartz watches from Japan and Hong Kong were capturing the mass market. Swatch set the price at US$ 40, a price at which people could buy multiple Swatches as fashion accessories. The low price left no profit margin for Japanese or Hong Kong-based companies to copy Swatch and undercut its price. Directed to sell the Swatch for that price and not a penny more, the Swatch project team worked backwards to arrive at the target cost, a process that involved determining the margin Swatch needed to support marketing and services and earn a profit.

Given the high cost of Swiss labor, Swatch was able to achieve this goal only by making radical changes in the product and production methods. Instead of using the more traditional metal or leather, for example, Swatch used plastic. Swatch's engineers also drastically simplified the design of the watch's inner workings, reducing the number of parts from one hundred fifty to fifty-one. Finally, the engineers developed new and cheaper assembly techniques; for example, the watch cases were sealed by ultrasonic welding instead of screws. Taken together, the design and manufacturing changes enabled Swatch to reduce direct labor costs from 30 percent to less than 10 percent of total costs. These cost innovations produced a cost structure that is hard to beat and let Swatch profitably dominate the mass market for watches, a market previously dominated by Asian manufacturers with a cheaper labor pool.

Q4. Are there any impediments to discourage the market from accepting your product? Addressing adoption hurdles early on ensures the successful actualization of your idea.

The remaining two principles address the execution risks of blue ocean strategy.

Blue Ocean Strategy Principle No. 5: Overcome Key Organizational Hurdles

Blue ocean strategy represents a significant departure from the status quo. It hinges on a shift from convergence to divergence in value curves at lower costs. That raises the execution bar. And consequently, like swimmers on the shore of a new sea, many corporate participants feel significant trepidation upon entering a blue ocean market. The challenges managers face are steep.

- **A cognitive hurdle:** Waking employees up to the need for a strategic shift. Red oceans may not be the paths to future profitable growth, but they feel comfortable to people and may have even served an organization well until now, so why rock the boat?

- **Limited resources:** The greater the shift in strategy, the greater it is assumed are the resources needed to execute it.
- **Motivation:** How do you motivate key players to move fast and tenaciously to carry out a break from the status quo?
- **Politics:** As one manager puts it, "In our organization, you get shot down before you stand up."

Although all companies face different degrees of these hurdles, and many may face only some subset of the four, knowing how to triumph over them is key to attenuating organizational risk. The conventional theory of organizational change rests on transforming the mass. So change efforts are focused on moving the mass, requiring steep resources and long time frames luxuries few executives can afford. Tipping point leadership, by contrast, takes a reverse course. To change the mass, it focuses on transforming the extremes: the people, acts and activities that exercise a disproportionate influence on performance.

How can you go about breaking through 'cognitive blinders'? Tipping point leaders let people see and experience harsh reality first hand. Don't let top brass, middle brass, or any brass hypothesize about reality. While numbers are disputable and uninspiring, coming face-to-face with poor performance can be shocking and inescapable, but actionable. The direct-experience approach exercises a disproportionate influence on tipping people's cognitive hurdles fast. Not only must you get your managers out of the office to see operational horror, but also you must get them to listen to their most disgruntled customers firsthand.

In order to jump over the resource hurdle, leaders must ask questions, such as, are we allocating resources based on old assumptions, or should we seek out and concentrate resources on hot spots? Where are our hot spots— that is, those activities that will have the greatest performance impact but are resource starved? Conversely, where are our cold spots— those activities that have scant performance impact but are consuming significant resources? The key is to redirect resources from cold spots to hot spots to maximize the return for each dollar. Also, leaders should consider appointing a 'horse trader' to trade the resources that aren't needed for those that are. Basically, the principle behind jumping the resource hurdle is in line with the logic of value innovation, i.e., pursuing breakthroughs in value at low costs.

In today's environment of shrinking bonuses and mass layoffs, how can leaders motivate employees? To achieve this, leaders must ask, who are our key influencers— our 'kingpins'? How can we focus the spotlight on and manage them based on fair process? By focusing on factors of disproportionate influence in motivating employees, including kingpins, managers can avoid the conventional pitfalls of launching massive top-down mobilization initiatives that are usually inefficient and ineffective, and instead execute a strategic transformation quickly and at low cost.

To overcome political hurdle, leaders should ask, who will fight me and who will align with the new strategy? Have I built coalitions with natural allies to 'encircle' dissidents? Do I have a 'consigliere' to remove the biggest land mines so that I don't have to focus on changing those who will not change? By focusing on three disproportionate influence factors— leveraging 'angels', silencing 'devils' and getting a consigliere on the top management team, leaders can leap over the political hurdle.

Blue Ocean Strategy Principle No. 6: Built Execution into Strategy

Kim and Mauborgne admit that creating a culture of trust and commitment that motivates people to execute the agreed plan of action is crucial in all types of strategies, but where blue ocean strategy is concerned, this challenge is heightened. A successful Blue Ocean launch thus requires extra effort from a unified group. To this end, the authors envision what they call a fair process, a set of elements (engagement, explanation and expectation clarity) that make people trust an adopted strategy so that they will comply with its requirements without being coerced.

Build a culture of trust and voluntary cooperation. Link the 3 E's: engagement, explanation and expectation with the actual process of developing a strategy and acting upon it at all levels of your organization.

Means involving individuals in the strategic decisions that affect them by asking for their input and allowing them to refute the merits of one another's ideas and assumptions. Encouraging refutation sharpens collective wisdom which in turn results in better strategy formulation and greater commitment from all involved to execute those decisions.

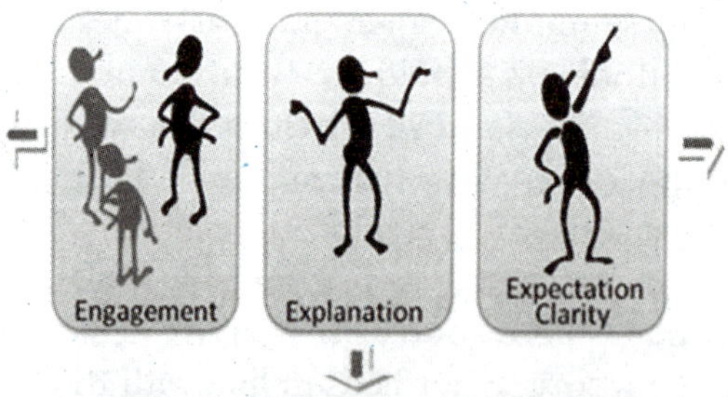

Requires that after a strategy is set, managers state the new rules of the game to their subordinates. Although the expectations may be demanding, employees should know up front what standards they will be judged by and the penalties for failure. When people clearly understand what is expected of them, political jockeying and favoritism are minimized and they can focus on executing the strategy rapidly.

Ensures that everyone involved and affected should understand why final strategic decisions are made as they are. An explanation of the thinking that underlies decisions makes people confident that managers have considered their opinions and have made decisions impartially in the overall interests of the company. Even if their own ideas have been rejected, explanation serves as a powerful feedback loop that enhances their learning.

Above all, blue ocean strategy is about risk minimization and not about risk taking

Of course, there is no such thing as a riskless strategy. Any strategy, whether red or blue, will always involve risk. Nonetheless, when it comes to venturing beyond the red ocean to create and capture blue oceans, there are six key risks companies face: search risk, planning risk, scope risk, business model risk, organizational risk, and management risk. The first four risks revolve around strategy formulation, and the latter two around strategy execution.

The six principles in Blue Ocean Strategy individually address how to mitigate each of these risks. The first blue ocean principle— reconstruct market boundaries— addresses the search risk of how to successfully identify commercially compelling blue ocean opportunities. The second principle— focus on the big picture, not the numbers— tackles how to mitigate the planning risk of investing lots of effort and lots of time but delivering only tactical red ocean moves. The third principle— reach beyond existing demand— addresses the scope risk of aggregating the greatest demand for a new offering. The fourth principle— get the strategic sequence right— addresses how to build a robust business model to ensure that you make a healthy profit on your blue ocean idea, thereby mitigating business model risk. The fifth principle— overcome key organizational hurdles— tackles how to knock over organizational hurdles in executing a blue ocean strategy addressing organizational risk. The sixth principle— build execution into strategy— tackles how to motivate people to execute blue ocean strategy to the best of their abilities, overcoming management risk.

Although the term blue oceans is new, their existence is not

Look back one hundred years and ask yourself, how many of today's industries were then unknown? The answer: many industries as basic as automobiles, music recording, aviation, petrochemicals, health care, and management consulting were unheard of or had just begun to emerge at that time. Now turn the clock back only thirty years. Again, a plethora of multibillion dollar industries jumps out—mutual funds, cell phones, gas- fired electricity plants, biotechnology, discount retail, express delivery, minivans, snowboards, coffee bars, and home videos to name a few. Just three decades ago, none of these industries existed in a meaningful way. Now put the clock forward twenty years or perhaps fifty years and ask yourself how many now unknown industries will likely exist then. If history is any predictor of the future, the answer is many of them.

Sustainability and Renewal

More often than not, a blue ocean strategy will go without credible challenges for ten to fifteen years, as was the case with Cirque du Soleil, Southwest Airlines, Federal Express, The Home Depot, Bloomberg, and CNN, to name just a few. This sustainability can be traced to the following imitation barriers rooted in blue ocean strategy:

- For a start, adopting a blue ocean creator's business model is easier to imagine than to do. Because blue ocean creators immediately attract customers in large volumes, they are able to generate scale economies very rapidly, putting would-be imitators at an immediate and continuing cost disadvantage. The huge economies of scale in purchasing that Wal-Mart enjoys, for example, have significantly discouraged other companies from imitating its business model.

- The immediate attraction of large number of customers can also create network externalities. The more customers eBay has online, the more attractive the auction site becomes for both sellers and buyers, giving users few incentives to go elsewhere.
- Further, when imitation requires significant political, operational, and cultural changes, organizational politics may impede a would-be competitor's ability to switch to a divergent business model. For instance, airlines trying to follow Southwest's example of offering the speed of air travel with the flexibility and cost of driving would have faced major revisions in routing, training, marketing, and pricing, not to mention culture. Few established airlines had the flexibility to make such extensive organizational and operating changes overnight.
- Cognitive barriers can be just as effective. When a company offers a leap in value, it rapidly earns brand buzz and a loyal following in the marketplace. Experience shows that even the most expensive marketing campaigns struggle to unseat a blue ocean creator. Microsoft, for example, has been trying for more than ten years to occupy the center of the blue ocean that Intuit created with its financial software product— Quicken. Despite all of its technical efforts and marketing investment, Microsoft has not been able to unseat Intuit as the industry leader.
- In other situations, attempts to imitate a blue ocean creator could conflict with the imitator's existing brand image. The Body Shop, for example, shuns top models and makes no promises of eternal youth and beauty. For other established cosmetic brands like L'Oreal, such an imitation is very difficult because it would signal a complete invalidation of their current images, which are based on promises of eternal youth and beauty.

Eventually, however, almost every blue ocean strategy will be imitated. As imitators try to grab a share of your blue ocean, you typically launch offenses to defend your hard-earned customer base. But imitators often persist. Obsessed with hanging on to market share, you may fall into the trap of competing, racing to beat the new competition. Over time, the competition, and not the buyer, may come to occupy the center of your strategic thought and actions. If you stay on this course, the basic shape of your value curve will begin to converge with those of the competition. The question now poses itself— When is the right time to venture out again? Kim and Mauborgne suggest doing this only when one's own value curve converges with the one of the competition. However, as long as the value curve shows focus, differentiability and a clear advertising message this should cease. The current income should, if possible, be enlarged, deepened and stretched. This can happen by optimization of the underlying business processes and through geographical expansions. The Blue Ocean should, therefore, only be swum through in its entirety.

Using BOS Tools & Frameworks

Given below are the strategy formulation analytics and frameworks that can help you in the practical development of blue ocean market-space.

I) Pioneer-Migrator-Settler Map

How can you determine if there is a possibility of creating a blue ocean for any of your current products or services? A PMS map allows you and your team to quickly capture, in one distinct picture, the overall strategic health of your business portfolio today, and more importantly, identify if you have future growth potential.

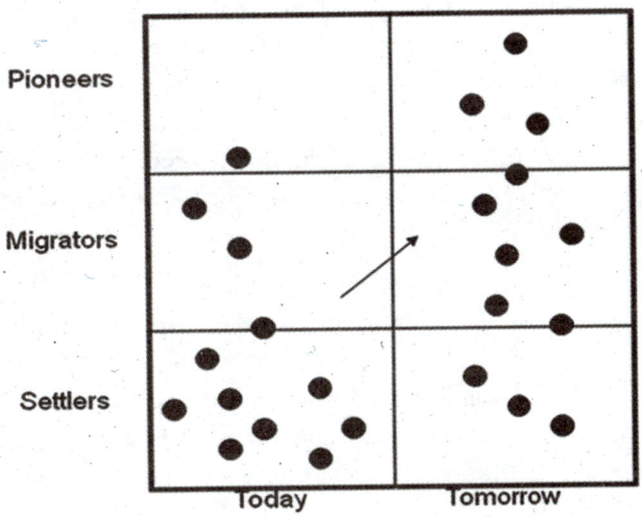

PMS Map is a 3-by-2 matrix where each row represents a business category— pioneers, migrators and settlers. With respect to the two columns, the first represents the business situation today, while the second column represents the business situation in the future. If your business offers unprecedented value, has a dramatically divergent value curve to the competition, and has a mass following, then plot this unit in the top section because it is a Pioneer. At the other extreme, if your unit's value curve converges with the competition, is a me-too offering, and is largely stuck in the red ocean then plot this business as a Settler. If your business is in between, providing relatively high value, maybe it is best in class yet only offers improved value, not innovative value then plot this business/product as a Migrator.

In case, both the current portfolio and the planned offerings consist mainly of settlers, the company has a low growth trajectory, is largely confined to red oceans, and needs to push for value innovation. Although the company might be profitable today as its settlers are still making money, it may well have fallen into the trap of competitive benchmarking, imitation, and intense price competition. Clearly, what companies should be doing is shifting the balance of their future portfolio towards pioneers. The PMS map above depicts this trajectory, showing the scatter plot of a company's portfolio of businesses, where the gravity of its current portfolio of twelve businesses, expressed as twelve dots, shifts from a preponderance of settlers to a stronger balance of migrators and pioneers.

II) The As Is Strategy Canvas

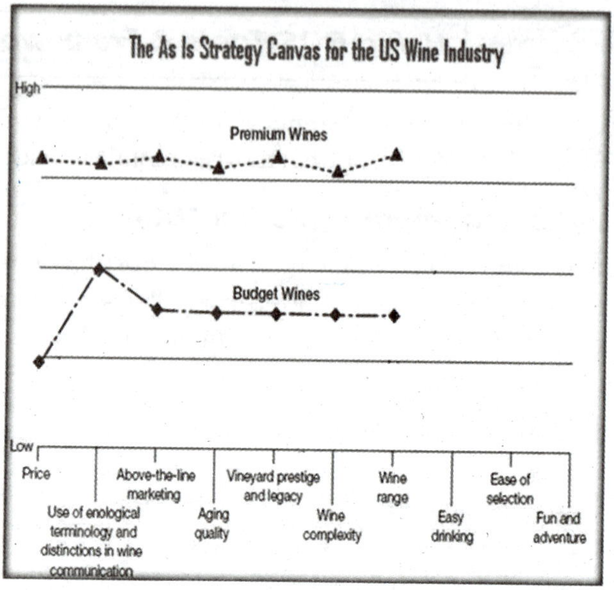

It captures the current state of play in the known market space and crisply communicates the three key elements of strategy: factors of competition, offering level buyers receive across these factors, and your and your competitions' strategic profile and cost structure. This allows you to understand where the competition is currently investing, the factors the industry currently competes on in products, service, and delivery, and what customers receive from the existing competitive offerings in the market. The horizontal axis captures the range of factors the industry competes on and invests in while the vertical axis of the strategy canvas captures the offering level that buyers receive across all these key competing factors. To create the strategy canvas, you simply plot points for the current performance of your company and all competitors, and then "connect the dots" to create a series of lines that represents the "value curve" for each company.

The authors point out that one of the problems with traditional strategic planning sessions is that the managers usually bring their own biases and perceptions of what is important to the table, leading to a lack of consensus on the organization's current situation. The result is often a lengthy, ponderous, hard to read document that isn't used to run the business. The visually compelling strategy canvas, in contrast, offers several advantages to executives:

- It enables you to quickly see areas where your strategy and those of your competitors converge (where everyone is following the same orthodoxy or set of assumptions on how business is done).
- It shows areas of divergence, where your company's strategy differs significantly from that of your competitors.
- It also helps you to see "white space" opportunities for innovation and competitive differentiation.

III) The Buyer Utility Map

Managers all too often focus on delivering more of the same utility at the same stage of the buyer's experience. That approach may be reasonable in emerging industries, where there's plenty of room for improving a company's current utility proposition. But in many existing industries, this approach is unlikely to produce market-shaping strategic moves. The Buyer Utility Map, to this end, lets managers identify the full range of utility propositions that a product or service can offer.

First, across the horizontal axis, we find the six stages of the Buyer Experience Cycle. A customer's experience can usually be broken down into a cycle of six distinct stages, running more or less sequentially from purchase to disposal. Each stage encompasses a wide variety of specific experiences. At each stage, managers can ask a set of questions to gauge the quality of buyer's experience.

Purchase →	Delivery →	Use →	Supplements →	Maintenance →	Disposal
How long does it take to find the product you need? Is the place of purchase attractive and accessible? How secure is the transaction environment? How rapidly can you make a purchase?	How long does it take to get the product delivered? How difficult is it to unpack and install the new product? Do buyers have to arrange delivery themselves? If yes, how costly and difficult is this?	Does the product require training or expert assistance? Is the product easy to store when not in use? How effective are the product's features and functions? Does the product or service deliver far more power or options than required by the average user? Is in overcharged with bells and whistles?	Do you need other products and services to make this product work? If so, how costly are they? How much time do they take? How easy are they to obtain?	Does the product require external maintenance? How easy is it to maintain and upgrade the product? How costly is maintenance?	Does use of the product create waste items? How easy is it to dispose of the product? Are there legal or environmental issues in disposing of the product safely? How costly is disposal?

Cutting across the stages of the buyer's experience are what the authors call the levers of utility— ways in which companies unlock utility for their customers. At each stage of buyer experience, a company can typically use these six levers (Customer Productivity, Simplicity, Convenience, Risk, Fun & Image, and Environmental Friendliness) to unlock exceptional buyer utility. The combination of six rows and columns gives a total of 36 cells. Each cell thus describes a different approach to inventing a new or improved product. By locating your proposed offering on the thirty-six spaces of the buyer utility map, you can clearly see how, and whether the new idea not only creates a different utility proposition from existing offerings but also removes the biggest blocks to utility that stand in the way of converting non-customers into customers.

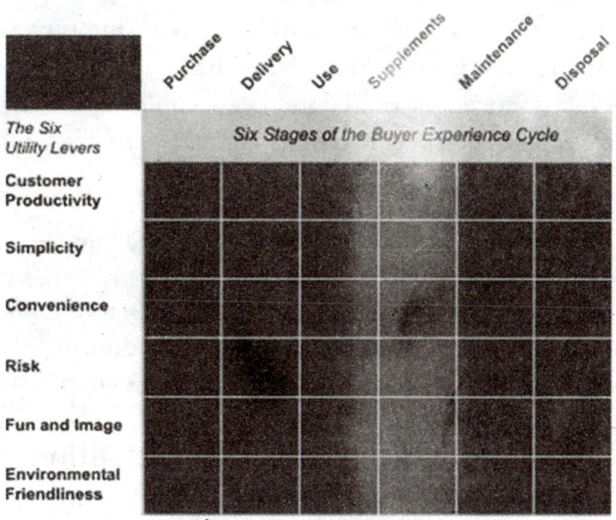

Let's now look at how successful innovators have staked out new spaces on the BUM.

Using a new utility lever at the same stage— Many successful innovations create new expectations for a familiar experience, Starbucks, which has revolutionized the American office-worker's coffee break, is a case in point. Traditionally, people bought coffee in delis or fast-food chains— businesses that competed by offering customers fast and cheap coffee. In terms of the map, those companies focused on delivering customer productivity in the purchasing experience. Starbucks, however, moved into a new space entirely. By establishing chic coffee bars that offer an exotic mix of brews, the company injected fun and cachet into the coffee-purchasing experience. As a result, middle class America has become coffee literate, and coffee bars have become American fixtures.

Using the same utility lever at a new stage— Companies can also innovate by extending a familiar utility to different parts of the customer's product or service experience. That's how Michael Dell changed the computer business. Computer manufacturers used to compete by offering faster computers with more features and software. In terms of the map, they offered customers more productivity in the use of the machines. Dell extended the same utility to the delivery experience. By bypassing dealers, Dell delivers PCs tailored to customer's needs faster than any other computer manufacturer.

Using a new utility lever at a new stage— In some industries, the most rewarding innovations do something completely new. A good example of this kind of innovation is the Alto, a disposable fluorescent bulb manufactured by European electronics giant, Philips. Most lightbulb manufacturers competed to offer customers more productivity in use; they did not pay much attention to the fact that bulbs had to be carted off to special dumping sites because of their harmful mercury content. By creating a fluorescent bulb that could be disposed of in an environment-friendly manner, Philips moved into and dominated a utility space largely ignored by its competitors. In the first year alone, the Alto poached more than 25% of traditional fluorescent lamp sales in the United States, while enjoying superior margins.

Beyond highlighting the differences between ideas that are genuine innovations and those that are essentially revisions of existing offerings, the buyer utility map reminds executives just how many unexplored innovation possibilities there are. Even the most productive innovators end up occupying only a small number of the 36 utility spaces. Think for a moment of your own industry. How many spaces does your company occupy?

IV) The Simultaneous Pursuit of Differentiation and Low Cost

One of the most commonly accepted dogmas of competition-based strategy is the value-cost trade-off. It is conventionally believed that companies can either create greater value to customers at a higher cost or create reasonable value at lower cost. As differentiation and low cost are seen as mutually exclusive pursuits, strategy is seen as a choice between them.

In contrast, companies that seek to create blue oceans, break this trade-off and pursue differentiation and low-cost simultaneously. Cost savings are made from eliminating and reducing the factors an industry competes on. Buyer value is lifted by raising and creating elements the industry has never offered. Over time, costs are reduced further as scale economies kick in, due to high sales volumes that superior value generates.

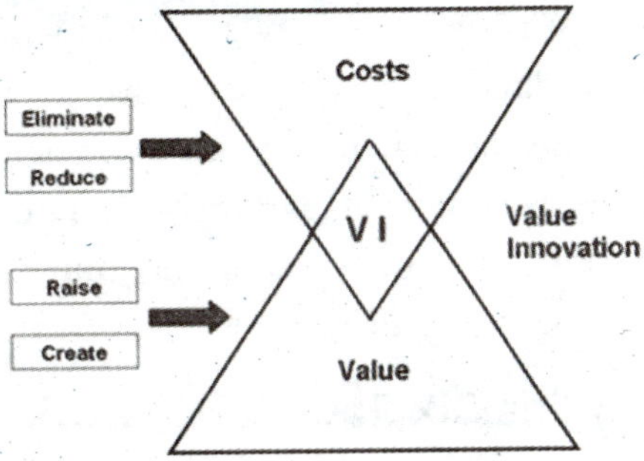

V) The Eliminate-Reduce-Raise-Create Grid (ERRC)

According to Kim and Mauborgne, the key for adding value to customers lies in a four-action-framework, where the following four questions are asked:

- Which to-date self-evident factors should be eliminated?
- Which factors should be reduced significantly?
- Which factors should be expanded significantly?
- Which factors unknown in the market till now should be newly created?

The ERRC framework ensures that we drive down costs by eliminating and reducing key competitive factors that the industry competes on, but do not add significant value. And it ensures that we dramatically raise buyer value well above the industry standard by reconstructing industry boundaries to raise and create new factors. Of particular importance are the actions of eliminating and creating, which push companies to go beyond value maximization exercises with existing factors of competition. Eliminating and creating prompt companies to change the factors themselves, hence making the existing rules of competition irrelevant.

Below are the steps Australian Casella wines took to create a blue ocean strategy—steps that any company can take to get out of the red ocean of competition:

1. **Eliminate:** Casella Wines recognized that most wineries touted aging and tanning qualities, two factors that intimidated customers. Casella decided to focus their efforts on different qualities.
2. **Reduce:** To avoid customer confusion; Casella Wines limited their offerings to just one white wine and one red wine.
3. **Raise:** Casella Wines raised the involvement of retailers with [yellow tail]'s success by giving retail employees Australian outback clothing that made [yellow tail] seem friendly instead of intimidating like other wines.
4. **Create:** Casella wines created new customer experiences for wine drinking: easy drinking, ease of selection, and a sense of fun and adventure.

While people are very good at identifying productive new things they should be doing, such as providing their customers with new services, they are notoriously bad at identifying things that can be eliminated, such as inefficient internal processes. In a tough economy, protection of the core, shedding of extraneous strategies and refocusing of available resources make you a more formidable competitor in the long run. Overall, what an organization decides to stop doing, or do less of, is just as important as what it needs to start doing.

VI) The Six Path Framework

These paths challenge the six fundamental assumptions on which most companies hypnotically build their strategies. Specifically, companies tend to do the following that keeps them trapped competing in red oceans:

- Define their industry similarly and focus on being the best within it.
- Look at their industries through the lens of generally accepted strategic groups (such as luxury automobiles, economy cars, and family vehicles), and strive to stand out in the strategic group they play in.
- Focus on the same buyer group, be it the purchaser (as in the office equipment industry), the user (as in the clothing industry), or the influencer (as in the pharmaceutical industry).
- Define the scope of the products and services offered by their industry similarly.
- Accept their industry's functional or emotional orientation.
- Focus on the same point in time—and often on current competitive threats—in formulating strategy.

If you're offering what your competitors offer, then you will always be fighting them for customers. How do you create new elements of value? Where do you start? There are six pathways or places you can look to find new factors of value to consider for your market:

Path 1: Look across alternative industries

The first path suggests engaging with alternative industries. This way one avoids definitions which resemble those of competitors. Alternative industries could either be substitutes (different form but same functionality like coffee & tea) or alternatives (different functions and forms, but same purpose like cinemas and restaurants since both cater to the same objective— people enjoying a night out). Customers frequently choose unconsciously between different alternatives when making purchasing decisions. Every vendor has to realize, that this choice frequently exceeds classic market limits. It is precisely at these gateways where the lever for value innovation can be found.

Take the example of Intuit's Quicken. To sort out their personal finances, people can buy and install a financial software package, hire a CPA, or simply use pencil and paper. The software, the CPA, and the pencil are largely substitutes for each other. They have very different forms but serve the same function: helping people manage their financial affairs. Instead of benchmarking the competition, Intuit created a blue ocean by looking to the pencil as the chief alternative to personal financial software to develop Quicken software. Intuit focused on bringing out both the decisive advantages that the computer had over the pencil— speed and accuracy; and the decisive advantages that the pencil had over computers— simplicity of use and low price— and eliminated or reduced everything else.

With Quicken's user-friendly interface resembling the familiar chequebook, it was faster and more accurate than the pencil, yet almost just as simple to use. The program eliminated the accounting jargon and the sophisticated features traditional financial software offered, offering only the few basic functions that most customers use. Moreover, simplifying the software cut costs. Quicken retailed at about $90, a 70% price drop. Neither the pencil nor other software packages could compete.

Path 2: Look across strategic groups within industries

The auto industry has luxury cars, mid-size cars and economy cars; the wine industry has budget and premium wines. These inter-industry strategic groups are typically defined by price and complexity. Japanese car makers combined two groups mid-size and economy cars to create a new, large market. What strategic groups can you combine or create within your industry? The key to creating a blue ocean across existing strategic groups is to understand which factors determine customers' decisions to trade up or down from one group to another, thereby combining the most attractive factors of both groups and eliminating or reducing everything else.

Consider how Ralph Lauren, the U.S. designer, created a blue ocean of "high fashion with no fashion" by understanding the factors that determine buyers' decisions to trade up or down from one strategic group to another. In creating Polo, Ralph Lauren combined the best features of haute couture (designer name, elegance of their stores, and fine materials) with the best features of lower-priced classical lines (classical look, lower prices) to not only capture share from both strategic groups, but to also draw new customers into the market.

Path 3: Look across the chain of buyers

Typically, an industry concentrates on who the single target buyer is. But in reality, there is a chain of "buyers" who are directly or indirectly involved in the buying decision— *purchasers, users and influencers*. Each hold different definitions of value.

- Challenging an industry's conventional understanding about which buyer group to target can lead to the discovery of new blue ocean.
- By looking across buyer-groups, companies can gain new insights into how to redesign their value curves to focus on a previously overlooked set of buyers.

Consider Bloomberg, the U.S. based financial information provider. In a little more than a decade, Bloomberg became one of the largest and most profitable business information providers in the world. Until Bloomberg's debut in the early 1980s, Reuters, Dow Jownes and Telerate dominated the online financial information industry, providing news and prices in real time to the brokerage and investment community. The industry focused on purchasers— IT managers—who valued standardized systems, which made their lives easier. This made no sense to Bloomberg. Traders and analysts, not IT managers, make or lose millions of dollars for their employers each day. So Bloomberg designed a system specifically to offer traders a leap in value, one with easy-to-use terminals and keyboards labelled with familiar financial terms. The systems also had two flat-panel monitors so that traders could see all the information they need at once without having to open and close numerous windows. Because traders must analyze information before they act, Bloomberg added a built-in analytic capability that worked with the press of a button. Before this, traders and analysts had to download data and use a pencil and calculator to perform important financial calculations. Now users could quickly run "what if" scenarios to compute returns on alternative investments, and they could perform longitudinal analyses of historical data. By focusing on users, Bloomberg was also able to see the paradox of traders' and analysts' personal lives. They have tremendous income but work such long hours that they have little time to spend it. Realizing that markets have slow times during the day when little trading takes place, Bloomberg decided to add information and purchasing services aimed at enhancing traders' personal lives. Traders could use these services to buy items such as flowers, clothing, and jewellery; make travel arrangements; get information about wines; or search through real estate listings.

By shifting its focus upstream from purchasers to users, Bloomberg created a value curve that was radically different from anything the industry had seen before. The traders and analysts wielded their power within their firms to force IT managers to purchase Bloomberg terminals.

Path 4: Look across complementary product and service offerings

Untapped value is often hidden in complementary products and services. The key is to define the total solution buyers seek when they choose a product or service. Phillips realized that when the Brits make tea, they first boil water, then they clean the lime scale (hard, off-white, chalky deposits found in kettles) out of the water, then they brew the tea. So it developed a tea-pot with a filter that would catch the lime scale and give tea drinkers a beverage without the pain of cleaning it.

- What is the context in which your product or service is used?
- What happens before, during, and after?
- Can you identify the pain points?
- How can you eliminate these pain points through a complementary product or service offering?

Barnes & Noble and Borders superstores in the U.S. redefined the scope of the services they used to offer. Instead of focusing solely on the moment a customer purchases a book— as the hundreds of bookstores were doing – they asked, what do customers do before, during, and after purchasing a book? They found that often before purchasing books, buyers want to sit and browse through several selections before making a choice, yet traditional bookstores did not offer a place to do so— in fact, they discouraged the practice. Then they observed that often after purchasing books or magazines, customers went to a coffee shop to spend some time alone reading. With these insights they transformed the product they sell from the book itself into the pleasure of reading and intellectual exploration, adding lounges, knowledgeable staff, and coffee bars to create an environment that celebrates reading and learning. In less than six years, B&N and Borders emerged as the two largest bookstore chains in the United States, with more than one thousand three hundred superstores between them.

Path 5: Look across functional or emotional appeal to buyers

If your product is an emotional one, what would happen if you stripped the emotion out and made it functional? If it is a functional product, what would happen if you made it emotional? Emotionally oriented industries offer many extras that add price without enhancing functionality. Stripping away those extras may create a fundamentally simpler, lower-priced, lower-cost business model that customers would welcome. Conversely, functionally oriented industries can often infuse commodity products with new life by adding a dose of emotion and, in so doing, can stimulate new demand.

QB House created a blue ocean in the Japanese barbershop industry and is rapidly growing throughout Asia. At the heart of QB House's blue ocean strategy is a shift in their product appeal from emotional to a highly functional one. In Japan, the time it takes to get a man's haircut hovers around one hour. Why? A long process of activities is undertaken to make the haircutting experience a ritual. Numerous hot towels are applied, shoulders are rubbed and massaged, customers are served tea and coffee, and the barber follows a ritual in cutting hair, including special hair and skin treatments such as blow drying and shaving. The result is that the actual time spent cutting hair is a fraction of the total time. Moreover, these actions create a long queue for other potential customers. The price of this haircutting process is 3,000 to 5,000 yen ($27 to $45). QB House changed all that. It recognized that many people, especially working professionals, do not wish to waste an hour on a haircut. So QB House stripped away the emotional service elements of hot towels, shoulder rubs, and tea and coffee. It also dramatically reduced special hair treatments and focused mainly on basic cuts. QB House then went one step further, eliminating the traditional time-consuming wash-and-dry practice by creating the "air wash" system—an overhead hose that is pulled down to "vacuum" every cut-off hair. This new system works much better and faster, without getting the customer's head wet. All these changes reduced the haircutting time from one hour to ten minutes. Moreover, outside each QB House shop, there is a traffic light system that indicates when a haircut slot is available. This removes waiting time uncertainty and eliminates the reservation desk.

In this way, QB House was able to reduce the price of a haircut to 1,000 yen ($9) versus the industry average of 3,000 to 5,000 yen ($27–$45) while raising the hourly revenue earned per barber nearly 50 percent, with lower staff costs and less required retail space per barber. QB House created this "no-nonsense" haircutting service with improved hygiene. It introduced not only a sanitation facility set up for each chair but also a "one-use" policy, where every customer is provided with a new set of towel and comb.

Path 6: Look across time

Does your industry show signs of a trend that is established, irreversible and has a clear trajectory? Ted Turner realized the demand for news at any time in any time zone, so he created CNN. Steve Jobs recognized the trend of people who so badly wanted a particular song, unbundled from an album, that they were illegally downloading them. What future trends do you see?

To create a blue ocean, one must look into the future and imagine what a developing trend will look like at its logical conclusion. Then work back from that point to see what can be changed today to meet that goal. Instead of this, what most companies do is adapt incrementally and somewhat passively as trends emerge. They focus on projecting the trend itself and pace themselves to keep up with the trend they are tracking.

VII) The To Be Strategy Canvas

While the *As Is Strategy Canvas* is the central diagnostic tool of Blue Ocean Strategy, the *To Be Strategy Canvas* is the primary action framework. Upon completion of the *ERRC grid*, you will have identified key competitive factors to eliminate from your current offering, other factors that you will reduce well below the current industry standard, factors to raise well above the current industry standard, and new factors that you will create that the industry has never offered. Now it's time to plot your new blue ocean strategy on the *To Be Strategy Canvas*. Consider the *To Be Strategy Canvas* for [yellow tail]. Spot the factors that they eliminated (enological terminology, above the line marketing, and aging quality), reduced (vineyard prestige, complexity and range), raised (easy drinking), and created (ease of selection, fun & adventure).

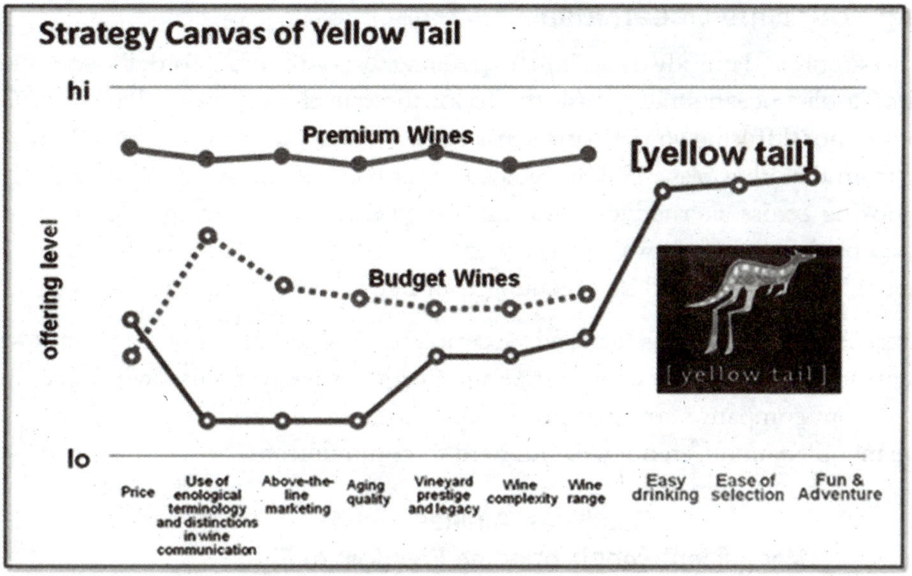

Likewise the *To Be Strategy Canvas* for CNN & The Body Shop will look something like this:

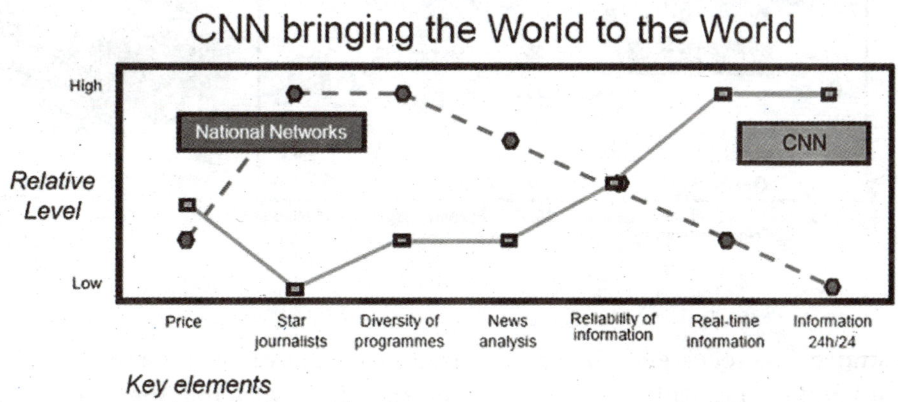

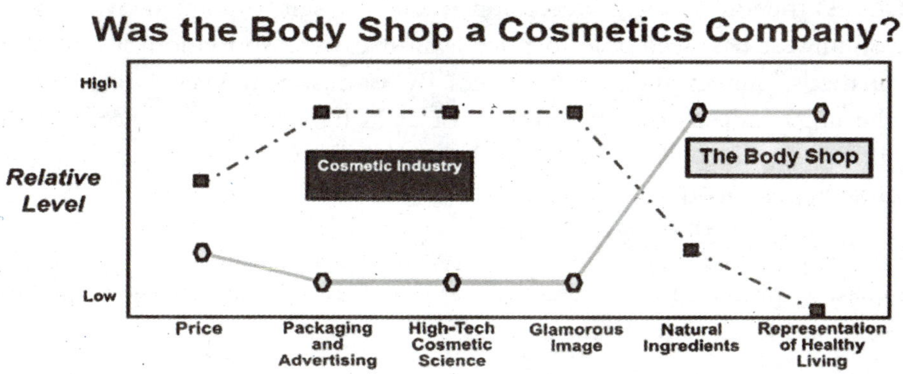

Testing Your Blue Ocean Idea

Finally, to simply and quickly do an initial screening test— if your "To Be" value curve has the three criteria of a blue ocean strategy, ask the following questions. Does it have focus? This indicates that you are not diffusing your efforts across all key factors of competition. Does your value curve diverge from the other players? This indicates that you are not benchmarking the competition but rather looking across alternatives. And can you give your new strategy a compelling tagline? This indicates a clear and distinct way to communicate your new offering to the mass of the population and your employees who will be executing your new "To Be" strategy.

Southwest Airline's profile is a perfect example of a good strategy, because it shows the three complementary qualities that characterize an effective strategy: focus, divergence, and a compelling tagline. If your company's strategic profile does not clearly reveal those qualities, your strategy will likely be muddled, undifferentiated, and hard to communicate.

Southwest Airlines
Magnificent People bringing Freedom to Fly

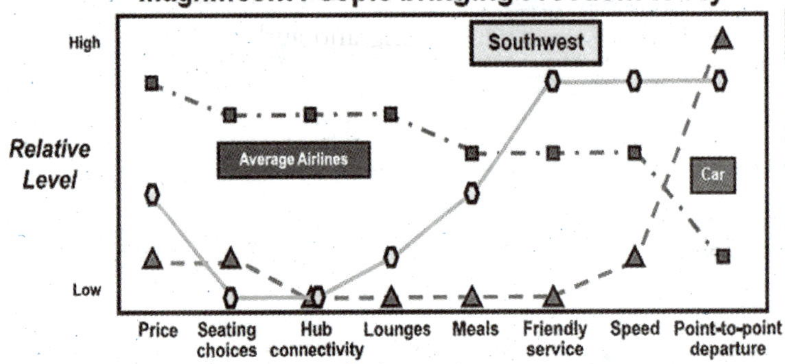

Focus

Every great strategy has focus, and a company's strategic profile, or value curve, should clearly show it. Looking at Southwest's profile, for example, you can see at once that the company emphasizes just three factors: friendly service, speed, and frequent point-to-point departures. By focusing in this way, Southwest has been able to price against car transportation; it doesn't make extra investments in meals, lounges, and seating choices. By contrast, Southwest's traditional competitors invest in all the airline industry's competitive factors, which makes it much more difficult for them to match Southwest's prices. Across-the-board investing is often a sign that competitors' moves are setting a company's agenda.

Divergence

When a company's strategy is formed reactively as it tries to keep up with the competition, it loses its uniqueness. Consider the similarities in most airlines' meals, seating choices and business-class lounges. On the strategy canvas, therefore, reactive strategists tend to share a profile. Indeed, in the case of Southwest, we find that the value curves of the company's competitors are virtually identical, which is why they share the same value curve in the exhibit. By contrast, the value curves of innovators' strategies always stand apart. They might eliminate or substantially reduce investments in certain factors, or they might dramatically increase investments in others. Sometimes, they even create new factors, thereby changing the industry's overall profile. Southwest, for instance, pioneered point-to-point travel between midsize cities; previously, the industry operated through hub-and-spoke systems.

Compelling tagline

The final test of a good strategy is how well it lends itself to a tagline. "The speed of the plane at the price of the car—whenever you need it." That's the tagline of Southwest Airlines, or at least it could be. What could Southwest's competitors say? Even the most proficient ad agency would have difficulty reducing the conventional offering of lunches, seat choices, lounges, and hub links with standard service, slower speeds, and higher prices into a memorable tagline. A good tagline must not only deliver a clear message, but also advertise an offering truthfully, or else customers will lose trust and interest. If you can't come up with a strong and authentic tagline, chances are you don't have a strong strategy, either.

"Blue Ocean Strategy is not about taking risks, but about learning how to open up and capture new markets. No company can afford to be a riverboat gambler."

—Renee Mauborgne

A Blue Ocean is a market space that is created by identifying an unserved set of customers, then delivering to them a compelling new value proposition. This is done by reconfiguring what is on offer to better balance customer needs with the economic costs of doing so. The problem is that most companies are too numbers-driven. They do lots of comparative industry analysis— especially on the competition— but that blinds them to the big picture. Blue ocean strategy offers an alternative. At its centre is the

four-step strategy visualization process any company or organization can apply. The first step is visual awakening. At this stage, executives are asked to draw their 'as is' strategy map— a visual representation of their company's strategy vis-à-vis the competition. This brings home the need for change. It serves as a forceful wake-up call for companies to challenge their existing strategies. The next step is what the authors call the visual exploration. Here managers go into the field to explore the six paths to new market space creation. The executives observe distinct differences of alternative products and services and zero down to which factors should be eliminated, created or changed in the company's offerings. The penultimate step is the visual strategy fair. Here executives begin to draw their 'to be' strategy map based on insights from the market exploration and test the same with customers, non-customers, and lost customers. After refining the 'to be' strategy canvas, the last step is to communicate it in a way that can be easily understood by any employee.

SOME OTHER KEY BLUE OCEAN CREATIONS

Ford Model T

Before the launch of Ford's Model T, the automobile industry was small and unattractive. More than 500 automakers in America competed in turning out handmade luxury cars that cost around $1,500 and were enormously unpopular with all but the very rich. Anti-car activists tore up roads, ringed parked cars with barbed wire, and organized boycotts of car-driving businessmen and politicians. Woodrow Wilson caught the spirit of the times when he said in 1906 that "nothing has spread socialistic feeling more than the automobile." He called it "a picture of the arrogance of wealth."

The Model T set 1908 as the historic year when Ford revolutionized not only the automobile industry but American society, and arguably all of Western culture. At that time, horse-drawn carriages were the primary means of local transportation across America. The carriage had two distinct advantages over cars. Horses could easily negotiate the bumps and mud that stymied cars especially in rain and snow on the nation's ubiquitous dirt roads. And horses and carriages were much easier to maintain than the luxurious autos of the time, which frequently broke down, requiring expert repairmen who were expensive and in short supply. It was Henry Ford's understanding of these advantages that showed him how he could break away from the competition and unlock enormous untapped demand.

Instead of creating fashionable, customized cars for weekends in the countryside, a luxury few could justify, Ford built a car that, like the horse-drawn carriage, was for everyday use. The Model

T came in just one color, black, and there were few optional extras. It was reliable and durable, designed to travel effortlessly over dirt roads in rain, snow, or sunshine. It was easy to use and fix. People could learn to drive it in a day. And like Cirque, Ford went outside the industry for a price point, looking at horse-drawn carriages ($400), not other autos. In 1908, the first Model T cost $850; in 1909, the price dropped to $609, and by 1924, it was down to $290. In this way, Ford converted buyers of horse-drawn carriages into car buyers—just as Cirque turned theater goers into circus goers. Sales of the Model T boomed. Ford's market share surged from 9% in 1908 to 61% in 1921, and by 1923, a majority of American households had a car.

Even as Ford offered the mass of buyers a leap in value, the company also achieved the lowest cost structure in the industry, much as Cirque did later. By keeping the cars highly standardized with limited options and interchangeable parts, Ford was able to scrap the prevailing manufacturing system in which cars were constructed by skilled craftsmen who swarmed around one workstation and built a car piece by piece from start to finish. Ford's revolutionary assembly line replaced craftsmen with unskilled laborers, each of whom worked quickly and efficiently on one small task. This allowed Ford to make a car in just four days—21 days was the industry norm—creating huge cost savings.

Apple iTunes

Apple observed the flood of illegal music file sharing that began in the late 1990s. Music file sharing programs such as Napster, Kazaa and LimeWire had created a network of Internet savvy music lovers freely, yet illegally, sharing music across the globe. By 2003, more than two billion illegal music files were being traded every month. While the recording industry fought to stop the cannibalization of physical CDs, illegal digital music downloading continued to grow. With the technology out there for anyone to digitally download music free instead of paying $19 for an average CD, the trend towards digital music was clear. This trend was underscored by the fast growing demand for MP3 players that played mobile digital music, such as Apple's hit iPod. Apple capitalized on this decisive trend with a clear trajectory by launching the iTunes online music store in 2003. In agreement with five major music companies—BMG, EMI Group, Sony, Universal Music Group and Warner Brothers Records—iTunes offered legal, easy-to-use, and flexible à la carte song downloads. iTunes allowed buyers to freely browse two hundred thousand songs, listen to thirty-second samples, and download an individual song for 99 cents or an entire album for $9.99. By allowing people to buy individual songs and strategically pricing them far more reasonably, iTunes broke a key customer annoyance factor: the need to purchase an entire CD when they wanted only one or two songs on it. iTunes also leapt past free downloading services, providing sound quality as well as intuitive navigating, searching and browsing functions. To illegally download music, you must first search for the song, album, or artist. If you are looking for a complete album, you must know the names of all the songs and their order. It is rare to find a complete album to download in one location. The sound quality is consistently poor because most people burn CDs at a low bit rate to save space. And most of the tracks available reflect the tastes of sixteen-year-olds, so although theoretically there are billions of tracks available, the scope is limited. In contrast, Apple's search and browsing functions are considered the best in the business. Moreover, iTunes music editors include a number of added features usually found in the record shops, including iTunes essentials such as Best Hair Bands or Best Love Songs, staff favorites, celebrity play lists, and *Billboard* charts. And iTunes sound quality is the best because iTunes encodes songs in a format called AAC, which offers sound quality superior to MP3s, even those burned at a very high data rate.

Customers have been flocking to iTunes ever since its launch in 2003. It is also a win-win situation for the recording companies and artists as they receive 65 percent of the purchase price of digitally downloaded songs, at last financially benefiting from the digital downloading craze. In addition, Apple further protected recording companies by devising copyright protection that would not inconvenience users who had grown accustomed to the freedom of digital music in the post Napster world, but would satisfy the music industry. The iTunes Music Store allows users to burn songs onto iPods and CDs up to seven times, enough to easily satisfy music lovers but far too few times to make professional piracy an issue. True to its corporate slogan, "Think different," Apple tried marketing music on the internet in a way no one had tried before, and it worked. Today the iTunes Music Store has surpassed Wal-Mart, Amazon and Target to become the largest music retailer in the US. With over 50 million customers, iTunes has sold over 4 billion songs and features the world's largest music catalog of over 10 million songs.

NetJets

NetJets created the blue ocean of fractional jet ownership. In just over twenty years, NetJets has grown larger than many airlines, with more than six hundred and ninety aircrafts, operating more than three hundred and seventy thousand flights to more than one hundred fifty countries. Purchased by Berkshire Hathaway in 1998, today NetJets is a multibillion-dollar business. NetJets' success has been attributed to its flexibility, shortened travel time, hassle-free travel experience, increased reliability, and strategic pricing. This is how NetJets crafted its own blue ocean strategy— The most lucrative mass of customers in the aviation industry are corporate travelers. NetJets looked at the existing alternatives and found that when business travelers want to fly, they have two principal choices. On the one hand, a company's executives can fly business class or first class on a commercial airline. On the other hand, a company can purchase its own aircraft to serve its corporate travel needs. The strategic question is, Why would corporations choose one alternative industry over another? By focusing on the key factors that lead corporations to trade across alternatives and eliminating or reducing everything else, NetJets reconstructed its market boundaries.

Why do corporations choose to use commercial airlines for their corporate travel?

Surely it's not because of the long check-in and security lines, hectic flight transfers, overnight stays, or congested airports. Rather, they choose commercial airlines for only one reason: costs. On the one hand, commercial travel avoids the high up-front, fixed-cost investment of a multimillion-dollar jet aircraft. On the other hand, a company purchases only the number of corporate airline tickets needed per year, lowering variable costs and reducing the possibility of unused aviation travel time that often accompanies the ownership of corporate jets. So NetJets offered its customers one-sixteenth ownership of an aircraft to be shared with fifteen other customers, each one entitled to fifty hours of flight time per year. Starting at $375,000 (plus pilot, maintenance, and other monthly costs), owners could purchase a share in a $6 million aircraft. Thus, customers get the convenience of a private jet at the price of a commercial airline ticket.

Comparing first-class travel with private aircraft, the National Business Aviation Association found that when direct and indirect costs—hotel, meals, travel time, expenses—were factored in, the cost of first-class commercial travel was significantly higher. In a cost-benefit analysis for four passengers on a theoretical trip from Newark to Austin, the real cost of the commercial trip was $19,400, compared with $10,100 in a private jet. As for NetJets, it avoids the enormous fixed costs that commercial airlines attempt to cover by filling larger and larger aircraft. NetJets' smaller airplanes, the use of smaller regional airports, and limited staff keep costs to a minimum.

To understand the rest of the NetJets formula, consider the flip side: Why do people choose corporate jets over commercial travel? Certainly it is not to pay the multimillion-dollar price to purchase planes. Nor is it to set up a dedicated flight department to take care of scheduling and other administrative matters. Nor it is to pay so-called deadhead costs—the costs of flying the aircraft from its home base to where it is needed. Rather, corporations buy private jets to dramatically cut total travel time, to reduce the hassle of congested airports, to allow for point-to-point travel, and to gain the benefit of having more productive and energized executives, who can hit the ground running upon arrival. So NetJets built on these distinctive strengths. Whereas 70 percent of commercial flights went to only thirty airports across the United States, NetJets offered access to more than five thousand five hundred airports across the country, in convenient locations near business centers. On international flights, your plane pulls directly up to the customs office. With point-to-point service and the exponential increase in the number of airports to land in, there are no flight transfers; trips that would otherwise require overnight stays can be completed in a single day. The time from your car to takeoff is measured in minutes instead of hours. For example, whereas a flight from Washington, D.C. to Sacramento would take 10.5 hours on a commercial airline, it is only 5.2 hours on a NetJets aircraft; from Palm Springs to Cabo San Lucas takes 6 hours commercial, and only 2.1 hours via NetJets. Perhaps most appealing, your jet is always available with only four hours' notice. If a jet is not available, NetJets will charter one for you. Last but not the least, NetJets dramatically reduces issues related to security threats and offers clients customized in-flight service, such as having your favorite food and beverages ready for you when you board. By offering the best of commercial travel and private jets and eliminating and reducing everything else, NetJets opened up a multibillion-dollar blue ocean wherein customers get the convenience and speed of a private jet with a low fixed cost and the low variable cost of commercial airline travel. And the competition? According to NetJets, in the past seven years, fifty-seven companies have set up fractional jet operations; of those, fifty-seven have gone out of business.

Nintendo Wii

When Nintendo was making their new game player, they could have done what Sony and Microsoft were doing. Make very powerful game machines that appeal to hardcore male gamers. Back then, that was the red ocean norm. Instead, Nintendo went back to the drawing board and decided to create a machine that was simple and fun. They wanted to create games that the whole family could enjoy, from little kids to grandparents. To do this, they created a much simpler controller, which was much more intuitive— few people want to learn how to press 12 different buttons to play a tennis game, but anyone can swing a controller to simulate the motion of a racquet. So what happened? While Sony and Microsoft were fighting it out tooth and nail for a narrow demographic, Nintendo brought in entirely new demographics to gaming, and the Wii has been an enormous success.

How the industry was deconstructed and reconstructed by Nintendo

All in all, Nintendo flipped the board and took the industry hostage with its new, holistic video game approach. No longer is high-definition capability the defining matter in video games; it would be absurd to deny its importance, especially in hardcore gamers, but for the casual gamer, it's almost a non-issue. When playing a Wii you know you're not watching a movie being rendered in real-time, and Nintendo realized that'd be just fine with people. Balls bounce just fine but if you're looking for real-time rendering of wind rustling through leaves look outside your window— this isn't something important enough to justify the added cost.

> "While some people put their money on the screen, we decided to put ours into the game experience, in an attempt to not just improve the market, but disrupt it."
> — Nintendo CEO, Satoru wata

Now gamers are playing with their families, their friends and not alone in the dark at night (which is the typical gamer concept until now). With its Wii Sports package, which comes bundled with the Console, and includes Baseball, Bowling, Boxing, Golf and Tennis, some people don't even find a reason to buy more games. The accessories (driving wheel, sword, blaster fishing rod) become the ways to unlock a more participative playing experience. The launch of Wii Fit was another media sensation and challenged the notion that video games help to create couch potatoes. Wii Fit is a balancing board (additional hardware) that comes with a full exercise program, equipped for fun (soccer headers, slalom), Fitness (jogging), Balance activities (Yoga), among others. The Wii Fit has even been praised for use as means of recovery through physical therapy for patients, being prescribed by doctors to regain strength and rehabilitation of certain injuries.

Strategy Canvas for Wii

Nintendo has never released the strategy canvas they used, but we can probably reverse engineer it. This canvas illustrates a range of factors that seem to be defining of the video game industry. Each of these factors holds part of the explanation about the strategic direction that Microsoft, Sony and Nintendo (as well as other competitors) have taken. Each one implies a certain amount of resource allocation and investment, and may well be the fruit of many years of strategic thinking and development. Together, they depict the factors that each company, through their products, chooses to differentiate themselves in the market.

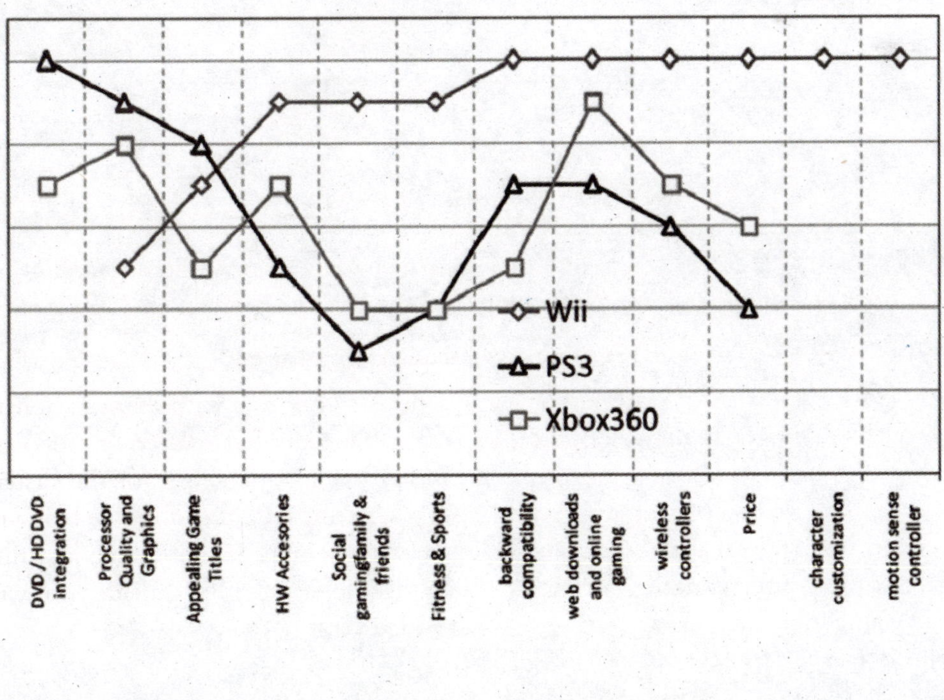

The difference with the Wii is that Nintendo chooses a path astray from the arms' race to better technology and builds a product that, although technically inferior, sets to capture the lion's share of the market by focusing its firepower on factors besides the technical prowess. Nintendo's mission seems to be "to encourage people around the world to play video games regardless of their age, gender or cultural background", capturing young and old alike.

The well-known end of the story

Nintendo came from a distant third to a solid first thanks to BOS. Nintendo's strategy didn't just win; it made the competition irrelevant.

IMPORTANT NOTE

This summary culls the content of the book - "Blue Ocean Strategy" down to its essence so that even an average reader can sensitize himself to it, sparing him with the time consuming details. In case you feel a need to further explore this topic, the author recommends reading the original work published by "Harvard Business Press".

"I feel a very unusual sensation - if it is not indigestion, I think it must be gratitude"

Well, to say this is my book would be totally untrue. I would instead call it a synergetic product of many minds. The whole purpose of writing this book was to celebrate & publicize the best of business bestsellers and most importantly the ideas that they each represent. So, heartfelt thanks to all those publishers and individual authors whose work has been showcased in my book. Without the insights from their chart-topping business literature, this book would never have been written.

Big hugs to my family & friends for putting up with my authorial nonsense and encouraging me all the way to become the writer my elementary school teachers always said I'd become. I love you more than a photosynthetic plant loves its color green.

Thanks are also due to the editor and the entire team at Unicorn Books Pvt. Ltd. They have been patient with my whining, accepting of nothing but my best, and above all, had the conviction to believe in my dream of promoting wisdom of the best books on business to the widest audience possible. The friendship we developed during this project has been an added bonus.

Finally, I would like to thank all my readers. If you are already here, it suggests you might have read through what came before it!